Marmalade SDK Mobile Game Development Essentials

Get to grips with the Marmalade SDK to develop games for a wide range of mobile devices, including iOS, Android, and more

Sean Scaplehorn

BIRMINGHAM - MUMBAI

Marmalade SDK Mobile Game Development Essentials

First published: November 2012

Production Reference: 2161112

Published by Packt Publishing Ltd.
Livery Place
35 Livery Street
Birmingham B3 2PB, UK.

ISBN 978-1-84969-336-3

www.packtpub.com

Cover Image by Neha Rajappan (neha.rajappan1@gmail.com)

Credits

Author
Sean Scaplehorn

Reviewers
Joshua Bycer
Tim Closs
Marc Evans
Jern-Kuan Leong
Ronald Tan Heng Neng
Francis Styck

Acquisition Editor
Kartikey Pandey

Lead Technical Editor
Dayan Hyames

Technical Editor
Charmaine Pereira

Copy Editors
Aditya Nair
Insiya Morbiwala

Project Coordinator
Amey Sawant

Proofreader
Maria Gould

Indexer
Tejal Soni

Graphics
Valentina D'silva

Production Coordinator
Prachali Bhiwandkar

Cover Work
Prachali Bhiwandkar

About the Author

Sean Scaplehorn is a programmer with 15 years of experience in the videogames industry, who has worked on projects for both console and mobile devices. He has worked on games published by companies including Sony, Electronic Arts, Konami, Square Enix, and Namco.

Sean got his first home computer while still at primary school, which kick-started his interest in programming. After learning to code from typing in listings printed in computer magazines, he went on to write his own games and shared them with his school friends. He knew then that writing games was what he wanted to do when he grew up.

However, on leaving university, Sean spent a couple of years writing software for printing check books. When he could stand it no longer, he made the leap into videogames development and hasn't looked back since.

He worked at Ideaworks3D, the company behind the Marmalade SDK, for four years. In this time he saw the Marmalade SDK evolve from an in-house technology to being a product in its own right, when it was launched as the Airplay SDK.

Sean now works from his home in the South of England as a freelance game coder.

I would like to thank the following people for their help and support while writing this book. To my wife Sandra and daughter Kara for their patience and understanding while Daddy "wrote his book", and to Marc Evans, a longtime friend and former colleague, for his invaluable feedback on my writing.

I would also like to thank Simon Pick for giving an eager young man the best first job in the games industry he could have wished for, and Tim Closs, CTO of Marmalade, for kindly taking the time to review this book during its development to ensure its accuracy.

About the Reviewers

Joshua Bycer is a game industry analyst with over 7 years of experience examining game design and the trends of the industry. He has been published locally on game sites Gamasutra and QuarterToThree, and internationally in *Igromania* Magazine. He has maintained the blog site `chronicgamedesigner.blogspot.com` since 2007 and is in the process of setting up his new site `game-wisdom.com`.

His goal is to expand critical writing on the industry, to better examine future trends, and raise the standard for critical analysis.

Tim Closs has over 20 years' experience of commercial software development, and joined Marmalade in 2004. As CTO, Tim has lead the creation and productization of the Marmalade SDK, and continues to drive the company's technology and product strategies. Tim holds a Mathematics degree and Theoretical Physics postgraduate diploma from Cambridge University.

Marc Evans has been developing software almost as long as he has been playing games, and is currently involved in improving the content creation experience for the artists and designers of major console games.

Jern-Kuan Leong has been interested in programming ever since he started playing computer games on his 286s. He spent the early part of his career in enterprise software development, and quickly jumped into the games industry when the opportunity came. He has worked with LucasArts for four years and more recently with NVIDIA. He continues to explore the joy of game programming and design to this day.

Ronald Tan Heng Neng has worked at Ubisoft, IBM, and is currently the producer at 12 Gigs, Inc. (`www.12gigs.com`), a cross-platform social mobile casino games network in the San Francisco Bay Area, with hit titles on Facebook, iOS, Android, and Amazon.

Since obtaining his BSc (Hons) in Business Information Technology at Birmingham City University (United Kingdom), Ronald has garnered more than a decade of professional program/project management experience. This valuable experience also led him back to his passion in games, with a focus on games production and execution. Ronald also holds the highly sought after Project Management Professional (PMP)® and Certified IT Project Manager (CITPM) certifications.

In his spare time Ronald enjoys reading, traveling, developing small games, and blogging occasionally on topics he's passionate about at `http://ronald-tan.com`.

Francis Styck has been developing games since his college days at UNLV, while pursuing an Engineering degree in the 1980s when games were written in Assembly language on the Atari 800 and Commodore 64. He continued with his education at UNLV and graduated with an MBA in 2001. Today, he is still writing games but now uses the power of C++, Marmalade, and cocos2d-x to support many platforms and devices. You can stay in touch with Francis using LinkedIn at `http://www.linkedin.com/in/styck`.

www.PacktPub.com

Support files, eBooks, discount offers and more

You might want to visit www.PacktPub.com for support files and downloads related to your book.

Did you know that Packt offers eBook versions of every book published, with PDF and ePub files available? You can upgrade to the eBook version at www.PacktPub.com and as a print book customer, you are entitled to a discount on the eBook copy. Get in touch with us at service@packtpub.com for more details.

At www.PacktPub.com, you can also read a collection of free technical articles, sign up for a range of free newsletters and receive exclusive discounts and offers on Packt books and eBooks.

http://PacktLib.PacktPub.com

Do you need instant solutions to your IT questions? PacktLib is Packt's online digital book library. Here, you can access, read and search across Packt's entire library of books.

Why Subscribe?

- Fully searchable across every book published by Packt
- Copy and paste, print and bookmark content
- On demand and accessible via web browser

Free Access for Packt account holders

If you have an account with Packt at www.PacktPub.com, you can use this to access PacktLib today and view nine entirely free books. Simply use your login credentials for immediate access.

Table of Contents

Preface

The modern mobile device is an immensely powerful piece of equipment. Technology has advanced to such an extent that the current generation of cell phones and tablets are able to host games and applications that are both graphically and sonically impressive, and can even be compared to the titles available on home consoles and computers.

However, writing a game that will run on the plethora of available devices is difficult. There are a number of different platforms to support (for example, Android and iOS) and each platform can have devices that range considerably in terms of capabilities and processing power.

This is where the Marmalade SDK comes to the rescue! Marmalade is a cross-platform solution that allows us to write the source code for a video game once in C++ (a language that most video game developers will already be familiar with) and then deploy it to a number of different platforms, including iOS, Android, and BlackBerry PlayBook.

In this book we shall be learning how to use the Marmalade SDK to implement all the features demanded of a modern mobile video game.

What this book covers

Chapter 1, Getting Started with Marmalade: We start our journey into the world of the Marmalade SDK by learning how to install the SDK and build a simple "Hello World" application. We will then discover how to deploy and run the finished program to a number of different mobile platforms.

Chapter 2, Resource Management and 2D Graphics Rendering: Most video games are media-rich experiences packed full of superb graphics and stunning sound effects and music. In this chapter we will first look at how Marmalade makes it easy for us to load graphics and other resources into memory by using the built-in resource handling system. We will then discover how to render simple two-dimensional graphics on the screen.

Chapter 3, User Input: Our games will need to allow the user to provide input to control the action; so in this chapter we will be looking at how to respond to keypad, touch screen, and accelerometer inputs.

Chapter 4, 3D Graphics Rendering: Mobile devices now feature graphics processing units that enable them to easily render beautiful 3D graphics. After a brief overview of the basics of 3D rendering, we will then learn how to use Marmalade to render a spinning cube, first by generating the 3D model data in code and later by discovering how we can use a 3D modeling package to create and export a 3D model that can be loaded and drawn in a Marmalade application.

Chapter 5, Animating 3D Graphics: Building on the foundation of the previous chapter, we will then cover how to make our 3D graphics more interesting by making them animated.

Chapter 6, Implementing Fonts, User Interfaces, and Localization: Before a user can even play the first level of our game, they will first need to navigate its menu system. This chapter covers Marmalade's support for font rendering, the ways in which a user interface can be constructed, and finishes up with a look at how to localize a game so it can support multiple languages.

Chapter 7, Adding Sound and Video: Sound and music are both very important aspects of a video game and can make a game feel much more immersive and exciting, so learning how to add these elements to a game is the main aim of this chapter. Marmalade. also allows us to display full motion video clips, so we'll take a brief look at this too.

Chapter 8, Supporting a Wide Range of Devices: Different mobile devices have different capabilities and can also vary in terms of both main processor and graphics rendering power. In this chapter we look at ways in which Marmalade helps us to support as wide a range of devices as possible by allowing our game to adapt to the hardware it is running on. We'll also look at using Marmalade's built-in support for compressing and decompressing files to reduce the size of our game's installation package.

Chapter 9, Adding Social Media and Other Online Services: Since most devices are now permanently connected to the Internet, this chapter explores some of the options available to us for adding online features to our games, from integration with Facebook to displaying adverts as a possible revenue stream.

Chapter 10, Extending Marmalade with the Extensions Development Kit (EDK): While the Marmalade SDK does a great job of standardizing most of the normal requirements of writing a videogame, such as displaying graphics or playing sounds, there sometimes comes the requirement to access a device feature that Marmalade does not support directly. This chapter shows how we can get access to the underlying SDK on Windows, iOS, and Android in order to access device features that we would otherwise not be able to.

What you need for this book

You will need the following in order to make full use of the content of this book:

- An Internet-connected PC with at least 1GB RAM running Windows XP Service Pack 2, Vista, or Windows 7
- Microsoft Visual Studio 2005/2008/2010 (C++ Express editions are suitable for this)
- A licensed copy of the Marmalade SDK

The first chapter will explain how to install a suitable version of Microsoft Visual Studio, and how to obtain Marmalade and purchase a license for it.

For making iOS deployments, you will also need to have signed up to Apple's iOS Developer Program; further details on this are also provided in the first chapter.

For the chapters on 3D graphics, it will also be beneficial if you have one of the supported modeling packages available. Marmalade provides direct support for Autodesk 3DS Max and Autodesk Maya, but a cheaper alternative is the open source Blender package.

Who this book is for

This book is intended to show you how to use Marmalade to implement the features required by a video game. It is not intended as a guide on how to write a video game, although there is sample code provided for a simple game that grows alongside each chapter of the book.

Since the Marmalade SDK is implemented in C++, you are expected to already be able to code in this programming language.

You are also expected to have a working knowledge of the concepts involved in both 2D and 3D graphics rendering. Brief overviews are provided in the relevant chapters, but they are intended merely as a refresher and to introduce terminology used in later parts of the book.

Conventions

In this book, you will find a number of styles of text that distinguish between different kinds of information. Here are some examples of these styles, and an explanation of their meaning.

Code words in text are shown as follows: "The value used for `platform` is normally just the name of the operating system."

A block of code is set as follows:

```
{OS=IPHONE}
Message="Hello iOS!"
{}
{OS=QNX}
Message="Hello BlackBerry!"
{}
```

When we wish to draw your attention to a particular part of a code block, the relevant lines or items are set in bold:

```
{OS=IPHONE}
Message="Hello iOS!"
{}
{OS=QNX}
Message="Hello BlackBerry!"
{}
```

Any command-line input or output is written as follows:

```
C:\PlayBook> blackberry-debugtokenrequest -cskpass <password> -keystore
sigtool.p12 -storepass <password> -deviceId 0x<device id> debugtoken.bar
```

New terms and **important words** are shown in bold. Words that you see on the screen, in menus or dialog boxes for example, appear in the text like this: "Click on the **Deploy All** button and an install package will be made."

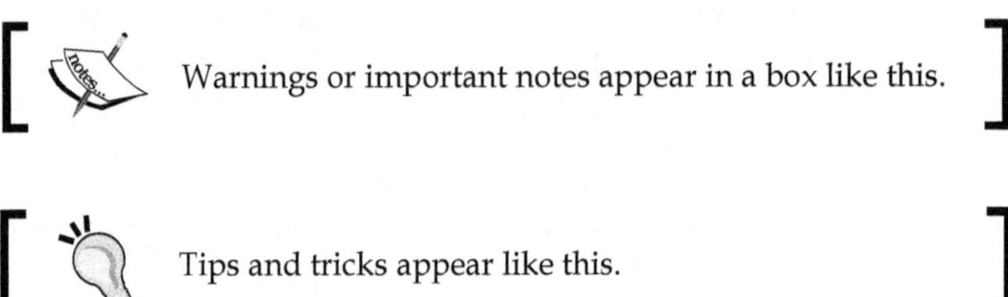

Warnings or important notes appear in a box like this.
Tips and tricks appear like this.

Reader feedback

Feedback from our readers is always welcome. Let us know what you think about this book—what you liked or may have disliked. Reader feedback is important for us to develop titles that you really get the most out of.

To send us general feedback, simply send an e-mail to `feedback@packtpub.com`, and mention the book title via the subject of your message.

If there is a topic that you have expertise in and you are interested in either writing or contributing to a book, see our author guide on `www.packtpub.com/authors`.

Customer support

Now that you are the proud owner of a Packt book, we have a number of things to help you to get the most from your purchase.

Downloading the example code

You can download the example code files for all Packt books you have purchased from your account at `http://www.PacktPub.com`. If you purchased this book elsewhere, you can visit `http://www.PacktPub.com/support` and register to have the files e-mailed directly to you.

Downloading the color images of this book

We also provide you a PDF file that has color images of the screenshots/diagrams used in this book. The color images will help you better understand the changes in the output. You can download this file from `http://www.packtpub.com/sites/default/files/downloads/3363OT_images.pdf`

Errata

Although we have taken every care to ensure the accuracy of our content, mistakes do happen. If you find a mistake in one of our books—maybe a mistake in the text or the code—we would be grateful if you would report this to us. By doing so, you can save other readers from frustration and help us improve subsequent versions of this book. If you find any errata, please report them by visiting `http://www.packtpub.com/support`, selecting your book, clicking on the **errata submission form** link, and entering the details of your errata. Once your errata are verified, your submission will be accepted and the errata will be uploaded on our website, or added to any list of existing errata, under the Errata section of that title. Any existing errata can be viewed by selecting your title from `http://www.packtpub.com/support`.

Piracy

Piracy of copyright material on the Internet is an ongoing problem across all media. At Packt, we take the protection of our copyright and licenses very seriously. If you come across any illegal copies of our works, in any form, on the Internet, please provide us with the location address or website name immediately so that we can pursue a remedy.

Please contact us at `copyright@packtpub.com` with a link to the suspected pirated material.

We appreciate your help in protecting our authors, and our ability to bring you valuable content.

Questions

You can contact us at `questions@packtpub.com` if you are having a problem with any aspect of the book, and we will do our best to address it.

1
Getting Started with Marmalade

In this chapter, we will first be learning how to get the Marmalade SDK set up for development. While Marmalade is available in both Windows and Mac versions, the Windows version is the most developed of the two and is what we shall be primarily covering in this book. By the end of this chapter, we will know how to do the following:

- Set up a Windows PC for development using the Marmalade SDK
- Create and build a "Hello World" project
- Deploy and run the "Hello World" project on several mobile platforms

So without further ado, let's get started!

Installing the Marmalade SDK

The following sections will show you how to get your PC set up for development using Marmalade, from installing a suitable development environment through to licensing, downloading, and installing your copy of Marmalade.

Installing a development environment

Before we can start coding, we will first need to install a version of Microsoft's Visual C++, which is the Windows development environment that Marmalade uses. If you don't already have a version installed, you can download a copy for free. At the time of writing, the Express 2012 version had just been released but the most recent, free version directly supported by Marmalade was still Visual C++ 2010 Express, which can be downloaded from the following URL:

`http://www.microsoft.com/visualstudio/en-us/products/2010-editions/visual-cpp-express`

Follow the instructions on this web page to download and install the product.

For the Apple Mac version of Marmalade, the supported development environment is Xcode, which is available as a free download from the Mac App Store. In this book, we will be assuming that the Windows version of Marmalade will be used, unless specifically stated otherwise.

Choosing your Marmalade license type

With a suitable development environment in place, we can now get on to downloading Marmalade itself. First, you need to head over to the Marmalade website using the following URL:

`http://www.madewithmarmalade.com`

At the top of the website are two buttons labeled **Buy** and **Free Trial**. Click on one of these (it doesn't matter which, as they both go to the same place!) and you'll see a page explaining the licensing options, which are also described in the following table:

License type	Description
Evaluation	This is free to use but is time limited (currently 45 days), and while you can deploy it to all supported platforms, you are not allowed to distribute the applications built with this version.
Community	This is the cheapest way of getting started with Marmalade, but you are limited to only being able to release it on iOS and Android, and your application will also feature a Marmalade splash screen on startup.
Indie	This version removes the limitations of the basic license, with no splash screen and the ability to target any supported platform.
Professional	This version adds dedicated support from Marmalade should you face any issues during development, and provides early access to the new versions of Marmalade.

When you have chosen the license level, you will first need to register with the Marmalade website by providing an e-mail address and password.

The e-mail address you register will be linked to your license and will be used to activate it later. Make sure you use a valid e-mail address when registering.

Once you are registered, you will be taken to a web page where you can choose the level of license you require. After confirming payment, you will be sent an e-mail that allows you to activate your license and download the Marmalade installer.

Downloading and installing Marmalade

Now that you have a valid license, head back to the Marmalade website using the same URL we used earlier.

1. If you are not already logged on to the website, do so using the **Login** link at the top-right corner of the web page.
2. Click on the **Download** button, and you will be taken to a page where you can download both the most recent and previous releases of the Marmalade installer. Click on the button for the version you require, to start downloading it. Once the download is complete, run the installer and follow the instructions. The installer will first ask you to accept the **End User License Agreement** by selecting a radio button, and will then ask for an installation location.
3. Next, enter the file location you want to install to. The default installation directory drops the minor revision number (so version 6.1.1 will be installed into a subdirectory called 6.1). You may want to add the minor revision number back in, to make it easier to have multiple versions of Marmalade installed at the same time.
4. Once the installer has finished copying the files to your hard drive, it will then display the Marmalade Configuration Utility, which is described in greater detail in the next section. Once the Configuration Utility has been closed, the installer will then offer you the option of launching some useful resources, such as the SDK documentation, before it exits.

It is possible to have more than one version of the Marmalade SDK installed at a time and switch between versions as you need, hence the advice regarding the installation directory. This becomes very useful when device-specific bugs are fixed in a new version of Marmalade, but you still need to support an older project that requires a different version of Marmalade.

Using the Marmalade Configuration Utility

The **Marmalade Configuration Utility** window appears at the end of the installation process, but it can also be launched from its shortcut icon:

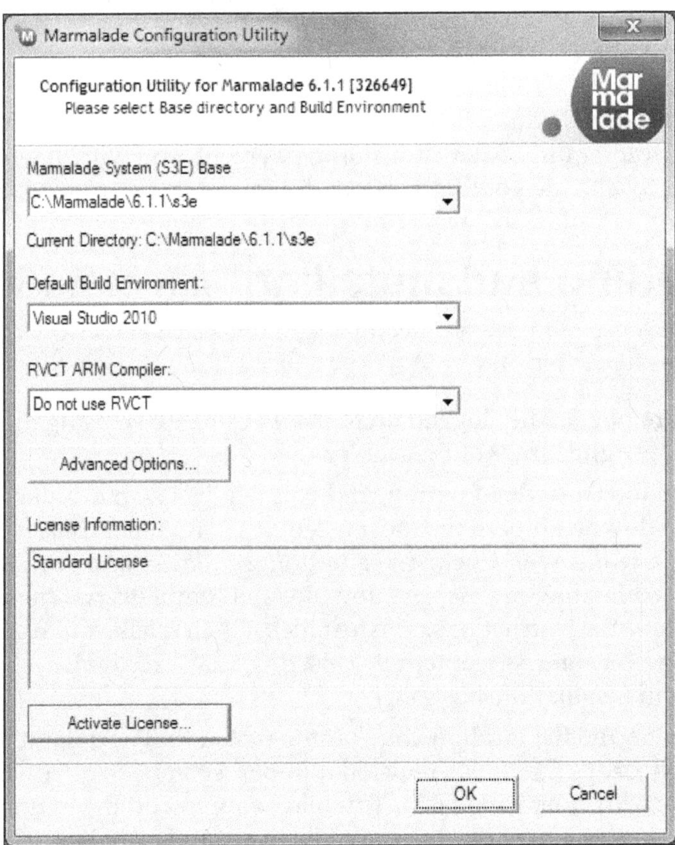

When launching the Marmalade Configuration Utility on Windows Vista or Windows 7, you should right-click on the icon and select the **Run as administrator** option, otherwise any changes that you make might not be applied.

The most important element is the **License Information** box. Below this is a button labeled **Activate License...** that allows you to activate your Marmalade installation. Follow these steps to get activated:

1. Click on the **Activate License...** button to display a dialog box that asks you to enter the e-mail address and password you used when obtaining your license.

2. The dialog box also has a drop-down box labeled **Machine ID (Ethernet MAC address)**, which you should make sure is set to the MAC address of an Ethernet port that will always be present on your computer. Normally you won't need to change this.
3. Click on the **OK** button to connect to the Marmalade licensing server. You will be asked to select the license you want to install. (Normally there will only be a single option available.) Do so and click on **OK**.
4. A summary of the **End User License Agreement** (**EULA**), appropriate to the type of license you are using, will be displayed, so click on **OK** to accept it. A reference to the full EULA is also provided in the dialog box.
5. You should now see a message confirming successful license installation. At this point Marmalade is ready to go!

Before we finish here though, let's look at the other available options. The first is labeled **Marmalade System (S3E) Base** and consists of a drop-down box that allows you to select the version of the Marmalade SDK you want to use, if you have more than one installed of course!

S3E is short for Segundo Embedded Execution Environment and this is the lowest layer of the Marmalade SDK. This naming convention was adopted by the SDK during its early days of development, and it remains to this day. As you will see later in this book, there are a great many APIs that are prefixed with this name.

The **Default Build Environment** lets you choose which development environment you wish to use, assuming you have more than one supported version of Visual C++ installed.

The drop-down box labeled **RVCT ARM Compiler** allows you to change the compiler that will be used when making a device build. (Most mobile devices contain an ARM CPU, so we must compile our code for this processor type.) Marmalade ships with the GCC compiler and uses this by default, but it can also make use of the RVCT C++ compiler from ARM, which is an additional purchase and can produce better optimized code. We normally do not need to change this setting and can leave it on the first option labeled **Do not use RVCT**.

The **Advanced Options...** button provides access to a more verbose project-building option and also some experimental parts of the SDK. You will not normally need to make any changes here.

Managing your Marmalade account and licenses

Before we get on to doing some actual coding, it is worth mentioning how you can manage your Marmalade license and account. If you head back to the Marmalade website and log on, you'll notice a link at the top-right corner of the site labeled **My Account**.

Hover your mouse pointer over this link, and a menu of options that allow you to change your account details and license usage will appear. The following sections provide further information on each of these options.

Viewing an overview of your account

The menu option called **Overview** takes you to a page where you can see your personal details along with a summary of the number of licenses and users you have set up under your account. From this screen, there are buttons that allow you to update your profile, modify registered user information, buy new licenses, and manage existing ones.

Updating your profile information

Clicking the **Profile** option in the **My Account** menu or clicking on the **Update Profile Information** button on the profile overview screen will display a page that allows you to alter information such as your name, contact information, address, and account login password. There is also a checkbox that allows you to sign up for e-mail news updates from Marmalade.

Managing your licenses

Clicking the **Licenses** link in the **My Account** menu or clicking on the button labeled **Manage** on the overview screen will take you to a page where you can upgrade the level of your license or buy further licenses for new team members.

The **Manage Licenses** section at the bottom of this page shows all the currently active licenses in your account, and also allows you to release a license that is currently in use so that it can be transferred to another computer.

Releasing a license is useful if you need to work on a different computer for some reason, or if you have a new development computer that you wish to transfer your license to. You can release a license as often as you like, but a single license can only be used on a single computer at a time.

Managing your user list

If you are working in a team then you will obviously need more than one Marmalade license, but you also need to manage who has access to those licenses. Clicking on the **Users** option in the **My Account** menu or clicking on the **Manage Users** button on the overview page allows you to do this.

This page shows a list of all the users assigned to your account, and also has an **Invite Users** section that allows you to add new users to your account. Enter their e-mail addresses in the boxes provided, and click the **Send invite** button to send them a mail telling them how to activate their own Marmalade account.

Creating a Marmalade project

With Marmalade installed, we can now get down to doing some coding, and what better place to start than with the classic example of a "Hello World" program.

Creating the "Hello World" project

To begin a new project, we must first create an MKB file, which is Marmalade's own project file format. We use MKB files to specify all the source files, libraries, and build options needed to build our project.

The MKB file is actually used to generate a Visual C++ project file, but whenever we want to add or remove a source file to our project, we must do so by editing the MKB file and regenerating the Visual C++ project file from it using Marmalade's make file builder script, which we'll be looking at in just a moment.

In addition to source files, the MKB file also allows you to list all the other datafiles and resource files that your application will need in order to run, as this information will be needed when it comes to deploying your application on different mobile platforms.

Marmalade does come with a small tool called the LaunchPad, which can be used to create a new project, but in the interest of learning how a Marmalade project is put together, we will go about creating everything from scratch instead.

Downloading the example code

You can download the example code files for all Packt books you have purchased from your account at `http://www.PacktPub.com`. If you purchased this book elsewhere, you can visit `http://www.PacktPub.com/support` and register to have the files e-mailed directly to you.

The MKB file for the "Hello World" project

Let's make a start on our "Hello World" project. Create a new directory to hold the project files, and then create a file called `Hello.mkb` in this directory and enter the following into it:

```
#
# Main MKB file for Hello project
#

# Modules used by this project
subprojects
{
  iwgx
}

# The files that make up the project (source, data etc.)
files
{
  [SourceCode]
  (source)

  Main.cpp
}

# Settings to configure the deployment process
deployments
{
  name="Hello"
  caption="Hello World"
}
```

The first section of `Hello.mkb` is the `subprojects` section, which lists all the additional code modules used by our application. In this instance, a code module is a library that can be added to our project either as a group of C or C++ source files or, alternatively, as pre-compiled, linkable object files accompanying header files. In the previous example, there is just one, `iwgx`, which is the Marmalade code module responsible for rendering graphics.

All the higher level modules within Marmalade are referenced in this manner, and you can also use this system to create your own modules to enable code re-use across projects. To create a subproject module we use an MKF file, which amounts to a little more than an MKB file with a different file extension! When we add an entry to the `subprojects` list, the Marmalade makefile builder script will search for a suitable MKF file that describes each subproject. We'll see detailed examples of how to do this later in the book.

The next section is labeled `files`, and this is where we list all the source code files for our project. It is possible to split your source files up into different directories. To make it easy, you simply put the directory name in brackets (`(source)` in our example) and then list all the source files in the directory below.

It is also possible to group the related files together into subsections, which we do using square brackets (`[SourceCode]` in our example). Any source files below this will be added to that section and will then appear in a separate folder in the Visual C++ Solution Explorer. There is no need for the directory and group names to match, and indeed you can have more than one directory in a group if you so wish.

Finally we have the `deployments` section, which is where various settings are made that control the process of deploying our application to different device types.

In our example we are making two settings. The `name` setting provides the filename of our final executable and is also used in file and directory names created for us by Marmalade, while `caption` sets the name that will appear under the application's icon when installed on a device.

Both the aforementioned settings are examples of general settings that apply across all device types, but there are also a great many other settings available, which are specific to particular platforms, such as iOS or Android. A full list of these can be found in the `Marmalade Documentation` help file that is installed as part of the Marmalade SDK, and we'll also be looking at this in *Chapter 8, Supporting a Wide Range of Devices*, of this book along with the additional sections of the MKB file that have not yet been shown for this example.

The use of whitespace in the MKB file is pretty much up to your own personal preference. Though most of the Marmalade examples tend to indent entries within blocks, tabs or spaces can also be used.

Comments can also be added using the hash (`#`) character. Everything after the hash character till the end of the current line is then considered a comment.

The source file for the "Hello World" project

We may now use the MKB file for our project but we still can't do anything with it yet, as we've told Marmalade that there is a source file called `Main.cpp`, which doesn't exist yet. If we were to try and use the MKB file to build the project, we would get an error reported about this missing file, so let's create it.

You will recall that we said that our `Main.cpp` file would reside in a directory called `source` in the MKB file, so first create this new subdirectory in the project directory. Now, create a file called `Main.cpp` in the source directory and enter the following into it:

```
//-----------------------------------------------------------
// Learning Mobile Game Development with Marmalade
// Chapter 1 - Hello
//-----------------------------------------------------------

// Marmalade SDK includes
#include "IwGx.h"
#include "s3eConfig.h"
#include "s3eDevice.h"

//-----------------------------------------------------------
// Main entry point
//-----------------------------------------------------------
int main()
{
  // Initialise Marmalade modules
  IwGxInit();

  // Set a default message, then check the ICF file to see if
  // a proper message has been specified
  char lMessage[S3E_CONFIG_STRING_MAX] = "Hello!";
  s3eConfigGetString("APP", "Message", lMessage);

  // Set screen clear colour to black
  IwGxSetColClear(0, 0, 0, 255);

  // Draw text at double default size
  IwGxPrintSetScale(2);

  // Loop until we receive a quit message
  while (!s3eDeviceCheckQuitRequest())
  {
    // Allow device to process its internal events
    s3eDeviceYield(0);

    // Clear the screen
    IwGxClear();
```

```
        // Display our message on screen
        IwGxPrintString(10, 10, lMessage);

        // Flush IwGx draw buffers to screen
        IwGxFlush();

        // Swap screen double buffer
        IwGxSwapBuffers();
    }

    // Terminate Marmalade modules
    IwGxTerminate();

    return 0;
}
```

The code should be fairly simple to follow, but here is a quick breakdown.

First we reference the include files to allow us to use the parts of Marmalade that are necessary for our application, and then we create our main entry point function `main`. This is equivalent to the `main()` function in a standard C or C++ program, except that it takes no parameters as Marmalade does not accept command-line parameters. It's quite hard to specify command-line parameters on mobile devices, so there really isn't any need!

The first thing our application needs to do is initialize Marmalade's rendering module with a call to `IwGxInit()`, which will initialize the screen and set up standard behavior such as double buffering of the display.

Next we allocate a character buffer that will contain the message that we will be displaying on screen. We initialize it to a default message to make sure that there is something to be shown, but we then use a call to the `s3eConfigGetString` function to see if another message has been specified in the application's configuration file, which will be explained in more detail shortly.

The following call to `IwGxSetColClear` sets the desired screen background color to black, and then the call to `IwGxPrintSetScale` tells Marmalade to display text using its built-in font (which is quite small in size) at double its default resolution.

We now enter our main processing loop that will continue until the `s3eDeviceCheckQuitRequest` function returns a true value, which will happen if the user quits the application or if the device sends a quit request to the application for any reason.

The first line of our main loop is a call to `s3eDeviceYield`. This is a very important function that must be called at regular intervals during our application, to allow the device's OS to perform important tasks such as handling events—user inputs, incoming phone calls, and so on. Under most circumstances, a single call to this function in the main loop is sufficient.

The value passed to `s3eDeviceYield` is the maximum time (in milliseconds) that our application will yield to the OS for. Normally this value is set to zero, which yields long enough for the device to process the events, but will return control to our application as soon as all the events have been processed.

Next, we call `IwGxClear` to clear the screen and then use `IwGxPrintString` to display a message on the screen. `IwGxFlush` causes the Marmalade engine to then process all our drawing requests to yield a final screen image that we can then display to the world using `IwGxSwapBuffers`.

Finally, outside the main loop, we call `IwGxTerminate` to shut down Marmalade's rendering engine, and finally return zero to indicate that our application was completed without any errors.

Building the "Hello World" project

Now that we have set up our project and written the necessary code, it is finally time to build it. To do this open a Windows Explorer window and navigate to the folder containing `Hello.mkb`, and then just double-click on the file. You might see a brief flash of a command-prompt window, but after a short delay, Visual C++ should automatically start up with our project.

The act of double-clicking the MKB file actually causes the Marmalade makefile builder script to be executed. This is actually a script written in the Python language, which takes the MKB file and outputs a Visual C++ solution file and other required elements. A file association is automatically set up when installing Marmalade, so you can either double-click the file, or alternatively use the command prompt to create your project by changing to the project directory and entering `Hello.mkb`.

Before we go on to compile and run the project though, let's take a quick look at what Marmalade has created for us.

If you look in the project directory, there should be two new directories, which are described in the following sections.

The build directory

One of the directories created by the MKB file will be named `build_hello_vcxx`, where the "xx" part is dependent on the version of Visual C++ you are using.

This directory is Marmalade's working directory and is where all the object files created during building are stored. It will also be the home to our deployment packages when it comes to making device builds.

A Visual C++ solution file created from the MKB file also lives in this directory, and while you can use these files to switch between projects, you should never add files or change project settings using the options in the Visual C++ IDE.

Always make project changes to the MKB file, then either close Visual C++ and double-click the MKB file to rebuild the solution, or alternatively perform a build inside Visual C++ to update the solution file with any changes. You should not make changes directly within the Visual C++ IDE as they will be lost the next time that the MKB file is used to recreate the project file.

The data directory

The MKB file will also generate a directory called `data`, and this is where Marmalade requires you to place any files that your application will need to load, such as images, 3D model data, sound files, and others. While you can create this directory and these files yourself, and it will not cause a problem, we might as well let the makefile builder do it for us!

If you take a look inside the `data` directory, you will see that the build process has also created two more files called `app.icf` and `app.config.txt`. These files are used to configure your application and are explained in the following sections.

The app.config.txt file

This file provides a list of all the application-specific settings that can be made in the `app.icf` file, along with a description of what each setting does and how it is used. There are two reasons for using this file:

1. Adding entries to this file keeps your project settings documented in a single place, so other coders can check this file to see what a particular setting does.
2. Any setting contained in the `app.icf` file that is not documented in the `app.config.txt` file will generate a runtime error message when you try to specify or access it in your program.

Additionally, the `app.config.txt` file also requires you to define a group name for your settings, which is specified by using square brackets.

If you look at the `s3eConfigGetString` function call in the "Hello World" project code, you will see an example of this. This call is trying to access a setting called `Message` from the group `APP`, so let's add this into the `app.config.txt` file now, to stop any asserts from firing when running our application. Edit the file and add the following lines to the bottom of it:

```
[APP]
Message        The message we want to display on screen
```

The app.icf file

The `app.icf` file is used to add the configuration settings to your application, and as already stated these must be either documented in your project's `app.config.txt` file or must alternatively be defined in a similar file within one of the subprojects used by your application.

Adding a configuration setting is simply a matter of adding the setting name followed by an equals sign and then the value you wish to use. You must also ensure that you add the setting to the correct group, using the same square bracket notation used in the `app.config.txt` file. Here's an example:

```
[APP]
Message="Hello World"
```

The settings made in the `app.icf` file can then be accessed in code using the `s3eConfigGetInt` and `s3eConfigGetString` functions.

The `app.icf` file also has another couple of tricks up its sleeve, as settings can also be made that are specific to a certain platform or even specific to an individual device. Here's how you achieve this:

- To limit the application to a particular platform add the line `{OS=platform}`, and any settings following this will only apply to that device platform. The value used for `platform` is normally just the name of the operating system, for example, `ANDROID`, `BADA`, or `WINDOWS`, although it is worth mentioning that you should use `IPHONE` to refer to iPhones, iPods, and iPads! If in doubt, you can use a call to `s3eDeviceGetString(S3E_DEVICE_OS)` to discover the value that you need to use for a particular operating system.

- To limit the application to a particular device or devices, add the line `{ID=platform id}`, and any following settings will only be applied when run on the specified device. The `platform` value is the same as that used previously, while the `id` is an identifier for a particular device. The format of the `id` value depends on the operating system, but you can discover what value to use for a particular device by calling `s3eDeviceGetString(S3E_DEVICE_ID)`. It is also possible to provide a comma-separated list of `id` values if you need the settings to apply to more than one device.

Note that both of these settings will continue to take effect until a new OS or ID value is specified. If you wish to return to applying all the settings globally, just add `{}` after your last OS- or ID-specific setting.

> It is good practice to ensure that your OS- or ID-specific sections always terminate with `{}`, as not doing so can lead to a major head-scratching session when you deploy to device and find that some setting you have just changed doesn't appear to be taking effect.

To illustrate the use of `{}` , let's add some settings to the "Hello World" project `app.icf` file. Open the file and add the following lines to the bottom of it:

```
[APP]
{OS=ANDROID}
Message="Hello Android!"
{}

{OS=BADA}
Message="Hello Bada!"
{}

{OS=IPHONE}
Message="Hello iOS!"
{}

{OS=QNX}
Message="Hello BlackBerry!"
{}

{OS=WINDOWS}
Message="Hello Windows!"
{}
```

You should be able to see from this that we have specified a different message string for each different platform type that we wish to support.

Building and running in the Windows simulator

Now it's time for us to see the "Hello World" project in action. It is just a simple matter of compiling the code in Visual C++ and running it.

To compile the code, simply select **Build** | **Build Solution** or press the *F7* key. Visual C++ will compile and link the `Main.cpp` file.

Now we can execute the program. Select **Debug** | **Start Debugging** or simply press *F5*. The Marmalade Windows Simulator will be launched, which will in turn load and execute our program. The following image shows what the "Hello World" project should look like when run in the Windows Simulator:

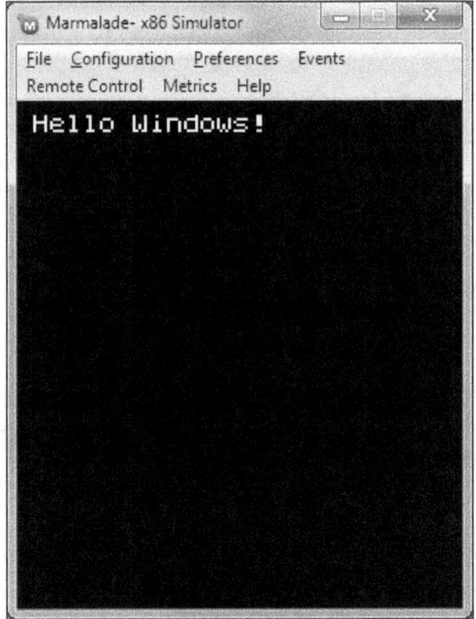

You will notice that the Windows Simulator contains a number of menu options. These allow you to make the Windows Simulator run in as close a manner to any device you choose as possible. The best way to see what you can change is to explore the menu options yourself, but here are a few of the more useful things you can do:

- Accelerometer: Testing accelerometer inputs on Windows would be impossible without **Configuration** | **Accelerometer...**. This brings up a dialog box that allows you to use the mouse to rotate a 3D image of a phone, to simulate the accelerometer input.

- OpenGL ES version: The Windows Simulator option **Configuration | GL...** allows you to emulate different versions of OpenGL ES, which makes it easy to see what your game may look like on different types of hardware. It also allows you to disable OpenGL ES support entirely, which will then force Marmalade to use its built-in software renderer.
- Screen resolution: Mobile devices have a wide range of supported screen resolutions, so **Configuration | Surface...** allows you to select any size for the screen that you desire.
- Emulation of device suspend and resume: It is easy to forget that the primary function of many devices is actually that of a telephone rather than of a gaming platform, which means your application could potentially be interrupted at any time by an incoming call. Marmalade takes care of most of the fiddly details of handling this automatically, but there may still be situations when you need to do something special under such circumstances. The Windows Simulator allows you to test whether your application responds correctly by way of **Events | Simulate Suspend** and **Events | Simulate Resume**.

Deploying a Marmalade project

We have now managed to create and run our first Marmalade application, but running it on Windows isn't our ultimate goal. The whole reason for the Marmalade SDK is to make it easy for us to develop our application once and then deploy it on a whole range of mobile device platforms.

Of course we might need to alter some of our assets, for example, because we are targeting a wide range of different screen resolutions and want our application to look its best at all times, the code itself should need no modification in order to run successfully.

To illustrate this, we will now take the "Hello World" project and get it running on a number of different mobile device platforms.

Compiling the "Hello World" project for the ARM CPU

Running our project in Windows meant we were compiling our code using the standard Visual C++ compiler and therefore generating Intel x86 code. However, it is a fact that the vast majority of mobile devices available today contain some version or other of the ARM processor, so the first thing we need to do is compile our code for ARM.

Luckily, Marmalade has made this incredibly easy for us. At the top of the Visual C++ window, you should see a drop-down box that defaults to a setting called **(x86) Debug**.

If you open the drop-down box, you will see several build types pre-configured for us, but the one we are interested in is the **GCC (ARM) Release** option. Select this and build the solution again (**Build | Build Solution** or press *F7*), and Visual C++ will use the GCC compiler to create an ARM version of our application.

Now we just need to get the code onto a device!

Deploying the "Hello World" project

Now that we have an ARM-compiled version of our code, we need to create an install package so we can test it on a real mobile device. To do this we need to use **Marmalade System Deployment Tool**. Follow these steps to go through the deployment process:

1. To launch the tool, make sure the **GCC (ARM) Release** build type is selected and the code has been compiled. Select **Debug | Start Debugging** (or press *F5*). Instead of running the code in the debugger (which would make little sense given that the Visual C++ debugger can only debug an Intel x86 executable), **Marmalade System Deployment Tool** will be launched instead.

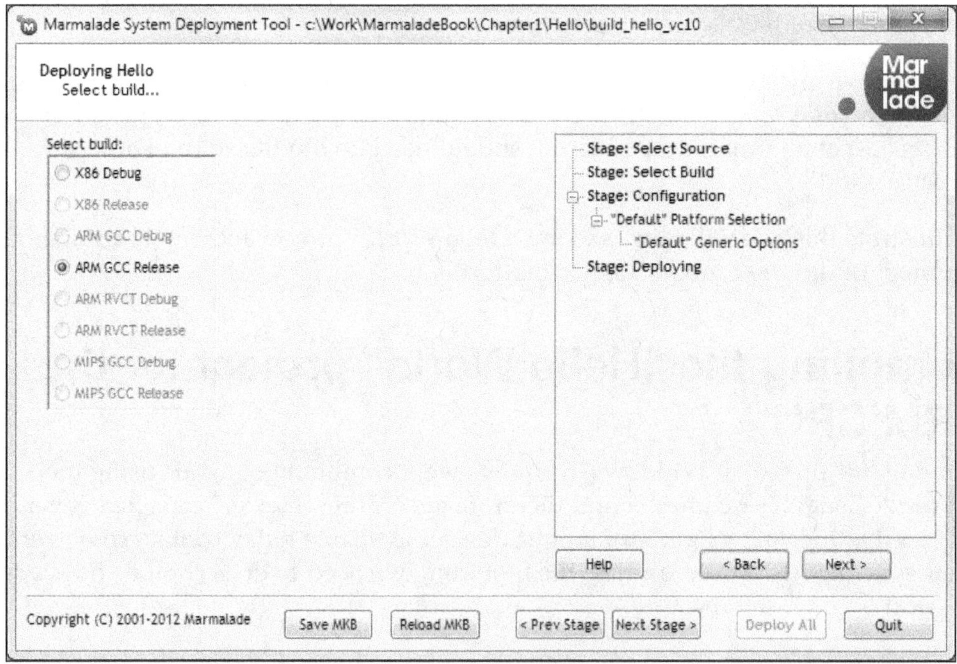

2. The program will first ask us to select the build type we wish to deploy and will have a number of radio buttons for the types available. Only those build types that are currently built will be selectable. In our case, we need to select the **ARM GCC Release** radio button and then click on the button labeled **Next Stage >**, to proceed to the next step.
3. The next page asks us to select a deployment configuration. We can specify the directory where we want our deployed package files to be created, and we also have a list of checkboxed items for the available deployment configurations that we can choose from. Marmalade allows us to create different configurations, which means we can deploy different resource packages to different devices. For now we won't concern ourselves with any of this, so just ensure that the **Default** setting is checked and then click on the **Next Stage >** button again.
4. We are now presented with a page listing all the device types that we can deploy to. Use the checkboxes to select which platforms to deploy to, and then click on **Next Stage >** once more to be taken to the final page.
5. At the top of this last page, we can see a brief description of the different deployment types we are about to make, with drop-down boxes for each, to specify whether we should just generate the necessary package files, ignore that build type completely, or optionally install and run the package as well.

The **Package and Install** options available in the Marmalade System Configuration Tool often rely on your system being set up with extra third-party software that isn't automatically installed as part of the Marmalade SDK. For this reason in this book, we will generally keep to using the **Package** option and install and run our deployment packages using manual methods.

6. Now that we have configured the type of deployment we want, just press the **Deploy All** button and Marmalade will make packages for all the different targets we selected.

The default location for the deployment packages is within the Marmalade `Build` directory. If you use Windows Explorer to look into this directory, you will see that a new directory called `deployments` has been created. In turn, this directory contains a folder called `default`, which comes from the deployment configuration we used.

It is possible to open Windows Explorer to the deployment folder by clicking on the **Explore...** button on the final page of the deployment utility.

The `default` directory contains subdirectories for each of our selected deployment platforms, and each of these will contain a `release` directory since it was the release build that we created the deployments from. Note that it is also possible to deploy a debug build, which can be useful when debugging. Go into the `release` folder and there you will find our freshly made deployment package.

All that is left to do now is to install and run it on a device.

Installing on Android devices

Let's start by looking at how to install an Android build.

Before being able to make an Android deployment with the deployment tool, there is a prerequisite that the Java JDK must be installed. You can download this from the following web page:

`http://www.oracle.com/technetwork/java/javase/downloads/index.html`

The Android package file for the "Hello World" project is called `Hello.apk`, and to install it we first need to copy it to an Android device. This can be done by copying the file to an SD card, or if your device has built-in storage memory, copying the file into that.

Before we can install our package, we first need to make sure that the Android device will allow us to do so. Go into your device's **Settings** program and select the **Applications** option. Here there is an **Unknown sources** option, which allows us to install our own packages. Make sure this option is ticked.

Next find the file manager application on your device. Different devices may have different names for this application, but it often has an icon with a picture of a filing cabinet folder on it. Navigate the directories to find the location where you copied the `Hello.apk` file, then tap on the file's entry in the list.

The screen will change to show a big list of things that the application is asking to access, along with the **Install** and **Cancel** buttons. Click on the **Install** button and the package will be installed. You can then choose the **Open** button to start your application, or the **Done** button if you don't want to run it now. Click on **Open** and we should then be greeted with our **Hello Android!** message.

By installing the Android SDK, it is also possible to speed up testing on the device by allowing the deployment tool to automatically package, install, and run the deployed package. Instructions on setting up the Android SDK so this will work can be found in *Chapter 10, Extending Marmalade with the Extensions Development Kit (EDK)* of this book.

Installing on iOS devices

If you've tried to create an iOS build of the "Hello World" project, you will have noticed that it currently fails to complete with a signing error. This is because you will need to provide Marmalade with some certificate files, which can only be generated by becoming a registered Apple developer.

Joining the **iOS Developer Program** currently costs $99 per year, and you can find more details about it at the following web page:

`https://developer.apple.com/programs/which-program/`

Once you've signed up, you'll be able to access the **iOS Dev Center** that will then allow you to create the required certificates. Normally you would require an Apple Mac to generate these certificates, but, handily, Marmalade provides a small utility called the **iPhone Sign Request Tool** that gets around this issue. Here is what you need to do:

1. Launch the Marmalade iPhone Sign Request Tool and fill in the fields as follows:
    1. **Certificate Request File**: Pick a location where this file will be saved. You will need to upload this to the iOS Dev Center shortly.
    2. **Key File**: Choose **developer_identity.key** from the drop-down box.
    3. **Common Name**: The name you used when registering with the iOS Developer Program.
    4. **Email Address**: The e-mail address you used when registering with the iOS Developer Program.
2. Now log on to the iOS Dev Center and click on the **iOS Provisioning Portal** link.
3. In the left-hand pane, click on the **Certificates** link. Click on the **Development** tab and then on the **Request Certificate** button to bring up a page of instructions. On this new page, press the **Choose File** button to upload the file you generated in step 1.
4. Click on the **Certificates** link in the left-hand pane again, and click on the link telling you to download the WWDR intermediate certificate. Save this file into the subdirectory `s3e\deploy\plugins\iphone\certificates` of your Marmalade SDK installation.
5. Refresh the **Certificates** page in your web browser until you see a **Download** button in the **Action** column. Click on this button and save the file into the directory from step 4, renaming it to `developer_identity.cer`.

6. In the left-hand pane, click on the **Devices** link to register your test devices with the iOS Dev Center by clicking on the **Add Devices** button and then entering a description for the device and its 40-character hex device ID. There is a link labeled **Finding the Device ID**, which tells you how to discover this value for a particular device.
7. Next click on the **App IDs** link and then on the **New App ID** button, and register a new App ID to use for your applications. You just need to enter a description (which can be anything you want) and a bundle identifier that is of the form `com.domainname.appname`. The `domainname` part can be pretty much anything you like (it doesn't necessarily have to relate to a real URL), while the `appname` part should either be the name of your application, or you can use an asterisk that then lets you use that App ID for any application.
8. Click on the **Provisioning** link and then click on the **New Profile** button. Enter a descriptive name for the profile and tick the checkbox next to your certificate name. Select the App ID you generated in step 7 from the drop-down box, and then tick all the checkboxes for any device that you want this provisioning profile to apply to.
9. Click on the **Provisioning** link again and keep refreshing this page until a **Download** button appears next to your new provisioning profile.

There is more information on this process in the Marmalade Documentation help file, and there are also **How To** tabs on most of the iOS Provisioning Portal pages explaining the processes involved, although most of these assume that you are using an Apple Mac to generate the various files.

With all those hurdles negotiated, we can then use **Marmalade System Deployment Tool** to generate a properly signed iOS install package, which will be named `Hello.ipa`. Now to get it installed onto a device!

It is possible to use iTunes to install your builds, but be warned that it tends to be a little bit of hit and miss as to whether it will work. Sometimes iTunes does not recognize that a new build is available and needs to be synched to the device. In my experience, a more reliable option is to use the **iPhone Configuration Utility**, which is a freely available Apple tool that can be downloaded from the following URL:

`http://support.apple.com/kb/DL1466`

First of all, you need to let the iPhone Configuration Utility know about your provisioning profile. Click on **Provisioning Profiles** in the far left pane and then click on the **Add** button in the toolbar. Navigate to the provisioning profile file you created in step 9 and click the **Open** button to add it to the list of available profiles. Alternatively, you can drag-and-drop the file into the list from Windows Explorer.

Next, click on the **Applications** entry in the left-hand panel and then click on the **Add** button. Find the `Hello.ipa` file in the deployment's `release` directory and click on **OK** to add it to the list of known applications, or again you can drag-and-drop the file from Windows Explorer into the list.

Now connect your iOS device to your computer using a USB cable. It should appear in the bottom of the left-hand pane after a short delay. Click on the name of your device and you should see five tabs appear in the main panel. Click the **Provisioning Profiles** tab and then click on the **Install** button next to your provisioning profile. Once done, this button will change to become a **Remove** button.

Our next step is to install the application itself, so click on the **Applications** tab to see a list of all applications that are either installed on the device already, or which can be installed. Find the entry labeled **Hello** and click on its **Install** button, which will change to read **Remove** once the application is installed.

After all that, we can finally run our application by finding its icon on the device and tapping on it. You should see the message **Hello iOS!**, which I admit may seem like something of an anticlimax after going through such a drawn-out process.

Installing on BlackBerry QNX devices

Marmalade can also deploy to BlackBerry QNX devices, the best known of which is the PlayBook tablet. In order to deploy to PlayBook, we need to do some setup work first. In the steps that follow, there are some commandlines that need to be entered. In these commandlines there are some arguments enclosed in angled brackets. After each set of commands, there is a table explaining what to replace the angle-bracketed arguments with.

1. First head over to the following URL to download the BlackBerry Native SDK, which contains some tools needed for signing builds:

   `https://developer.blackberry.com/native/download/`

2. Run the installer by right-clicking on its icon in Windows Explorer and selecting the **Run as Administrator** option to avoid permission problems when installing the SDK.
3. After the installation is complete, head over to the following URL to request some signing keys:

   `https://www.blackberry.com/SignedKeys/nfc-form.html`

4. We need to request a **Device Code Signing Key**, so select the first radio button to request this key type and then enter the personal information requested (your name, company name, and so on). You will also be asked to enter a PIN value consisting of eight alphanumeric characters. Ensure that you remember what you enter at this stage because you will need it to complete the registration of the keys.
5. Make sure the checkbox labeled **For BlackBerry PlayBook OS and BlackBerry 10 and Higher** is checked before ticking the license agreement checkbox and clicking on the **Submit** button.
6. The key files will be e-mailed to you, but there can be a delay of a few hours before they arrive. When you have the key files, create an empty folder on your PC and save them into it. We'll be assuming a folder called `C:\PlayBook` for the following steps.

7. Open a command-prompt window and change the current directory to be the one you created in step 6, and enter the following commands. The first command sets up the `PATH` environment variable so that the other commands can be executed. These commands register your key files with the BlackBerry signing servers and allow your PC to generate debug tokens:

```
C:\PlayBook> C:\bbndk-2.0.1\bbndk-env.bat

C:\PlayBook> blackberry-keytool -genkeypair -keystore sigtool.p12
-storepass <password> -dname "cn=<company name>" -alias author

C:\PlayBook> blackberry-signer -csksetup -cskpass <password>

C:\PlayBook> blackberry-signer -register -csjpin <pin> -cskpass
<password> <RDK file>

C:\PlayBook> blackberry-debugtokenrequest.bat -register -cskpass
<password> -csjpin <pin> <PBDT file>
```

Argument	Value to enter
`<company name>`	The company name you specified when requesting the key files in step 4.
`<password>`	A password of your choosing. Use the same value in each command.
`<PBDT file>`	The filename of the PBDT key file that was e-mailed to you in step 6. This filename should be of the form `client-PBDT-1234567.csj`, where the numeric part will be unique to your key file.
`<pin>`	The PIN value you specified when requesting the key files in step 4.
`<RDK file>`	The filename of the RDK key file that was e-mailed to you in step 6. This filename should be of the form `client-RDK-1234567.csj`, where the numeric part will be unique to your key file.

8. We can now generate a debug token file with the following commandline:

```
C:\PlayBook> blackberry-debugtokenrequest -cskpass <password>
-keystore sigtool.p12 -storepass <password> -deviceId 0x<device
id> debugtoken.bar
```

Argument	Value to enter
`<device id>`	The device ID of your BlackBerry device. As an example, you can find out this value on a PlayBook by going into the settings screen, clicking on the **About** item in the left-hand pane, and selecting the **Hardware** option in the drop-down box. The value labeled **PIN** is the device ID. When you specify this value in the commandline, make sure you prefix it with `0x`, as you would in C++ source code, to indicate a hexadecimal value.
`<password>`	This is the same password you used in the previous set of commands.

9. To install the debug token on to the device, first ensure that the device is connected via WiFi to the same network as your PC and then look at the device settings to determine the IP address assigned to it. This can be found by going to the **About** panel and selecting **Network** in the drop-down box.
10. Next we must enable development mode on the device, which can be done in the settings screen. Choose the **Security** panel and then click on the **Development Mode** entry on that screen. Set the toggle control next to **Use Development Mode** to **On**. You will be asked to enter a password for using development mode, so enter one into the edit boxes and click on the **Upload Debug Token** button.
11. Now we have to enter one more commandline to install the debug token on the device.

```
C:\PlayBook> blackberry-deploy -installDebugToken debugtoken.bar
-device <ip address> -password <device password>
```

Argument	Value to Enter
`<device password>`	The device password you set in step 10.
`<ip address>`	The IP address of the device as discovered in step 9.

12. Now we have to add the following two lines to the `deployments` sections of the MKB file, to allow us to make a valid deployment package:

```
playbook-author="<company name>"
playbook-authorid="<author id>"
```

Argument	Value to Enter
`<company name>`	The company name value you specified when requesting the key files in step 4.
`<author id>`	Finding the value for this is a little convoluted. First make a copy of the `debugtoken.bar` file generated in step 8, renaming it with the extension `.zip`. You can now use an archiving program to look inside this file. Enter the `META_INF` directory and extract the `MANIFEST.MF` file. Open this file in a text editor and look for an entry called `Package-Author-Id`. The string of characters following this entry is the value you need to put in the MKB file.

13. If Visual C++ is open, shut it down. Double-click the project MKB file to rebuild it with the changes made previously and start up Visual C++. Perform a **GCC (ARM) Release** build of the project and then press *F5* to launch the deployment tool.
14. In the deployment tool, change the settings to create a BlackBerry QNX deployment. When you reach the page labeled **Deployment Summary**, change the drop-down box to the **Package and Install** option before clicking the **Deploy All** button.
15. The final page in the deployment tool will be displayed, which for BlackBerry deployments has two additional fields. The first is labeled **Device hostname (or IP address)** for which you should supply the IP address of the device that you want to install the package to. The other field is labeled **Device password**, and you should enter the password you set up in step 10. Click on the **Deploy All** button again and the deployment will be made and installed to the device over WiFi.

The build should now be installed on the device, so breathe a sigh of relief and then look for its icon in the applications list. Touch the icon to run the program, and you should be greeted with the merry little message **Hello BlackBerry!**

Installing on Bada devices

Installing a build on to a Bada device is one example where using the **Package, Install and Run** option in **Marmalade System Deployment Tool** is actually a very good idea, as it is not possible to copy the package to a Bada device manually to install it.

To begin with, you need to install some device drivers for your Bada device so that the deployment tool can connect to it. Marmalade does ship with some drivers for Bada, but working out which of the three possible drivers matches your device can be hard to work out. For this reason, it is better to first install the Samsung Kies utility, which comes with a number of drivers and will install the correct one for you automatically. You can download Kies from the following web address:

`http://www.samsung.com/uk/support/usefulsoftware/KIES/JSP`

After installing Kies, connect your device to your computer with a USB cable and run the deployment tool. When you get to the platform selection page, you will see that there are four possible options for Bada. You must select the correct one for your device, which is based on both the version of Bada your device has and also its screen resolution.

Having chosen the correct Bada platform option, click on the **Next Stage >** button and then choose **Package, Install and Run** in the drop-down box at the top of the window. Click on the **Deploy All** button and an install package will be made, which is installed on to your device and executed, and you should then see the **Hello Bada!** message in all its monochrome glory!

Summary

The "Hello World" project may have been very simple, but it has served to demonstrate a surprising amount of the power of Marmalade. We now know how to create a new Marmalade project, build it, and create and apply our own application-specific settings to it.

We then ran our project in the Windows simulator and learned how to deploy and run it on a number of different mobile platforms.

Displaying some text on the screen isn't the most exciting thing in the world though, so in the next chapter we will learn how we can use the Marmalade SDK to draw simple 2D images on the screen. We'll also be finding out how Marmalade makes it easy for us to use bitmapped images.

2
Resource Management and 2D Graphics Rendering

Unless you happen to be writing an old school text adventure game (and perhaps even if you are), chances are that you will want more than just text in a simple debug font to appear on screen. Drawing nice-looking graphics demands that we should also be able to load those graphics into memory in order to display them; so in this chapter we will be looking at the following:

- Using Marmalade's resource manager to load games resources
- Extending the resource management system with our own custom classes
- The programming choices we have available to us for rendering purposes
- How to display a bitmapped image on screen using the IwGx API

The Marmalade ITX file format

An ITX file is Marmalade's built-in file format that can be used for loading all kinds of data into our program. The extension ITX is short for Ideaworks TeXt; Ideaworks being the original name of the company that created the SDK before they rebranded themselves as Marmalade.

ITX files have a simple text format and are used as the basis for resource loading. While it is possible to load resources ourselves, it is a bit like reinventing the wheel when Marmalade already provides a great deal of support for this truly tedious aspect of coding.

Marmalade has an API called IwUtil that contains a wide range of useful utility functions ranging from memory management and debugging through to the serialization of objects and random number generation. It also contains a class called `CIwTextParserITX`, which allows us to load and process an ITX file.

To add this functionality to our own project, we just need to add `iwutil` to the `subprojects` list of the MKB file and then add a call to `IwUtilInit` at the start of our program, and `IwUtilTerminate` in our shutdown code.

Before we can use the text parser, we will need to create an instance of it by using `new CIwTextParserITX`. This class is a singleton class, so we can create an instance of it at the start of our program and then reuse it as much as we like in the rest of our code (don't forget to release it on shutdown!). The instance can be accessed using the `IwGetTextParserITX` function, and we can then load and parse an ITX file using the following code:

```
IwGetTextParserITX()->ParseFile("myfile.itx");
```

An ITX file is little more than a big collection of class definitions. An instance of a class is defined by first putting the name of the class followed by a list of parameters for that instance enclosed in curly braces. Let's say we had a class called `WidgetClass` that was defined as follows (don't worry about the `CIwManaged` class and the `IW_MANAGED_DECLARE` macro for now, we'll come to these in a bit):

```
class WidgetClass : public CIwManaged
{
public:
  IW_MANAGED_DECLARE(WidgetClass)
  WidgetClass();
private:
  uint8          mColor[3];
  int32          mSize;
  bool           mSparkly;
  WidgetClass*   mpNextWidget;
  uint32         mNextWidgetHash;
};
```

Here is an example of how we might instantiate this class from within an ITX file:

```
WidgetClass
{
  name     "red_widget"
  color    { 255 0 0 }
  size     10
  sparkly  true
}

WidgetClass
{
  name     "green_widget"
  color    { 0 255 0 }
```

```
    size     20
    sparkly  false
    next     "red_widget"
}
```

This sample declares two instances of `WidgetClass`, and initializes those instances with a name, color value, size, and a flag indicating whether the widget in question is sparkly or not. Each of these settings is called an attribute, and they can be of any type we desire—string, integer, floating point, boolean, or an array of values (the `color` attribute provides an example of this).

Hopefully, you are looking at this and thinking how exactly this format can be magically loaded and instanced by the Marmalade text parser, since it obviously knows nothing about `WidgetClass`. A good question! The answer is that any class that you wish to parse from an ITX file must first be derived from the Marmalade class `CIwManaged`.

The CIwManaged class

The `CIwManaged` class is the base class used throughout the Marmalade SDK and by our own classes whenever we want to be able to create instances of them by loading from a file.

The class provides some virtual methods that we can override to allow the parser to recognize our own custom classes, and also to serialize them into a binary format and resolve any references to other classes or resources. It also provides the coding glue required to instantiate copies of our class at runtime.

This facility is really useful for us as it allows us to make our code more data-driven. Say we have a class that describes an item that the player can collect. We might have lots of different item types in our game, so rather than creating instances of them all in the source code, which only a programmer can then change, we could instead instantiate them from an ITX file, which a game designer with no coding knowledge can then edit.

Instantiating a class with the class factory

The first thing `CIwTextParserITX` will encounter in the ITX file is the class name, which it will use to create a brand new instance of our class. It achieves this by using the class factory, which is another part of the IwUtil API.

A class factory is a programming pattern that allows us to generate new instances of objects at runtime by asking another class (the so-called factory) to create a relevant class instance for us.

The Marmalade class factory system allows us to add our own classes to those provided by the SDK itself by registering a unique hash value identifying the class and a method that creates a new instance of it.

The hash value is normally derived by converting the name of the class into a number by passing its name as a string to the IwUtil API's function `IwHashString`. While this isn't guaranteed to produce a unique number, it is usually good enough for our purposes and clashes with hash values from other class names are rare.

To add our own custom `CIwManaged` derived class to the class factory, we just need to do the following (if you want to see a full example of this and indeed the things we'll be covering in the next few sections, take a look at the source code for the ITX project that accompanies this chapter):

1. Add the `IW_MANAGED_DECLARE(CustomClassName)` macro to the public section of the class. This declares a method called `GetClassName`, which will return the name of the class as a string, and also adds a couple of type definitions to allow the class to be used more easily with the `CIwArray` class, which is yet another piece of functionality provided by IwUtil.
2. Add the macro `IW_MANAGED_IMPLEMENT_FACTORY(CustomClassName)` to the source file for the class. This macro implements the `GetClassName` method and also creates the necessary class factory function that will be used to create a new instance of our class.
3. Finally, we have to register our class with the class factory itself by adding the macro `IW_CLASS_REGISTER(CustomClassName)` somewhere in our initialization code.

With this done, we can now include our class in an ITX file. The `CIwTextParserITX` class can now create a brand new instance of it with a call to the class factory function `IwClassFactoryCreate("CustomClassName")`.

Parsing a class

With the creation of a new instance of our class taken care of, the next step is to allow `CIwTextParserITX` to configure that instance by modifying its members. This is done with the following `CIwManaged` class' virtual methods:

Method	Description
`ParseOpen`	This method gets called when the text parser reaches the open curly brace of the class definition. It can be used to initialize anything that might be needed internally during the process of parsing an object. It is important that you do not use this method to initialize all the member variables of your class to some default values. The class constructor is a far better place to do this, as it is guaranteed to be called however the instance ends up being created.
`ParseAttribute`	This method is called whenever an attribute is encountered in the object definition. The attribute is passed as a standard C-style string to this method, which can then process it as needed. The text parser can be used within this method to extract any data elements in a variety of different ways, including strings, integers, and Boolean values.
`ParseClose`	This method is called when the closing curly brace of the class definition is encountered.

`ParseCloseChild`	It is possible to embed class definitions inside other class definitions in an ITX file. If a class does not implement the `ParseClose` method then when its closing curly brace is encountered, the `ParseCloseChild` method will be called on the parent class with a pointer to the child class.
	
	In this case parent and child do not refer to class inheritance hierarchies, but rather to how the classes have been defined in the ITX file. For example:
	
	`ParentClass`
	`{`
	    `name "parent"`
	
	    `ChildClass`
	    `{`
	        `name "child"`
	    `}`
	`}`

When overriding any of these methods, you should normally call the version of the method from the superclass, be that `CIwManaged` or some other class derived from it. For example, the `name` attribute is parsed by `CIwManaged::ParseAttribute`, which not only reads the name for the class but also generates a hash value of the name. The hash value is very important when it comes to serializing and resolving class instances later.

The following diagram shows an example of how an instance of `WidgetClass` defined earlier in this chapter would be processed by the ITX parser:

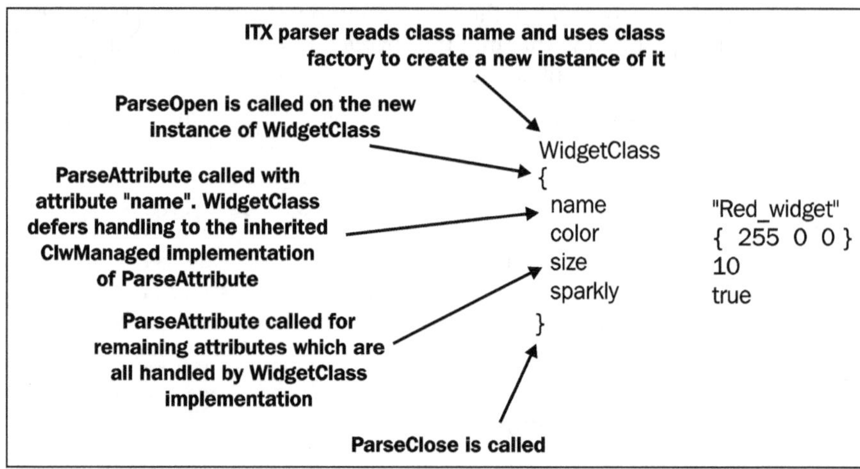

For `WidgetClass` the only method we would definitely need to implement is the `ParseAttribute` method, which might look like the following code:

```
bool WidgetClass::ParseAttribute(CIwTextParserITX* apParser,
const char* apAttribute)
{
  if (!stricmp(apAttribute, "color"))
  {
    apParser->ReadUInt8Array(mColor, 3);
  }
else if (!stricmp(apAttribute, "size"))
  {
    apParser->ReadInt32(&mSize);
  }
else if (!stricmp(apAttribute, "sparkly"))
  {
    apParser->ReadBool(&mSparkly);
  }
else if (!stricmp(apAttribute, "next"))
  {
  CIwStringL lNextWidget;
  apParser->ReadString(lNextWidget);
  mNextWidgetHash = IwHashString(lNextWidget.c_str());
  }
```

```
else
    return CIwManaged::ParseAttribute(apParser, apAttribute);
return true;
}
```

Serializing a class

Serializing an object instance is the process of converting the current state of the object into (or from) a binary format.

While not strictly necessary when parsing an ITX file, it is still very much a useful part of the functionality provided by `CIwManaged`, and forms an integral part of the resource handling process that we will be seeing later in this chapter.

The serialization functionality can also be useful when it comes to saving out things such as current game progress or high score tables, though of course we can still use normal file handling operations to do this if we prefer.

Serialization of our class is handled by overriding the virtual method `Serialise`. This method can then use the serialization functions provided by IwUtil, which all start with the prefix `IwSerialise`.

For example, `IwSerialiseInt32` will serialize an `int32` value. All these functions make use of the Marmalade type definitions for the basic variable types, as these are far more explicit when it comes to the memory footprint of a variable. Take a look at the header files `IwSerialise.h` and `s3eTypes.h` in the Marmalade SDK installation for more information on the `IwSerialise` functions and the variable types respectively.

We must make sure to call our superclass implementation of `Serialise` as well to ensure every part of the object is serialized. Normally this would be the first thing we do in our implementation of `Serialise`, but it does not have to be so as long as it is called at some point.

We can serialize our objects to a file of our choosing by calling `IwSerialiseOpen`. This allows us to specify the filename and a Boolean flag that indicates whether we are reading or writing the file. We then call the `Serialise` method of each object we want to serialize, and finally call `IwSerialiseClose` to finish the process.

One nice feature of the `IwSerialise` functions is that, in most cases, we do not have to worry about whether the `Serialise` method has been called to write data to a file or if it has been called to read data from a file. We just call the function and it will read or write the value, as appropriate.

There are times that we will care about reading or writing values to a file; for example, if we need to allocate a block of memory to read some values into. The functions `IwSerialiseIsReading` and `IwSerialiseIsWriting` allow us to make the appropriate decisions.

The following code snippet illustrates how the serialization functions are used by showing what the `Serialise` method might look like for `WidgetClass`:

```
void WidgetClass::Serialise()
{
  CIwManaged::Serialise();
  IwSerialiseUInt8(mColor[0], 3);
  IwSerialiseInt32(mSize);
  IwSerialiseBool(mSparkly);
}
```

Resolving a class

The act of resolving a class instance is to fix up any parts of our class that are not initialized correctly when parsing the object from an ITX file or having created it from the serialization process.

When might this happen? The most frequent reason for needing to resolve our instances is when the instance requires a pointer to another class that may not exist when it is first created.

This is best illustrated by an example. Let's say our class contains a pointer to another instance of our class in order to implement a linked list. When we read in our instances, it is possible we might refer to an instance that has not yet been created and so we can't create the linked list yet.

To solve this problem we instead store a value in our data that will allow us to look up the required instance later. This might be a string representing the name of the instance or perhaps a unique identifier number.

Once all the instances have been read in, we can then call the `CIwManaged` class' virtual method `Resolve` on each instance in turn and obtain the required pointer to the correct instance using whatever methodology we see fit. For example, we might maintain a list of all instances of our class that gets added to whenever a new instance is created. We can then use this list to look up the required instance.

It is not always necessary to create our own implementation of `Resolve`, but if we do we must be sure to call the inherited version of the method from our superclass.

We'll take one more look at `WidgetClass` to wrap this all up. You may remember that it had a member `mpNextWidget` that points to another instance of `WidgetClass`. In the ITX file, we supplied a value for this member by specifying the name of another `WidgetClass` instance. In the `ParseAttribute` method, we read in this name and calculated a hash value from it which was stored in the `mNextWidgetHash` member variable.

We can implement the `Resolve` method and look up a pointer to the correct instance but we'll also need to maintain a list of all `WidgetClass` instances in order to do this. One way of doing this is to implement `ParseClose` and store each instance in a list. The following code shows how this could be achieved:

```
void WidgetClass::ParseClose(CIwTextParserITX* apParser)
{
  // Add this instance to a list.  gpWidgetList is an instance of a
  // Marmalade class called CIwManagedList which is very useful
  // for storing lists of objects derived from CIwManaged!
  gpWidgetList->Add(this);
}

void WidgetClass::Resolve()
{
  // Look up an instance of WidgetClass with the given hash
  if (mNextWidgetHash)
  {
    mpNextWidget = static_cast<WidgetClass*>
                    (gpWidgetList->GetObjHashed(mNextWidgetHash));
  }
}
```

The Marmalade resource manager

Most bitmap art packages are capable of saving images in a number of different file formats, but we really need access to the actual bitmap data itself, which may well be stored in a compressed format with any particular file format.

Marmalade makes the task of loading images simple by way of the IwResManager API. This API relies upon the ITX file format we have just discussed, and is not just limited to loading images. It can also be used to load in data such as 3D models and animations, and we can also use it to keep track of our own custom classes.

Earlier we had to create our own instance of `CIwTextParserITX` in order to parse an ITX file. IwResManager creates its own instance of `CIwTextParserITX` when it needs it, so we don't need to worry about creating our own instance.

Adding IwResManager to a project

To make the IwResManager API available to a project, all that needs to be done is to add `iwresmanager` to the subprojects list in the MKB file.

To initialize the API just add a call to `IwResManagerInit`, which will create a singleton instance of the Marmalade resource manager class `CIwResManager`. This class is used to load, free, and of course access our projects resources, whatever they may be. The singleton can be accessed using the function `IwGetResManager`.

When our project terminates we should call `IwResManagerTerminate`, which will destroy the resource manager singleton and any resources it may still have loaded in memory.

Specifying resources with a GROUP file

Marmalade allows us to collect different types of resources together into a resource group. We are free to mix images, sounds, 3D models, and any other data types we might need to use.

Why would we want to group resources together? Well, let's say you are writing a game with a number of different levels. Each level will have some common resources (for example, the player graphics) but might have unique elements specific to that level, so it would make sense to only have these resources in memory when the level is being played. You could therefore create one resource group for the player graphics, and individual ones for each level.

In order to load a resource group into our program, we first need to create a GROUP file. A GROUP file is actually an ITX file with the extension `.group` that allows us to list all the resources we want to gather together.

Let's start by taking a look at a sample GROUP file:

```
CIwResGroup
{
  name  "game_resources"

  "./images/titlescreen.png"
```

```
    "./sounds/sounds.group"
    "./levels/levels.itx"
}
```

The first line of this file is defining a new `CIwResGroup` class instance, which is the class used to implement a resource group, and the first thing we do inside the curly braces of the definition is to give the resource group a name. This name will be used later to allow us to access the resource group.

A GROUP file should only contain a single `CIwResGroup` definition. The Marmalade SDK documentation states that behavior is undefined should you specify more than one. In practice this is not a problem since the GROUP file is the lowest level block of resources that can be loaded at a time, so there would be no real benefit in specifying more than one `CIwResGroup` anyway.

The remaining lines of the example definition specify the resources we want to include in this group, and most often these will just be filenames for the resources in question. As we progress through this book we will see some extra functionality that the group file provides us with, but for now we'll just concentrate on the main task of loading resources.

In the example, we are specifying three files that we want to be part of this resource group. The first is a bitmapped image saved in the PNG file format. The next resource is a reference to another GROUP file. When this GROUP file is loaded, the `sounds.group` file will be loaded into memory as well.

The final file we are including is `levels.itx`, which is a standard ITX file and would be used to create instances of our own classes.

Loading groups and accessing resources

To load a GROUP file in our program, we do the following:

```
CIwResGroup* pResGroup;
pResGroup = IwGetResManager()->LoadGroup("groupfile.group");
```

This will look in the project's `data` directory for the specified GROUP file, and then load it into memory. The `LoadGroup` method returns a pointer to the `CIwResGroup` instance that was created, which we can store away somewhere so we can release the resource group and all its resources later.

With the resource group in memory, we can access the individual resources in one of two ways. The first way is to ask the `CIwResGroup` instance itself to locate a particular resource for us. Here's how we do this:

```
CIwResource* pResource;
pResource = pResGroup->GetResNamed(name, type, flags);
```

In the call to `GetResNamed`, the `name` parameter is a null terminated string containing the name of the resource we want to access. This is the value that is specified using the `name` attribute in an ITX file. If no `name` value is explicitly specified, the name of the first resource encountered in the GROUP file (minus any extension) will be used for the name. In the example GROUP file in the previous section this name would become `titlescreen`, since the first resource in the file is the `titlescreen.png` file.

The `type` parameter indicates the class of the resource that we are trying to locate. This parameter is also a string and is simply the class name of the resource type.

Finally there is the `flags` parameter that we can normally leave out entirely as it defaults to a value of zero. There are various flags we can use that alter the way the search for our resource is performed. For example, `IW_RES_PERMIT_NULL_F` will prevent an assert from being fired if the required resource could not be found. Check the Marmalade documentation for more information on these flags, though in most cases the default value of zero is what we need to use.

If the resource can't be found, the `GetResNamed` call will return `NULL`, otherwise it returns our resource as a pointer to a `CIwResource` instance, which we can then cast to the required class type.

The second way of accessing a resource is to ask the resource manager to find it by searching through all the currently loaded groups. This can be very useful since it means we don't have to know exactly which resource group to search in. Obviously a full search of all currently loaded resource groups will be slower, but it means we don't have to keep track of every resource group we load. After all, that's what the resource manager is for! The call required to search all loaded groups for a particular resource is as follows:

```
CIwResource* pResource;
pResource = IwGetResManager()->GetResNamed(name, type, flags);
```

The parameters are exactly the same as calling the `CIwResGroup::GetResNamed` method.

Finally, we can remove a resource group and everything it contains from memory by making the following call:

```
IwGetResManager()->DestroyGroup(pResGroup);
```

We should destroy a group whenever we no longer need those resources in memory (for example, a group containing resources for a particular level of a game only needs to be in memory when playing that level). It isn't strictly necessary to destroy all groups on shutdown however, as Marmalade will ensure everything that has been allocated will be freed whenever an application is terminated.

The CIwResource class

We've already seen how the `CIwManaged` class can be used to allow us to easily create instances of our own classes by loading them out of a file. This functionality is improved further by the `CIwResource` class, which allows us to include our own classes into a resource group.

In the GROUP file example shown in the previous section, we specified the `levels.itx` file that may contain definitions of our own classes. If our custom classes used `CIwResource` as their base class (or of course another class that was in turn derived from `CIwResource`) then all of our resources can be added to the resource group, saving us the bother of keeping track of them ourselves.

GROUP file serialization

It is great that we can load different types of resources so easily, but ultimately we probably do not want to deploy our application with a collection of easily recognized or editable files. There are several reasons for this:

- Loading speed: Parsing a text file and converting it into a class is a slower operation than just loading in a ready parsed serialized version. It is also possible that we might need to do some sort of conversion on the original data to make it usable in the game, so if we can avoid doing this we will improve the loading time of our game.
- To prevent hacking: If we ship a collection of text files and common file formats such as PNG files, we make it very easy for someone to hack and modify our game or make unauthorized use of the game's resources.
- Smaller code size: If we are loading resource data that is already in a form that our game code can use directly, there is no need to include any code for converting the original data format into our own internal one. This makes the code size smaller and also helps guard against hackers a little more.
- Deployment size: Text files are often much larger than their serialized binary equivalents, so shipping a binary version could reduce the size of our install package.

Marmalade tackles all these issues by automatically converting every GROUP file we load into its binary equivalent using the serialization functionality provided by the `CIwManaged` class.

After the resource group has been fully loaded, the resource manager will call the `Serialise` method on every instance of every resource contained within the group, creating a file with `.bin` added to the original GROUP's filename. For example, the resources in a file called `images.group` would be serialized to a file called `images.group.bin`.

Once the serialized version of the GROUP file has been created, the resource manager destroys the resource group and then recreates it from the newly serialized version. This step is present as it makes catching problems, such as forgetting to serialize a member variable of a class, easier to spot.

There is a useful ICF setting that controls the resource building process. Simply add the following to the ICF file (refer back to *Chapter 1, Getting Started with Marmalade,* for a discussion of what an ICF file is):

```
[RESMANAGER]
ResBuild=1
```

When set to `1`, the `ResBuild` setting will ensure that the resource manager always loads the GROUP file and serializes it. By setting it to `0`, the GROUP file parsing stage is skipped and instead any existing serialized version of the GROUP file will be loaded directly. This can be very useful during development, to both increase application startup time when no resources have been added or changed, and also to match more closely the loading process on the device.

If you've made changes to the resources for your game but they aren't appearing when you run it, the `ResBuild` flag is always a good first port of call. It's amazing how easy it is to make a resource change and forget that you've disabled resource building!

Resource handlers

There is one final part of the IwResManager API that is worth mentioning, and this is the concept of **resource handlers**.

You may have wondered how the resource manager is able to load and process files of different types. It's great that we can just list a bunch of filenames in a GROUP file, but how exactly does a PNG format image file end up being loaded into a form that we can use for rendering? Resource handlers, of course!

A resource handler is a subclass of `CIwResHandler` that is used to load and process resources of a particular type, identified by one or more filename extensions.

When the text parser comes across a filename in the GROUP file, it looks at the file extension and then checks to see if a resource handler has been registered for that extension. If no suitable handler is found an error will be raised, otherwise the filename is passed to the relevant resource handler class that will then do whatever needs to be done to the file to make it usable in our code.

The entire resource manager system in Marmalade relies on resource handlers in order to work. GROUP files, ITX files, and bitmapped image files are all processed by classes derived from `CIwResHandler`, and we can create our own custom resource handlers should we want to make use of some other file type not supported by the core Marmalade SDK.

We will be coming back to the subject of resource handlers when we talk about implementing sound in *Chapter 7, Adding Sound and Video* of this book, since Marmalade does not have support for any sound file formats as part of the core SDK.

Graphics APIs provided by the Marmalade SDK

Now that we are familiar with resource management, we can get on to the more interesting task of showing a picture on the display.

Marmalade spoils us by providing several different ways in which we can draw graphics on the screen. The following sections provide an overview of the different options available to us.

The s3eSurface API

The lowest level of display access is the `s3eSurface` API. This provides access to the display by using a memory pointer that you can then use to directly read or alter pixels.

You can discover the width and height of the display in pixels and also the pitch, which is the number of bytes that you need to skip through memory to get to the next row of the display image.

The pitch is affected by the pixel format of the display (16-, 24-, or 32-bit displays are all possible) and often extra padding bytes are also added to allow each row to begin on a word-aligned memory address, which can improve display memory access times.

In practice this API is very rarely used, partly because it provides no support for drawing bitmapped images or lines, but mostly because it is incredibly slow on many modern devices due to the display being drawn by a **Graphics Processing Unit (GPU)**, which may place restrictions on how and when this memory can be accessed by the CPU.

We will not be using this API anywhere in this book, but if you wish to use it there is nothing you have to add to your project as it is always available in any Marmalade project.

The IwGL API and OpenGL ES

As mentioned above, most mobile devices available today contain a GPU that is used to speed up drawing operations and free the CPU for other tasks, such as updating the current state of a game. The standard API that has been adopted across most mobile platforms is OpenGL ES.

The OpenGL ES API is a derivative of the OpenGL API, which has been used on many desktop systems for many years. OpenGL ES was conceived as a cut-down version of OpenGL designed for embedded systems (hence the ES part of the name!).

There are two main versions of the OpenGL ES. The 1.x standard is intended for devices that have fixed, function rendering pipelines, which means that while control is provided in how a 3D point is transformed to 2D coordinates, and how a polygon and its associated textures (if any) are rasterized to the screen, you are completely limited to the options provided by the hardware.

The 2.x standard of OpenGL ES is intended for GPU hardware where the act of both transforming 3D points and rasterizing the resultant polygons can be programmed by way of **shaders**. A shader is a short program that can be applied very quickly to either transform 3D points (a vertex shader) or work out the required color of a rendered pixel (a pixel or fragment shader).

In most cases a device supporting OpenGL ES 2.x will also support OpenGL ES 1.x, but the two cannot be mixed. When initializing OpenGL, you request one or the other of these interfaces to be created as the OpenGL context. The context is really nothing more than a big structure which stores all the information that OpenGL needs in order to operate, such as the current frame buffer, pixel blending mode, and available shaders.

So what exactly is the IwGL API? Put simply, it is a wrapper for OpenGL ES that allows us to make normal OpenGL ES function calls directly, but it also provides some other very useful functionality:

- IwGL simplifies the process of initializing OpenGL ES to a single function call—`IwGLInit`. This function call will initialize the frame buffer and set up the OpenGL context so that it is ready and raring to go, with settings that should be optimal for the type of hardware available. Fine control over initialization is also provided to allow display and depth buffer formats to be chosen using settings made in the application's ICF file.
- It provides context state caching functions, such as keeping a copy of all textures currently uploaded to OpenGL ES. In the event of your application being suspended (for example, by an incoming call) all its textures and other resources could be lost, and normally it would be your responsibility to reload everything you need. IwGL automatically takes care of all this for us.
- Any OpenGL ES extension functions (extra functionality that a particular GPU may provide over and above the required base level of OpenGL ES) become mapped to functions that can be called directly and will not cause an error if that function is not actually supported. Normally you would need to specifically check if an extension exists before trying to call it.
- It also provides a Virtual Resolution system that makes it easy to take existing code that was hardcoded to a particular resolution or screen orientation and make it run at a different resolution or orientation by resizing or rotating the rendered image.

IwGL is an invaluable part of the Marmalade SDK when you are porting existing code written using OpenGL ES, as it allows you to take advantage of Marmalade's ability to deploy to multiple platforms without having to completely recode the entire project.

However, we won't be using IwGL in this book either. While there is nothing to stop us from using this API to develop a new project, it does mean we are limited to targeting only devices that feature GPUs (or support a software emulated version of OpenGL), and we still need to take care of things like loading textures ourselves.

You can use the IwGL API in your own project by adding `iwgl` to the `subprojects` section of the MKB file.

The Iw2D API

Given that this is a chapter about 2D graphics rendering, the Iw2D API must surely be the way to go, right?

Well, yes and no. It certainly has a lot going for it, like the following:

- It provides us with the ability to render flat shaded primitives such as lines, arcs, rectangles, and polygons, either as outlines or filled shapes.
- It allows us to easily load bitmapped images and render them on screen and also apply scaling or rotational transforms to those images.
- It makes it easy for us to draw text on screen that looks substantially better than the default debug font we've currently seen.
- It provides certain optimizations that allow us to speed up rendering. For example, it can batch together several requests to draw a particular image into a single call, which can yield good performance increases on many devices.

However, as you've probably already inferred from the tone of this section, we won't be using Iw2D in this book either.

If you are only interested in rendering 2D graphics, Iw2D may well be perfectly adequate for your needs, but if you ever want to make the jump to 3D graphics you will eventually find that the Iw2D API just doesn't do everything you need, such as rendering textured polygons of any shape, not just rectangular.

Since we will be tackling 3D graphics later in this very book, it makes sense for us to begin our journey into rendering with Marmalade by using 3D graphics itself.

If you want to use this API in your own project, just add `iw2d` to the `subprojects` section of the MKB file.

The IwGx API

Finally we come to the API that we will be using in this book; in fact we have already used a very small part of it in the creation of our "Hello World" project. Ladies and gentlemen, I give you the IwGx API!

This API is extremely flexible and boasts the following functionalities:

- It supports both hardware and software rendering pipelines, so your code can potentially run unaltered on modern hardware featuring a GPU yet still fall back to a software-based renderer for older or less capable hardware. You can even mix the two pipelines, so you could use the GPU for rasterization but still use the CPU for transform and lighting operations.

- It takes care of the nitty-gritty for us, such as initializing the display and texture management, in a similar way to the IwGL API.
- It allows us to use features such as texture mapping and flat or gouraud shading on arbitrary polygons.
- It provides some debugging functionality, such as simple text rendering (as in our "Hello World" project) and rendering shapes like rectangles and circles.
- It makes targeting OpenGL ES 2.x devices much easier, as it provides the necessary shader programs to emulate the fixed function pipeline of Open GL ES 1.x while still allowing us to provide our own custom shaders when we want to.

By using IwGx for rendering 2D graphics from the start, we will find it a whole lot easier to move on to drawing 3D polygons later, as the techniques involved are incredibly similar.

With Version 6.1 of Marmalade, the IwGx API underwent a little modernization and standardized using floating point values for specifying polygon information. Prior to this version, some information (for example, texture UV values) was specified in fixed point integer formats. There was also a software-based rendering engine for targeting old devices with no GPU hardware. If you have existing code that still needs the old fixed point way of doing things, you can revert back by adding `define IW_USE_LEGACY_MODULES` to the project MKB file.

It should come as no surprise by now that we can use IwGx in our project simply by adding `iwgx` to the `subprojects` section of the MKB file.

Using IwGx to render 2D graphics

Now that we know how to load resources, we can get on with the fun stuff. We're going to look at how we can draw a bitmapped image on screen.

IwGx initialization and termination

We've already seen how to do this in the "Hello World" project of *Chapter 1, Getting Started with Marmalade*. We just call `IwGxInit` to set up IwGx at the start of our program and `IwGxTerminate` to close it down again at the end.

Rendering a polygon

In IwGx, the most commonly used polygon types are lines, triangles, and quads (basically two triangles that share a common edge).

Also supported are sprites, which are always rectangular in shape and do not allow any scaling of textures, and n-polys, which can contain up to 63 vertices.

Sprites are rarely used since triangles and quads are more flexible, though they can be faster to draw especially in software rendering mode. The n-poly can also be faster to draw for the software renderer than a series of triangles, but they are generally best avoided since they need to be converted into triangles on the fly in order to be drawn using hardware rendering.

To render a polygon on screen, we at least need to specify where we want it to appear on screen and what color we want it to be in. Additionally, we might want to draw the polygon using a bitmapped image. The following sections show how we can provide this information.

Materials and textures

First we let IwGx know what color (or indeed colors) and image we want applied to our polygon. We do this by specifying the material we want to use, which is an instance of the `CIwMaterial` class that groups together this information. To set the material we want to use, we must provide IwGx with a pointer to the relevant `CIwMaterial` instance using the following function call:

```
IwGxSetMaterial(pMaterial);
```

If we are drawing a polygon with no image applied to it, then the very minimum information the material will need to provide is the color we want to use.

A material actually contains four different colors that, if you are at all familiar with 3D graphics rendering, you will probably recognize. They are the ambient, diffuse, emissive, and specular colors. For 2D rendering purposes, it is only the ambient color that we are concerned with. We'll look into the others when we move on to 3D rendering in *Chapter 4, 3D Graphics Rendering*.

The material also specifies the texture we want to apply. A texture specifies a bitmapped image that we want to apply to our polygon, and is represented in Marmalade by the `CIwTexture` class.

The `CIwTexture` class is actually a wrapper for the `CIwImage` class that actually stores the pixel information for an image. `CIwTexture` adds functionality to control how the image is actually rendered, with support for enabling and disabling features such as bilinear filtering and mipmapping.

Materials also provide control over other polygon rendering features, such as whether the polygon is rendered flat or gouraud shaded, and how it should be blended with the current screen contents when it is drawn.

Materials can either be created in code or they can be instanced by the resource manager. The following sections illustrate this.

Creating materials in code

Creating a material in code requires little more than making a new instance of `CIwMaterial` and using the available methods to set the color, textures, and other settings. For example, to create a material that will render bright red, semi-transparent polygons we could use the following code:

```
CIwMaterial* lpRedMaterial = new CIwMaterial;
lpRedMaterial->SetColAmbient(255, 0, 0, 128);
lpRedMaterial->SetAlphaMode(CIwMaterial::ALPHA_BLEND);
```

Note that Marmalade will raise an assert message if you try to create a local `CIwMaterial` instance on the program stack. This happens because rendering does not happen the moment you make a drawing function call, so by the time rendering does occur, the material data will likely have been trashed by other functions reusing the same area of stack space.

Creating materials using an MTL file

While creating materials in code is simple enough, there is an easier way, especially when it comes to specifying materials with textures. This involves yet another use of our friend, the ITX file.

A material file has the extension `.mtl` and again uses the same formatting rules as an ITX file. We can create any number of `CIwMaterial` instances in an MTL file and initialize them with the required colors, textures, and other settings.

As a bonus, any texture we refer to in the MTL file will also be loaded automatically, meaning we don't have to list it separately in a GROUP file. In order for this to work, all the source image files must reside in a subdirectory named `textures`, which is located in the same directory as the MTL file, or alternatively they must already have been loaded into memory either from another GROUP file or in the same GROUP file prior to referencing the MTL file.

Marmalade natively supports the PNG, TGA, GIF, and BMP image file formats. If you want to load any other type of bitmap, you will need to provide your own custom resource handler to do so.

Here is an example of what an MTL file might look like:

```
CIwMaterial
{
  name        "red"
  colAmbient  { 255 0 0 128 }
  alphaMode    BLEND
}

CIwMaterial
{
  name        "grid"
  colAmbient  { 128 128 128 128 }
  texture0     "grid.png"
  alphaMode    ADD
  shadeMode    FLAT
  filtering    false
}
```

This example generates a semi-transparent red material equivalent to that created in the previous section, and also a material using a texture named `grid.png`, which is drawn flat shaded with additive transparency at half the original image brightness and without bilinear filtering.

> You may have noticed that the image is specified using an attribute called `texture0`. Marmalade materials can actually be assigned two textures that can be blended together when rendering a polygon and they are referred to as `texture0` and `texture1`. In this book we will only be concerned with single texture materials.

There are far too many attribute names to list here, so for a complete list take a look at the Marmalade documentation page for the `CIwMaterial` class. This page lists all of them.

To make these materials available in our code, we just need to reference the MTL file inside a GROUP file that we are loading. We can then get hold of the materials by searching for them by name using the resource manager functions described earlier in this chapter.

> It is recommended that when materials are created using an MTL file, you do not modify any of their settings using the methods in the `CIwMaterial` class. Instead, make a copy of the material using the `CIwMaterial::Copy` method. While it is possible to do so, problems can occur if the same material is used to render several different things, since rendering does not occur as soon as a drawing function call is made. The end result is therefore unpredictable as it would depend on how the `CIwMaterial` happens to be configured when rendering finally occurs.

Vertex streams

In order to display a polygon on screen, we need to specify a list of screen coordinates that define the corner points. Since we are only rendering in 2D at the moment, each coordinate is specified as a `CIwSVec2` instance, which is a vector class defined in another Marmalade API called **IwGeom**. Any list of data items used when rendering polygons, be it vertices, colors, or whatever, is often referred to as a **stream**, so a list of vertices is called a **vertex stream**.

While we can specify this API to be part of our project by adding `iwgeom` to the `subprojects` section of the MKB file and calling `IwGeomInit` and `IwGeomTerminate`, there isn't actually a need to, since IwGx relies on this API itself.

The `CIwSVec2` class defines a two-component vector using signed 16-bit integers, so it is perfect for specifying screen coordinates.

The default screen coordinate system in IwGx places the origin at the top-left corner of the screen, with the x component increasing horizontally to the right and the y component increasing vertically downwards. It is possible to change the position of the origin, however, by passing a `CIwSVec2` instance containing the desired position of the origin to the function `IwGxSetScreenSpaceOrg`.

The following diagram illustrates how we could specify the coordinates for a triangle on a standard iPhone resolution screen (320 x 480 pixels). The top left of the screen is the origin and has a coordinate position of **(0,0)**, while the bottom-right corner has a position of **(320,480)**.

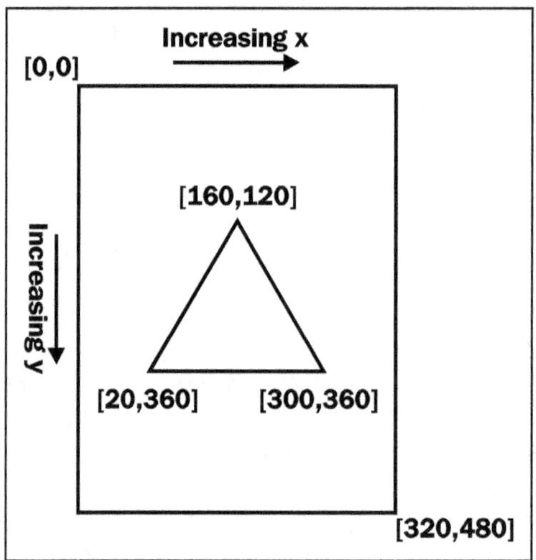

To render this triangle all we have to do is fill in an array of `CIwSVec2` with the coordinates and submit them to IwGx, as follows:

```
CIwSVec2* v = new CIwSVec2[3];
v[0].x = 160;     v[0].y = 120;
v[1].x = 20;      v[1].y = 360;
v[2].x = 300;     v[2].y = 360;
IwGxSetVertStreamScreenSpace(v, 3);
```

The function call, `IwGxSetVertStreamScreenSpace`, allows us to specify a list of screen space (that is, pixel) coordinates we want to use for rendering, but we must also explicitly state how many vertices we are submitting. In the case of our triangle, this is three.

It is also possible to specify our coordinates using sub-pixel positioning with the function call `IwGxSetVertStreamScreenSpaceSubPixel`. It may be getting a bit on the long side to type, but using sub-pixel positioning does provide the advantage of smoother movement on screen, as we are no longer limited to only moving things around the screen in terms of whole pixels.

Using sub-pixel coordinates can also improve the quality of the final rendered image, as slow moving objects won't appear to jump between pixel positions if we are rendering using bilinear filtering.

IwGx only supports eight sub-pixel positions per pixel; so to convert our coordinates to use sub-pixel positioning, all we need to do is multiply the screen coordinates by eight or use the bitwise shift operator to shift left by three places.

Color streams

If we want to draw a polygon using flat shading, so that every pixel rendered is the same color, we can just set the ambient color of our material and our work is done.

However, if we want to render a polygon using gouraud shading, we need to specify a color to be used at each vertex. This can't be done with a material, so we need to override the material's color information by providing our own color stream.

We do this by creating an array of `CIwColour` objects, which is Marmalade's chosen method of representing a color. This class has four public member variables of type `uint8` (an unsigned byte) called `r`, `g`, `b`, and `a`, which (probably not surprisingly) represent the red, green, blue, and alpha values of a color.

Note that because Marmalade was developed in the UK, all instances of the word *color* in the API will actually be spelled *colour*.

`CIwColour` also provide several methods to make setting and manipulating colors easier.

Returning to the triangle defined in the earlier diagram, if we wanted to color the top of it red, the bottom-right corner green, and the bottom-left corner blue, we can use the following code:

```
CIwColour* c = new CIwColour[3];
c[0].Set(255, 0, 0, 255);
c[1].Set(0 255, 0, 255);
c[2].Set(0, 0, 255, 255);
IwGxSetColStream(c);
```

Note that `IwGxSetColStream` does not require us to specify the number of colors in our stream. This is because IwGx expects to find the same number of colors as there are vertices. If we do not want to specify a color stream, we can just pass `NULL` into the `IwGxSetColStream` function and the selected material's colors will be used instead.

UV streams

When rendering a polygon with a texture, we need to somehow indicate how that texture should be mapped to the polygon. We do this by specifying a UV stream that allows us to state which part of the texture should appear at each vertex. The part of the texture required for each rendered pixel can then be worked out by the rendering engine by interpolating the UV values across the surface of the polygon.

In IwGx, UV coordinates are specified using floating point numbers. An individual UV value is often written as (u, v) and is represented in IwGx using the `CIwFVec2` class, which is a floating point equivalent of `CIwSVec2` that we came across earlier. The x component of the vector represents **u**, and the y component represents **v**.

UV values are mapped to a texture so that **(0.0, 0.0)** is the top left of the image and **(1.0, 1.0)** is the bottom-right corner. We can repeatedly tile a texture up to a maximum of eight times across our polygon by using values larger than one.

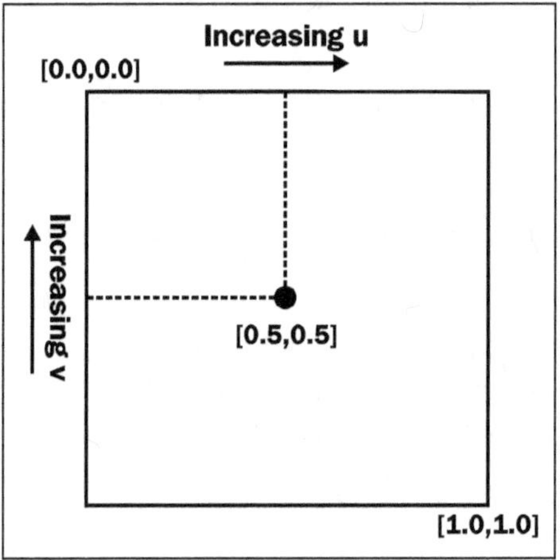

Prior to Marmalade version 6.1, UV values were given as 16-bit signed integers using a 12-bit fixed point representation. The value 4096 is equivalent to 1.0, 8192 is equivalent to 2.0, and 2048 is equivalent to 0.5. The IwGeom API provides us with the define `IW_GEOM_ONE`, which we can use to avoid having nasty-looking magic numbers throughout our code. This functionality can still be used by reverting to the legacy version of the IwGx API, as detailed earlier in this chapter.

By mapping UV values in this way, we make them independent of the actual size of the texture image. If we change the size of the image for any reason, it won't mess up rendering as our UV values do not need to change.

As with vertex streams, all we have to do to specify a set of UV values is allocate an array of CIwSVec2, populate the array, and submit it to IwGx. We don't need to specify the number of UV values we are submitting, as IwGx expects to see the same number of UVs as there are vertices. Here is some sample code that we might want to use to apply a texture to a triangle:

```
CIwSVec2* uv = new CIwSVec2[3];
uv[0].x = IW_GEOM_ONE / 2;      uv[0].y = 0;
uv[1].x = 0;                    uv[1].y = IW_GEOM_ONE;
uv[2].x = IW_GEOM_ONE;          uv[2].y = IW_GEOM_ONE;
IwGxSetUVStream(uv, 0);
```

The second parameter of IwGxSetUVStream indicates which texture the UV values apply to. If the material we are using only has a single texture, we can just leave this parameter out entirely as it will default to 0, but if the material does have a second texture, we need to supply a UV stream to be used with it by changing the second parameter of IwGxSetUVStream to 1. This UV stream could be the same as the stream for the first texture or it could be a completely different set of UV values.

If our material does not have a texture applied to it, there is no need to set the UV stream to NULL as it will be ignored completely.

Drawing a polygon

We've now seen how to set just about all the information we need to specify how we want our polygon to appear, so we can finally instruct IwGx to draw it. To do so, we need to let IwGx know how our various input streams should be interpreted by using the following function call:

```
IwGxDrawPrims(polygon_type, indices, num_indices);
```

The polygon_type parameter indicates whether we are drawing triangles, quads, lines, sprites, or n-polys, while the indices parameter is an array of uint16 values showing the order in which the elements of our input streams should be accessed. This is called an **index stream**. The num_indices parameter is just a count of how many elements are in the indices array.

The following diagram shows the types of polygons supported by IwGx. Note that it is possible to draw more than one polygon at a time by providing longer streams of data. This is something we should try to do as much as possible, since it prevents the GPU from idling while it is waiting to be supplied with new polygon information.

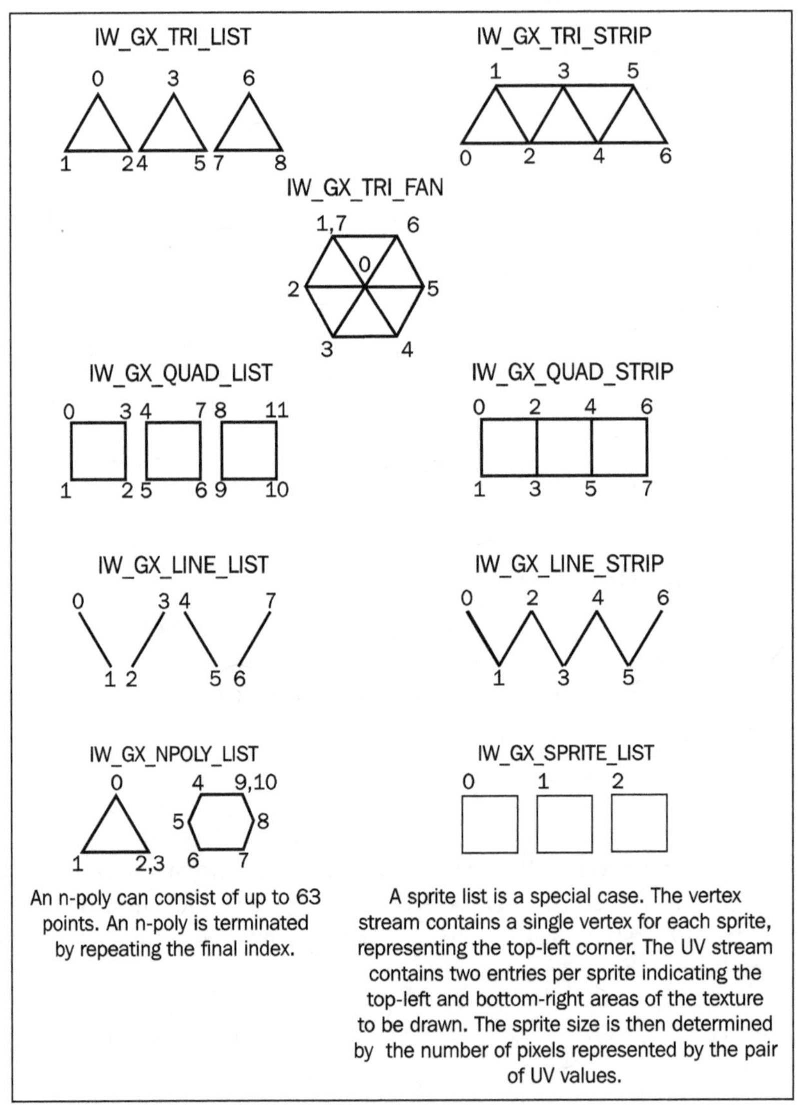

The numbers labeling the vertices in the diagram correspond to the elements of the index stream. When rendering, the `indices` array is traversed in the order shown for each polygon type, and the values it contains indicate which element of the various input streams should be used to render each vertex.

To draw the triangle we've been building up to, we can use the following code snippet:

```
uint16* indices = new uint16[3];
indices[0] = 0;  indices[1] = 1;  indices[2] = 2;
IwGxDrawPrims(IW_GX_TRI_STRIP, indices, 3);
```

We could simplify this a little more as the index stream isn't actually necessary in this instance since our input streams are accessed one element at a time in the order they occur in the stream, so we can just specify `NULL` for the `indices` parameter like this:

```
IwGxDrawPrims(IW_GX_TRI_STRIP, NULL, 3);
```

When creating the index stream there is one other point to bear in mind, which is the order in which we supply our vertices. Because IwGx can also be used to render 3D polygons on screen, it supports back face culling, which prevents any polygon that is facing away from the viewer from being rendered.

How is a polygon classified as facing toward or away from the viewer? If we label each vertex of a polygon with an incrementing number, starting with zero for the first vertex and following around the edges of the polygon from vertex to vertex, then a polygon is facing the viewer if its vertices form an anti-clockwise pattern when rendered on screen and considered in ascending numerical order. The order the vertices are supplied in is called the **winding order**, and the following diagram shows this more clearly:

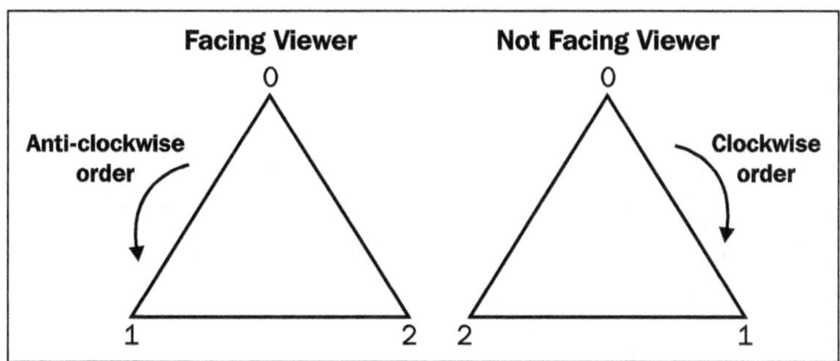

Putting the vertices in the correct order is not the only way to solve this problem, but it is worth getting in the habit of ordering the vertices in this way for when we progress to rendering 3D polygons. We can disable or reverse the back face culling operation on a per material basis by calling the `CIwMaterial::SetCullMode` method with one of the following enumeration values: `CULL_FRONT`, `CULL_BACK`, or `CULL_NONE`. The default is `CULL_BACK`.

If you are trying to draw a polygon and you just can't get it to appear, the first thing to do is double-check the winding order of your vertices. They may just be getting culled by the GPU and not being drawn!

Our polygon information has now been submitted for rendering; but we won't see it appear on screen just yet.

Displaying the rendered image

The final step in making something appear on screen is to flush all the drawing requests to the screen, and then display the final image.

IwGx automatically provides us with a double-buffered display setup. All this means is we do all our rendering to an off-screen buffer and then switch to displaying this buffer when all the drawing is complete. If we did not do this, we would likely see an incomplete, flickering screen display as our graphics could be displayed in an incomplete state if we drew straight to the visible display.

To complete the cycle of drawing, all we have to do is add the following two lines of code:

```
IwGxFlush();
IwGxSwapBuffers();
```

That's it! We've drawn our first polygon!

Example code

If you download the code package for this chapter, you will find three projects that illustrate the use of the Marmalade functionality we have learnt about in this chapter.

The ITX project

The ITX project demonstrates use of the ITX text parser and the `CIwManaged` class.

The example first creates custom instances of our own class by parsing an ITX file, then serializes those instances out to a file. All the instances are then destroyed and re-created by loading the serialized file back in.

The example also demonstrates the use of two more parts of the IwUtil API, which we haven't covered in depth, but are very useful to know about. First is the class `CIwManagedList`, which is used for maintaining a list of objects derived from `CIwManaged`, and the second is the `IwTrace` system that allows us to log information to a file (and to the standard output) in order to aid debugging.

The Graphics2D project

The Graphics2D project pulls everything we've learnt in this chapter together to render a rotating, textured polygon on screen. The following screenshot depicts this project in action:

The Skiing project

Throughout this book, we will be building up an entire game example that puts the things we have learnt into real practice. The game in question will be a simple version of that old favorite, the slalom skiing game, where the player guides a skier down a mountain, attempting to pass through as many flags as possible while avoiding obstacles.

In this chapter we kick things off by having a skier graphic at the top of the screen that moves from side to side, while some random trees scroll up the edges of the screen.

The following screenshot shows the project as it currently stands:

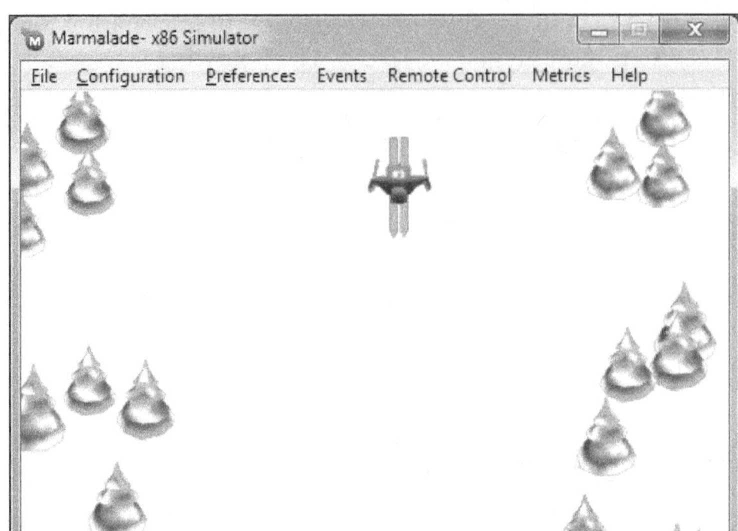

While this book is not intended to teach you the ins and outs of programming a game (it's assumed you already know how to do that) it might still be worthwhile providing a few notes on how the sample game is put together.

The GameObject class

The `GameObject` class is the base class for anything that makes up a part of the game world. Currently there are two classes which inherit from this class, `Skier` and `Tree`. No prizes for guessing what they represent!

`GameObject` provides two virtual methods that can be overridden by child classes to implement the behavior of an in-game object. The `GameObject::Update` method provides support for changing the position of an object by applying a velocity to it, while the `GameObject::Render` method allows a size and a material to be defined, and it will draw a textured polygon at the object's current position using this information.

The ModeManager and Mode classes

The main flow of most games is often represented internally as some kind of state machine. Even the simplest game will normally have at least a title screen and the main game screen, but add to this things such as pause modes, high score tables, options screen, and the like, and you soon end up with a large number of states that your game could be in.

Often these states are completely mutually exclusive, but sometimes we might want several states active, or at least visible, at the same time. For example, quite often the pause mode will appear on top of the game screen. Only the pause mode will be accepting input, but both it and the game screen need to be drawn.

One approach (and this is purely my own personal preference; your own may vary wildly) is to create a separate class which handles a single part of the game. For want of a better word, I represent these using a base class called `Mode`.

The `Mode` class is similar to the `GameObject` class in that it provides two virtual methods called `Update` and `Render`. A mode can be made active, which means its `Update` method will be executed in each frame, and it can be visible, which means its `Render` method will be called. These two states are completely independent of each other.

When a `Mode` instance is created, it is automatically added to a list maintained by a singleton class called `ModeManager`. The `ModeManager` class uses the list of `Mode` instances to update all active modes and render all visible modes on each iteration of the main game loop.

Currently the project only consists of a single mode called `ModeGame`, which is responsible for loading and freeing the required resources and also initializing, updating, and rendering all the `GameObject`s that make up the game world.

Summary

In this chapter we've learnt about Marmalade's powerful resource management system. We know how to use it at a simple level to just load and release resources such as bitmapped images or our own custom classes; we also have a good idea of how the resource management system is put together, and how we can extend it with our own functionality.

We've also covered the options available for rendering on-screen images, and seen how to use one of these, IwGx, to render polygons on the screen.

In the next chapter we'll be learning how we can start using the various input options available on modern mobile devices, since the whole point of games is that they are interactive.

3
User Input

A video game is not going to be a whole lot of fun to play if the user has no way of controlling the events that happen, so in this chapter we will be looking at the various ways in which we can add interactivity to our programs by using Marmalade. By the end of this chapter you will know how to detect the following types of input:

- Key presses
- Touch screen and pointer inputs
- Detection of gestures such as swipes and pinches
- Changes in device orientation using accelerometers

Detecting key input

We'll start our journey into the world of player input methods with the simplest method possible—pressing keys, which we detect by using the s3eKeyboard API. To use these functions in our code, we just need to include the `s3eKeyboard.h` file.

While the touch screen may now rule supreme as the primary method of interacting with many modern devices, it is still worthwhile to know how to detect key presses. Android devices, in particular, have keys that are intended to be used for quick access to menus and for navigation around a program. Quite often these are not even physical buttons, just an area at the bottom of the touch screen, but they are still reported as key presses.

Key press detection is also extremely useful when debugging your code in the Windows simulator, as Marmalade allows full access to your computer's keyboard too. This makes it really easy to add a debugging functionality triggered by a key press.

The s3eKeyboard API allows us to detect key input either by key state or by character input. It also provides functionality that allows us to determine what kind of keyboard support the device we are running on has available.

Initialization and update of key information

There is a function called `s3eKeyboardGetInt` that allows us to find out what kind of keyboard our device has. We can use this information to provide different input methods to our program should we want to. For example, entering a user's name on a high score might allow the user to enter their name directly if the device has a full alphabetic keyboard, but could fall back to a method using arrow keys to cycle through characters if the device does not feature a full keyboard.

The `s3eKeyboardGetInt` function call takes a single parameter from the `s3eKeyboardProperty` enumeration, and returns an integer value. Details of the available properties are provided in the following table:

Property name	Description
`S3E_KEYBOARD_HAS_NUMPAD`	Returns `1` if the device has a numeric keypad, otherwise returns `0`.
`S3E_KEYBOARD_HAS_ALPHA`	Returns `1` if the device has an alphabetic keypad, otherwise returns `0`.
`S3E_KEYBOARD_HAS_DIRECTION`	Returns `1` if the device has directional controls (up, down, left, right, and a **Select** or **OK** button), otherwise returns `0`.
`S3E_KEYBOARD_NUMPAD_ORIENTATION`	If the device has a numeric keypad, this property will return the orientation of the keypad relative to how the user is holding the device (if this is possible to detect).
`S3E_KEYBOARD_GET_CHAR`	Returns `1` if the device supports the character code input method or `0` if it does not.

The final value in this table can also be used with the function `s3eKeyboardSetInt` to show and hide the virtual keyboard on Android and iOS devices, which will then allow us to use the character code input method on these types of devices. The following function call will display the virtual keyboard:

```
s3eKeyboardSetInt(S3E_KEYBOARD_GET_CHAR, 1);
```

To hide the virtual keyboard, pass in `0` instead of `1`.

Given that this feature is limited to just Android and iOS, and there is no way of determining whether the functionality is supported at runtime, this approach is probably best avoided if you intend to support a wide range of devices.

In order for our program to keep receiving updates on key presses, we must call the function `s3eKeyboardUpdate` in our code, once per game frame. The s3eKeyboard API keeps its own internal cache of the current key press states, which is updated when calling this function; so if we don't call `s3eKeyboardUpdate` frequently, we risk missing key press events.

Detecting key state

The most useful method of key detection for most arcade style games is to be able to discover the up or down state of any key on the device. The s3eKeyboard API provides two ways in which we can do this, these being polling the current key state and by registering a callback function.

Detecting key state changes using polling

We'll start with the simplest approach of polling for the current state of a key. It may be the simplest approach, but in most cases it is also the best approach as far as game coding is concerned, since often all we want to know is whether a key is currently pressed or released so that we can update our game state accordingly.

To detect the current state of any key on our device we make a call to `s3eKeyboardGetState`, which takes a value from the `s3eKey` enumeration (take a look at the `s3eKeyboard.h` file for a full list, but you can normally guess the name of the enumeration fairly easily—for example, `s3eKeyUp` is the up arrow key, `s3eKey4` is the number *4* key, and so on) to identify the key we are interested in. The function returns an integer value that is a bit mask representing the current state of that key. The following key states can be detected by performing a bitwise AND operation on the return value:

Bit mask name	Description
`S3E_KEY_STATE_DOWN`	The key is currently being held down.
`S3E_KEY_STATE_PRESSED`	The key went from being up to down in the last call to `s3eKeyboardUpdate`.
`S3E_KEY_STATE_RELEASED`	The key went from being down to up in the last call to `s3eKeyboardUpdate`.

If the value returned from the function is zero, then the key can be assumed to currently be in the up position (that is, not being held) and has not just been released either.

The following code snippet shows how we would detect whether the number 3 key has just been pressed:

```
if ((s3eKeyboardGetState(s3eKey3) & S3E_KEY_STATE_PRESSED) != 0)
{
  // Number 3 key has just been pressed!
}
```

Detecting key state changes using callbacks

It is also possible to be informed whenever a key is pressed or released by using a callback function. Callbacks are preferred by many coders since they force us into writing smaller, more manageable functions that often yield a more concise and reusable solution. The polled approach to key detection may seem easier at first glance but it is easy to end up with a codebase that has key state checking logic spread across many source files. Using the callback approach will tend to ensure key handling code is implemented in a more structured way.

To set up a callback function that detects key state changes, we use the `s3eKeyboardRegister` function. We provide this function with the enumeration value `S3E_KEYBOARD_KEY_EVENT` to identify the type of callback we are setting up, a pointer to a function that will be the callback, and a void pointer that can be used to pass in our own custom data to the callback function.

When a key is pressed or released, the function we specified will be called. The callback function is passed a pointer to an `s3eKeyboardEvent` structure, which details the key press or release and is also provided with the custom data pointer we specified when registering the callback.

When we no longer wish to receive key state notifications, we can call `s3eKeyboardUnRegister` to disable the callback mechanism. We just need to pass the `S3E_KEYBOARD_KEY_EVENT` enumeration and the pointer to our callback method to stop the callbacks from occurring any more.

Here's a code snippet to illustrate how we might detect state changes to the number 3 key:

```
// Callback function that will receive key state notifications
int32 KeyStateCallback(s3eKeyboardEvent* apKeyEvent,
                       void* apUserData)
{
  if (apKeyEvent->m_Key == s3eKey3)
  {
    if (apKeyEvent->m_Pressed)
    {
```

```
        // Number 3 key has just been pressed
      }
      else
      {
        // Number 3 key has just been released
      }
    }
  }

// We use this to register the callback function…
s3eKeyboardRegister(S3E_KEYBOARD_KEY_EVENT,
                    (s3eCallback) KeyStateCallback, NULL);

// …and this to cancel notifications
s3eKeyboardUnRegister(S3E_KEYBOARD_KEY_EVENT,
                      (s3eCallback) KeyStateCallback);
```

The method of key press detection to be used is really down to project requirements and personal preference. Since a call to `s3eKeyboardUpdate` will cache the state of every key for us, a polled approach may be best if we need to detect the current state of several keys at any time. A callback approach may be better if we just want to respond immediately to a key press and are less interested in tracking the key's state beyond this.

Detecting character code input

The s3eKeyboard API also provides support for reading character codes from the keyboard. With this approach, we don't receive any notification of when a key was pressed or released. Instead, we receive a stream of character codes which automatically take into account any special modifier keys; so if a user pressed the *Shift* key, followed by the *A* key, then released both these keys, we would only receive the character code for a capital letter A.

This approach is probably less useful for most games due to it not being an immediate form of notification, especially since fewer and fewer devices now feature physical keys that can be pressed.

Not all devices support this input method, so you should use a call to `s3eKeyboardGetInt(S3E_KEYBOARD_GET_CHAR)` to determine if it can be used.

For the sake of completeness though, let us look at how we can receive character codes using either polling or callbacks.

Detecting character code input using polling

To find out if a key that generates a character code has been pressed, all we have to do is call the following function:

```
s3eWChar lCharCode = s3eKeyboardGetChar();
```

The `s3eWChar` type is just an alternate type definition for the standard C++ type `wchar_t`, a wide character. While this type can vary in size, it is assumed to be a 16-bit value in Marmalade. When a key is pressed, its character code will be added to the back of a queue. Calling this function will return the character to the front of the queue, or `S3E_WEOF` if the queue is empty. We often call this function in a loop in order to try and keep the queue empty and not risk losing key presses.

The character codes returned will depend on the device you are running on, but in most cases the standard alphabet A through Z, numbers, and punctuation characters will be ASCII codes, just stored in a 16-bit value.

Detecting character code input using callbacks

Using the callback method of receiving character codes takes the same approach as the callback method for receiving key state changes.

We again use `s3eKeyboardRegister` and `s3eKeyboardUnRegister` to start and stop notifications from occurring, but we use the enumeration value `S3E_KEYBOARD_CHAR_EVENT` to indicate that it is a character code event we want to receive.

The callback function we provide will now be sent a pointer to an `s3eKeyboardCharEvent` structure that contains a single member of type `s3eWChar` named `m_Char`. This member will contain the character code that was generated by the user.

Character code input is really only recommended if you are running on a device with a physical keyboard, as using virtual keyboards on touch screen devices can be unreliable with many key presses going unnoticed, particularly when characters outside the normal ASCII character set are entered (for example, Chinese or Japanese text entry).

Inputting strings

We've already seen how we can use the s3eKeyboard functionality to read character codes, but if we want to allow the user to enter a string and we don't mind our program forsaking its own user interface in favor of a standard modal string entry dialog, then we have a shortcut available to us.

The `s3eOSReadString` API makes string entry really simple; but it is not actually supported on every platform. To use this API we include the file `s3eOSReadString.h`, and then make a call to the function `s3eOSReadStringAvailable` to see if string entry functionality is available for use.

If we are able to use the API, then we have two functions at our disposal. The first is `s3eOSReadStringUTF8`, which will display a string entry dialog and return a UTF-8 encoded string as a `const char` pointer. The second method is `s3eOSReadStringUTF8WithDefault`, which allows us to also specify a UTF-8 string that will be used to populate the string dialog when it appears.

UTF-8 is a widely used character format that allows full multilingual character support. It is often used when memory concerns are foremost, as single-byte characters such as the standard ASCII character set can still be represented in a single byte. Characters from outside the ASCII set (for example, Japanese Kanji) are encoded with two, three, or more bytes of information. One big advantage of UTF-8 is that you can continue to use null-terminated strings since it is guaranteed that a zero byte will never form part of a valid character code.

Both functions otherwise work in the same way. They both return a pointer to the string entered by the user (the API will take care of freeing this memory), or NULL if the user canceled the dialog.

They both also take an optional last parameter that can customize the layout of the string entry dialog. If the parameter is omitted or the value zero is passed, no restrictions are applied. The following table shows the other values that can be used:

Value	Description
`S3E_OSREADSTRING_FLAG_EMAIL`	Indicates that we are expecting an e-mail address to be entered.
`S3E_OSREADSTRING_FLAG_NUMBER`	Indicates that we are expecting a numeric value to be entered.
`S3E_OSREADSTRING_FLAG_PASSWORD`	Indicates that the application will use the OS method for entering a password, possibly hiding characters as they are entered.
`S3E_OSREADSTRING_FLAG_URL`	Indicates that we are expecting a URL to be entered.

When using these functions in an application, it is possible that the user may enter characters that we are then unable to process or display; this should be kept in mind, as generic string input may not always be a good choice (for example, you may be unable to display every possible character that can be entered using your game's font!).

Using this API will also likely break the look and feel of the game as its super whizzy UI is suddenly overlaid or replaced by a drab and boring system dialog.

These reasons, combined with the fact that it is not supported by all platforms, may mean that it is a better decision to implement our own in-game string entry routines. That being said, it is still a useful API to know about, if only for debugging purposes.

Detecting touch screen and pointer input

There aren't many devices released these days that don't feature a touch screen. Most new devices have adopted this as the primary input method and have dropped physical buttons almost entirely.

In Marmalade we detect touch screen events using the **s3ePointer** API, which I have to admit is perhaps not the most obvious name for an API that handles touch screen input. To use this API in our own program we just need to include the `s3ePointer.h` file.

The reason for this slightly bizarre naming is that when this API was first developed, touch screens were not commonplace. Instead, some devices had little joystick-style nubs that were able to move a pointer around the screen, much like a mouse on a computer.

Due to the fact that touch screen input is primarily concerned with a screen coordinate and that it was unlikely that a device would arrive that had both touch screen and pointer inputs, the Marmalade SDK simply adapted the existing s3ePointer API to accommodate touch screens as well, since your finger or stylus is effectively a pointer anyway.

For the purpose of this chapter, whenever we talk about a position being "pointed at", we mean either an on-screen cursor has been moved to that position or a touch screen has had a contact made at that position. Positions are always returned as pixel positions relative to the top-left corner of the screen, as shown in the following diagram that shows what to expect on a device with a portrait HVGA screen size, such as a non-retina display iPhone:

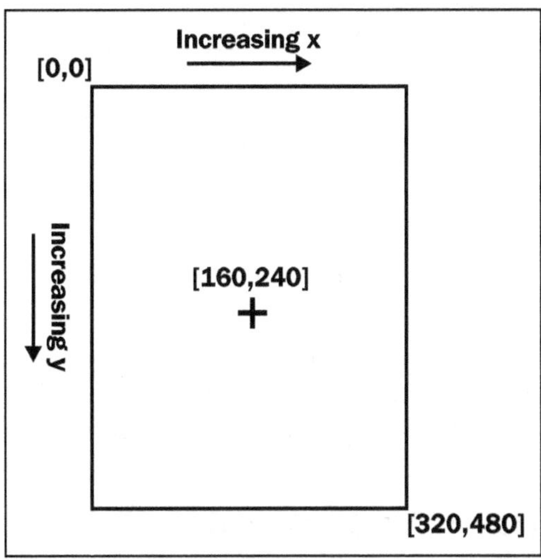

In the following sections, we will learn how to discover the capabilities available for use on the device we are running on and how to handle both single and multi-touch screens.

Determining available pointer functionality

We use the function `s3ePointerGetInt` to determine the properties of the hardware we are running on. We pass in one of the values in the following table, and we can then use the result to tailor our input methodology accordingly.

Property	Description
`S3E_POINTER_AVAILABLE`	Returns `1` if we can use the s3ePointer API on the device, or `0` if we can't.
`S3E_POINTER_HIDE_CURSOR`	If the system has some kind of mouse pointer-like cursor displayed on screen, this property will return 1 if the pointer is currently visible, otherwise it returns `0`. This property can also be used in the `s3ePointerSetInt` function to show and hide the cursor.
`S3E_POINTER_TYPE`	This will return the type of pointer we have at our disposal. See the next sub-section for more information on this.

Property	Description
S3E_POINTER_STYLUS_TYPE	This will return the type of stylus our device uses. See the next sub-section for more information on this.
S3E_POINTER_MULTI_TOUCH_AVAILABLE	If the device supports multi-touch (being able to detect more than one press on the touch screen at a time) the value 1 will be returned. Single touch devices will return 0.

For most game code, it is usually enough to first use the S3E_POINTER_AVAILABLE property to see if we have pointer capability available and the S3E_POINTER_MULTI_TOUCH_AVAILABLE property to configure our input methodology appropriately.

Determining the type of pointer input

When supplying the property type S3E_POINTER_TYPE to s3ePointerGetInt, the return value is one from the s3ePointerType enumeration.

Return Value	Description
S3E_POINTER_TYPE_INVALID	Invalid request. The most likely cause is that the s3ePointer API is not available on this device.
S3E_POINTER_TYPE_MOUSE	Pointer input is coming from a device that features an on-screen cursor to indicate position. The cursor may be controlled by a mouse or some other input device, such as a joystick.
S3E_POINTER_TYPE_STYLUS	Pointer input is from a stylus-based input method, most likely a touch screen of some sort.

In the majority of cases this distinction is not normally that important, but it might be relevant if you need to track the movement of the pointer.

With a mouse, our code will receive events whenever the pointer is moved across the screen, whether a mouse button is held or not. On a touch screen, we will obviously only receive movement events when the screen is being touched.

This is most notable when running on the simulator, as we will receive pointer events whenever the mouse pointer is moved within the bounds of the simulator window.

Determining the type of stylus input

If we use s3ePointerGetInt with the property S3E_POINTER_TYPE and get the return type S3E_POINTER_TYPE_STYLUS, we can interrogate a little further to find out what type of stylus we will be using by calling s3ePointerGetInt again with the property S3E_POINTER_STYLUS_TYPE. The return values possible are in the following table:

Return Value	Description
S3E_STYLUS_TYPE_INVALID	Call was invalid; most likely because we are not running on a hardware that uses a stylus.
S3E_STYLUS_TYPE_STYLUS	Inputs are made by touching a stylus to the input surface.
S3E_STYLUS_TYPE_FINGER	Inputs are made by touching a finger to the input surface.

This is probably not a distinction that we will need to worry about in most cases, but it might be useful to know so that games can be made more forgiving about inputs when they are made with a finger, since a stylus has a much smaller contact surface and should therefore allow for a far more accurate input.

Updating current pointer input status

In order to keep the s3ePointer API up-to-date with current touch screen inputs, it is necessary to call the s3ePointerUpdate function once per frame. This will update the cache of the current pointer status that is maintained within the s3ePointer API.

Detecting single touch input

If the s3ePointer API is available on our device, we are guaranteed to be able to detect and respond to the user touching the screen and moving their stylus or finger about, or moving an on-screen cursor around and pressing some kind of selection button.

Even if our hardware supports multi-touch, we can still make use of single touch input if our game has no need to know about multiple simultaneous touch points. This may make it a little simpler to code our game, as we don't need to worry about issues such as two buttons on our user interface being pressed at the same time.

As with key input, we can choose to use either a polled or callback-based approach.

Detecting single touch input using polling

We can determine the current on-screen position being pointed at (either by the on-screen cursor or a touch on the screen) by using the `s3ePointerGetX` and `s3ePointerGetY` functions, which will return the current horizontal and vertical pixel positions being pointed at.

In the case of a touch screen, the current position returned by these functions will be the last known position pointed at if the user is not currently making an input. The default value before any touches have been made will be (0,0) – the top-left corner of the screen.

To determine whether an input is currently in progress, we can use the function `s3ePointerGetState`, which takes an element from the `s3ePointerButton` enumeration and returns a value from the `s3ePointerState` enumeration. The following table shows the values that make up the `s3ePointerButton` enumeration:

Value	Description
`S3E_POINTER_BUTTON_SELECT`	Returns the status of either the left mouse button or a touch screen tap.
`S3E_POINTER_BUTTON_LEFTMOUSE`	An alternative name for `S3E_POINTER_BUTTON_SELECT`, which you may prefer to use if detecting other mouse buttons as well.
`S3E_POINTER_BUTTON_RIGHTMOUSE`	Returns the status of the right mouse button.
`S3E_POINTER_BUTTON_MIDDLEMOUSE`	Returns the status of the middle mouse button.
`S3E_POINTER_BUTTON_MOUSEWHEELUP`	Used to determine if the user has scrolled the mouse wheel upwards.
`S3E_POINTER_BUTTON_MOUSEWHEELDOWN`	Used to determine if the user has scrolled the mouse wheel downwards.

The next table shows the members of the `s3ePointerState` enumeration, which indicate the current status of the requested pointer button or touch screen tap:

Value	Description
`S3E_POINTER_STATE_UP`	The button is not depressed or contact is not currently made with the touch screen.
`S3E_POINTER_STATE_DOWN`	The button is being held down or contact has been made with the touch screen.

Value	Description
S3E_POINTER_STATE_PRESSED	The button or touch screen has just been pressed.
S3E_POINTER_STATE_RELEASED	The button or touch screen has just been released.
S3E_POINTER_STATE_UNKNOWN	Current status of this button is not known. For example, the middle mouse button status was requested but there is no middle mouse button present on the hardware.

With this information we now have the ability to track the pointer or touch screen position and determine when the user has touched or released the touch screen or pressed a mouse button.

Detecting single touch input using callbacks

It is also possible to keep track of pointer events using a callback-based system. For single touch input, there are two event types that we can register callback functions for; these are button and motion events.

We can start receiving pointer events by calling the `s3ePointerRegister` function, and we can stop them by calling `s3ePointerUnRegister`. Both functions take a value to identify the type of event we are concerned with, and a pointer to a callback function.

When registering a callback function, we can also provide a pointer to our own custom data structure that will be passed into the callback function whenever an event occurs.

The following code snippet shows how we can register a callback function that will be executed whenever the touch screen or a mouse button is pressed or released:

```
// Callback function that will receive pointer button notifications
int32 ButtonEventCallback(s3ePointerEvent* apButtonEvent,
                          void* apUserData)
{
  if (apButtonEvent->m_Button == S3E_POINTER_BUTTON_SELECT)
  {
    if (apButtonEvent->m_Pressed)
    {
      // Left mouse button or touch screen pressed
    }
    else
```

```
    {
      // Left mouse button or touch screen released
    }
  }
  return 0;
}

// We use this to register the callback function…
s3ePointerRegister(S3E_POINTER_BUTTON_EVENT,
                   (s3eCallback) ButtonEventCallback, NULL);

// …and this to cancel notifications
s3ePointerUnRegister(S3E_POINTER_BUTTON_EVENT,
                     (s3eCallback) ButtonEventCallback);
```

The button event callback's first parameter is a pointer to an `s3ePointerEvent` structure that contains four members. The button that was pressed is stored in a member called `m_Button` that is of the type `s3ePointerButton` (see the table in the *Detecting single touch input using polling* section earlier in this chapter for more details on this enumerated type).

The `m_Pressed` member will be `0` if the button was released and `1` if it was pressed. You might expect this to be of type `bool` rather than an integer but it isn't, because this is a C-based API, not C++-based and `bool` is not a part of the standard C language.

We can also discover the screen position where the event occurred by using the structure's `m_x` and `m_y` members.

It is also possible to register a callback that will inform us when the user has performed a pointer motion. We again use the `s3ePointerRegister`/`s3ePointerUnRegister` functions, but this time use `S3E_POINTER_MOTION_EVENT` as the callback type.

The callback function we register will be passed a pointer to an `s3ePointerMotionEvent` structure that consists of just `m_x` and `m_y` members containing the screen coordinate that is now being pointed at.

Detecting multi-touch input

A multi-touch capable display allows us to detect more than one touched point on the screen at a time. Every time the screen is touched, the device's OS will assign that touch point an ID number. As the user moves their finger around the screen, the coordinates associated with that ID number will be updated until the user removes their finger from the screen, whereupon that touch will become inactive and the ID number becomes invalid.

While Marmalade does provide a polling-based approach to handling multi-touch events, the callback approach is possibly the better choice as it leads to slightly more elegant code and is a little more efficient.

Detecting multi-touch input using polling

Marmalade provides us with a set of functions to allow multi-touch detection. The functions `s3ePointerGetTouchState`, `s3ePointerGetTouchX`, and `s3ePointerGetTouchY` are equivalent to the single touch functions `s3ePointerGetState`, `s3ePointerGetX`, and `s3ePointerGetY`, except that the multi-touch versions take a single parameter—the touch ID number.

The s3ePointer API also declares a preprocessor define `S3E_POINTER_TOUCH_MAX` that indicates the maximum possible value for the touch ID number (plus one!). As the user touches and releases the display, the touch ID numbers will be re-used. It is important to bear this in mind.

The following code snippet shows a loop that will allow us to process the currently active touch points:

```
for (uint32 i = 0; i < S3E_POINTER_TOUCH_MAX; i++)
{
  // Find position of this touch id.  Position is only valid if the
  // state for the touch ID is not S3E_POINTER_STATE_UNKNOWN or
  // S3E_POINTER_STATE_UP
  int32 x = s3ePointerGetTouchX(i);
  int32 y = s3ePointerGetTouchY(i);

  switch(s3ePointerGetTouchState(i))
  {
    case S3E_POINTER_STATE_RELEASED:
     // User just released the screen at x,y
     break;
    case S3E_POINTER_STATE_DOWN:
     // User just pressed or moved their finger to x,y
     // We need to know if we've already been tracking this
     // touch ID to tell whether this is a new press or a move
     break;
    default:
     // This touch ID is not currently active
     break;
  }
}
```

The biggest issue with this approach is that Marmalade never sends us an explicit notification that a touch event has just occurred. The `s3ePointerGetTouchState` function never returns `S3E_POINTER_STATE_PRESSED`, so instead we need to keep track of all touch IDs we have seen active so far when handling `S3E_POINTER_STATE_DOWN`. If a new touch ID is seen, we have detected the just-pressed condition.

While this code will work, I hope you will find that the callback-based approach that we are about to consider leads to a slightly more elegant solution.

Multi-touch input using callbacks

As with the polling approach, multi-touch detection using callbacks is almost exactly the same as the single touch callback method. We still use `s3ePointerRegister` and `s3ePointerUnRegister` to start and stop events being sent to our code, but instead we use `S3E_POINTER_TOUCH_EVENT` to receive notifications of the user pressing or releasing the screen, and `S3E_POINTER_TOUCH_MOTION_EVENT` to find out when the user has dragged their finger across the screen.

The callback function registered to `S3E_POINTER_TOUCH_EVENT` will be sent a pointer to an `s3ePointerTouchEvent` structure. This structure contains the screen coordinates where the event occurred (the `m_x` and `m_y` members), whether the screen was touched or released (the `m_Pressed` member, which will be set to `1` if the screen was touched), and most importantly the ID number for this touch event (the `m_TouchID` member), which we can use to keep track of this touch as the user moves their finger around the display.

The `S3E_POINTER_TOUCH_MOTION_EVENT` callback will receive a pointer to an `s3ePointerTouchMotionEvent` structure. This structure contains the ID number of the touch event that has been updated and the new screen coordinate values. These structure members have the same names as their equivalent members in the `s3ePointerTouchEvent` structure.

Marmalade provides us with no way of adjusting the frequency of touch events. Instead, it is really just dependant on how often the underlying operating system code dispatches such events.

Hopefully you can see that the callback-based method is a little neater than the polled method. Firstly, we can say goodbye to the truly nasty loop needed in the polled method to detect all currently active touches.

Secondly, with careful coding we can use the same code path to handle both single and multi-touch input. If we code first for multi-touch input, then making single touch work is simply a case of adding a fake touch ID to incoming single touch events and passing them through to the multi-touch code.

Recognizing gesture inputs

The arrival of the touch screen to mobile devices brought with it a new set of terminology related to making inputs to our programs. For years we have been using a mouse, clicking and dragging to interact with programs, and now with touch screens we have quickly become comfortable with the idea of swiping and pinching.

These methods of interaction have become known as **gestures** and users have become so used to them now that if your application doesn't respond as they expect, they may get quickly frustrated with your application.

Unfortunately, Marmalade does not provide any support for detecting these gestures, so instead we have to code for them ourselves. The following sections aim to provide some guidance on how to easily detect both swipes and pinches.

Detecting a swipe gesture

A swipe occurs when the user touches the screen and then slides that touch point quickly across the screen before releasing the screen.

To detect a swipe we must therefore first keep track of the screen coordinates where the user touched the screen and the time at which this occurred. When this touch event comes to an end due to the user releasing the screen, we first check the time it lasted for. If the length of time is not too long (say less than a quarter of a second), we check the distance between the start and end points. If this distance is large enough (perhaps a hundred pixels in length, or a fraction of the screen display size), then we have detected a swipe.

Often we only want to respond to a swipe if it is in a certain direction. We can determine this by using the dot product, the formula for which is shown in the following diagram:

$$|a| . |b| . \cos\theta = a_x \cdot b_x + a_y \cdot b_y$$

The dot product is calculated by multiplying the x and y components of the two vectors together and summing the results, or by multiplying the length of the two vectors together and then multiplying by the cosine of the angle between the two vectors.

To check if the user's swipe lies in a particular direction, we first make the direction of the swipe into a unit vector, then dot product this with a unit vector in the desired swipe direction. By using unit vectors we reduce the formula on the left-hand side of the previous diagram to just the cosine of the angle between the vectors, so it is now very simple to see if our swipe lies along the desired direction.

If the dot product value is very close to 1, then our two direction vectors are close to being parallel, since *cos(0°) = 1*, and we've detected a swipe in the required direction. Similarly, if the dot product is close to -1, we've detected a swipe in the opposite direction, as *cos(180°) = -1*.

Detecting a pinch gesture

Pinch gestures can only be used on devices featuring multi-touch displays, since they require two simultaneous touch points. A pinch gesture is often used to allow zooming in and out to occur and is performed by placing two fingers on the screen and then moving them together or apart. This is most easily achieved using the thumb and index finger.

Detecting a pinch gesture in code is actually quite simple. As soon as we have detected two touch points on the screen, we calculate a vector from one point to the other and find the distance of this vector. This is stored as the initial distance and will represent no zooming.

As the user moves their fingers around the screen, we just keep calculating the new distance between the two touch points, and then divide this distance by the original distance. The end result of this calculation is a zoom scale factor. If the user moves their fingers together, the zoom factor will be less than one; if they move them apart, the zoom value will be greater than one.

The pinch gesture is complete once the user removes at least one finger from the display.

Detecting accelerometer input

The final input method we will be considering in this chapter is the **accelerometer**, which allows us to detect the orientation that the user is currently holding the device at. An accelerometer is a sensor that can measure the forces applied to a device, be they static forces such as gravity, or dynamic forces generated by waving the device around.

Most devices will have three accelerometers aligned perpendicularly to each other, as shown in the following diagram. This configuration allows us to discover exactly how the user is holding the device at any time and so provides a method of controlling our game.

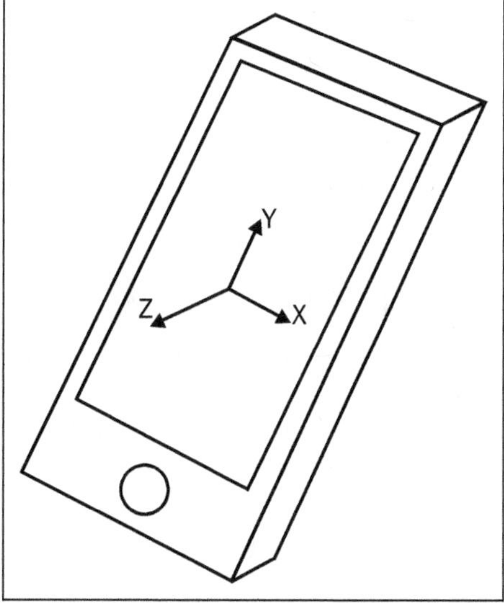

The directions of the arrows in the previous diagram show the directions in which acceleration will yield a positive value. This means that if you hold the device level with the display upwards in front of you, tipping it to the right will yield a positive value on the x axis accelerometer, tipping it away from you will generate positive y axis values and moving the device vertically upwards will generate a positive z axis value.

The Marmalade SDK provides us with access to the accelerometers of a device using the s3eAccelerometer API, which we can use in our code by including the `s3eAccelerometer.h` file.

Starting and stopping accelerometer input

Before attempting to use the accelerometer in our program, we must first check to see if accelerometer input is available on our device. If support is available, then we can start receiving accelerometer input. We do this with the following check:

```
if (s3eAccelerometerGetInt(S3E_ACCELEROMETER_AVAILABLE) != 0)
{
  // Accelerometer is available!  Start receiving input.
  s3eAccelerometerStart();
}
```

When we have finished using the accelerometers, we just make a call to `s3eAccelerometerStop` and we will receive no further inputs.

It is good practice on mobile devices to ensure that we only enable parts of the hardware when we are actually using them, since this helps to conserve battery power. In the case of accelerometers, the power use is probably so small that it is insignificant, but this is an area of mobile game programming that is always worth keeping in mind.

Reading accelerometer input

Finding the current accelerometer input values is really very simple. Marmalade provides three functions which return the current accelerometer value for each axis. These functions are called `s3eAccelerometerGetX`, `s3eAccelerometerGetY`, and `s3eAccelerometerGetZ`. Unsurprisingly, they return the current value of the accelerometer for the specified axis.

The values returned by these functions use a value of 1000 (though we should use the handy definition `S3E_ACCELEROMETER_1G` to avoid magic numbers in our code!) to represent an acceleration equivalent to normal Earth gravity.

When a sharp, quick movement is made to the device, the forces being applied to it will be greater than the normal gravitational force. In this case, the magnitude of the vector formed from the accelerometer values will be greater than `S3E_ACCELEROMETER_1G`. This can be a useful way of detecting whether the user has been shaking the device.

If the device were to be horizontally on a table, we should get a value of `0` returned for both the X and Y axes, and `-1000` for the z axis, since gravity acts downwards! As we rotate the device, the values returned will form a vector showing the direction in which gravity is acting, and we can then use this to determine the orientation of the device.

Using some trigonometry, we can work out the angle of tip around the x axis (forward/backward) and Y-axis (left/right). The angle around the X-axis can be found by taking the arc tan of the Y-accelerometer value divided by the Z value.

The angle around the y axis is a little trickier. First we have to find the length of the accelerometer vector projected onto the YZ plane, then we can find the arc tan of the X-accelerometer value divided by the projected length.

If all this sounds like too much scary math, the following code snippet does it all for us. Note than when calculating the rotation around the x axis using the `IwGeomAtan2` function, we negate both the Y- and Z-accelerometer values in order to yield a more usable result range, with 0 degrees returned when the device is level and increasing values when tipped away from the user.

```
iwangle xAngle = IwGeomAtan2(-accY, -accZ);
int32 lYZProjection = (int32) sqrtf((float) ((accY * accY) +
                                              (accZ * accZ)));
iwangle yAngle = IwGeomAtan2(accX, lYZProjection);
```

Smoothing accelerometer input

One problem we will encounter when using the accelerometer for input is that the values returned from it tend to be a bit "jumpy". Even the steadiest hand will be unable to hold the device still enough to see a steady value being returned from the accelerometer. This can cause your game to register movements when you don't want it to.

A common approach for solving this problem is to smooth the accelerometer values by combining the current readings with the previous readings. The easiest way of doing this is shown in the following code:

```
int32 accX = 0, accY = 0, accZ = 0;
int32 lSmoothFactor = IW_GEOM_ONE / 4;
// The following loop shows how we generate the smoothed accelerometer
// inputs.  In a real application the code within the loop would be
called once
// per game frame.
while (TRUE)
{
  int32 deltaX = s3eAccelerometerGetX() - accX;
  int32 deltaY = s3eAccelerometerGetY() - accY;
  int32 deltaZ = s3eAccelerometerGetZ() - accZ;
  accX += IW_FIXED_MUL(lSmoothFactor, deltaX);
  accY += IW_FIXED_MUL(lSmoothFactor, deltaY);
  accZ += IW_FIXED_MUL(lSmoothFactor, deltaZ);
}
```

The variables `accX`, `accY`, and `accZ` are the smoothed accelerometer values that we will use in our program for input. The `lSmoothFactor` value determines how much smoothing we are applying to the inputs. If it is set to `IW_GEOM_ONE`, no smoothing will be applied and the results will be exactly what is coming in from the accelerometers.

Lower values for the smoothing factor will generate less jittery input values, but this will be at the expense of adding a certain amount of lag to the inputs. The degree of lag depends on how often the smoothing code is executed, which in turn depends on the frame rate of your game.

Working out a good value to use for the smoothing factor is really just a case of trial and error. You just need to keep tweaking the value until you achieve a suitable result.

`IW_FIXED_MUL` is a useful function provided by Marmalade for doing fixed point multiplication where `IW_GEOM_ONE` (4096) is equivalent to one. It multiplies the two parameters together and then shifts the result back down to be in the correct range.

Testing accelerometer input on the Windows simulator

Given that computers don't tend to feature accelerometer inputs of any kind, testing this form of input in the Windows simulator may appear to be impossible. Fortunately, Marmalade does provide us with a way of doing so.

When running an application in the simulator, select the menu item **Configuration | Accelerometer...** and a window showing a small 3D representation of a mobile device will be displayed:

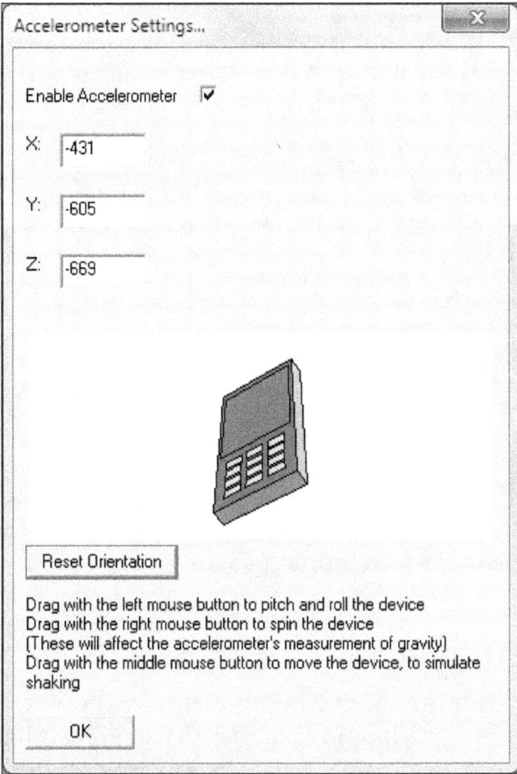

By clicking and dragging on this virtual device, we can alter the accelerometer inputs being fed into the simulator. It's a little tricky to use for playing a game but it normally suffices, so you can at least test applications that rely solely on accelerometer inputs.

The window also provides some edit boxes that show the current values of the accelerometer inputs as you rotate the 3D device about. These can also be used to enter exact values should you have need to do so.

Example code

The code package for this chapter contains three projects that demonstrate the things we've learnt in this chapter.

The Gesture project

This project demonstrates the use of the s3ePointer API by showing the screen coordinates pointed at by the user. If a multi-touch display is available, it will show multiple touch points.

The project also demonstrates a simple approach for detecting swipes and pinches and how it is possible to use the same gesture detection code with both single- and multi-touch capable displays.

The Slide project

The Slide project shows how to use the s3eAccelerometer API to read the current accelerometer values, apply a smoothing algorithm to them, and generate the angles of tip around the X- and Y-axes.

It also demonstrates something a little more game-like by allowing you to move a little red box around the screen by tipping the device.

The Skiing project

Our skiing game becomes interactive in this chapter, allowing you to rotate the skier left and right and have him move across the screen and affect the speed of scrolling. The skier can be controlled either by key presses and touch screen or accelerometer input.

We also have more of a game-like flow with the addition of a title screen mode that allows the input method to be selected, and a game over mode, which is triggered when the player goes into the trees at the edge of the game world.

The following sections highlight some of the new classes added to the project.

Player rotation

Rotation of the player has been achieved by including a number of different animation frames, each showing the player at a different angle of rotation. This makes it easy to slot into our existing `GameObject` code, which expects to draw a square image that is not rotated.

While this solution is very simple, it is perhaps not the best option. We could instead have extended `GameObject` to support rotated images, which would have both saved memory (we would not have needed to store all the extra animation frames) and yielded smoother rotation results, as the skier currently steps between frames at 10-degree rotation increments.

The ModeTitle and ModeGameOver classes

These classes implement the title screen and game over modes of the game. These have been added to make the project feel a little more like a game, although they are very basic to look at.

More importantly, these classes show how we can switch between game modes by making them active and visible. Take particular note of the `ModeGameOver` class, which stops the normal game mode from updating, but still allows it to render so we can see the game world along with the game over message.

The Camera class

The `Camera` class has been added to the project to allow us to specify a viewing point in the world. When rendering, we now use the camera position as the origin's location on the screen. So when we move the camera, the entire screen display will move relative to it. This makes it possible to do a horizontal scrolling effect without having to update the x coordinate of everything in the game world.

Another reason for making this change is to make our life easier when we upgrade the game to use 3D models in the next chapter, since this is closer to the way 3D graphics are rendered.

The Input Manager classes

Three new singleton classes have also been added to the project to make access to key, touch screen, and accelerometer inputs a little tidier. They are called `KeyManager`, `TouchManager`, and `AccelerometerManager` respectively.

These classes wrap the functionality provided by Marmalade into a simpler interface, which makes our game code easier to read. It also means that we can make changes to the inputs at a later date without having to change the game code. For example, the `KeyManager` class provides methods to indicate if the left or right arrow keys have been held. If we want to remap those keys or provide alternate possible keys, we can do so in the `KeyManager` code and our game code will work just fine.

The SkierController class

In order to add a layer of abstraction between the `Skier` class and the various input managers, the `SkierController` class has been added. This class provides a "steering" value, which is an integer number ranging from – `IW_GEOM_ONE` to +`IW_GEOM_ONE` that indicates how much the user is attempting to steer left (a negative value) or right (a positive value). The `Skier` class can just use this value to rotate the skier without needing to consider how this value is derived.

Internally, the `SkierController` class generates the steering value using the selected input method from the title screen.

For keyboard input, the left and right arrow keys modify the current steering value a little bit each frame.

Touch screen input uses the horizontal position of the player's finger on the screen to generate the value; so it is -1 when the player is touching the left-hand side of the screen and +1 when they are touching the right-hand side.

Finally, accelerometer input just scales the x axis accelerometer value into the required range.

Summary

In this chapter, we've covered how to make our programs interactive by detecting key and touch screen presses and by using the accelerometers of modern mobile devices. We've also seen how we can build on the basic functionality provided in order to detect swipe and pinch gestures.

In the next chapter, we'll be returning to things more graphical by showing how we can use Marmalade to render 3D graphics in our games.

4

3D Graphics Rendering

The graphics hardware inside the average smartphone is now capable of rendering 3D graphics of a surprisingly high quality for a device that is small enough to fit into your pocket.

The Marmalade SDK makes using 3D graphics in your own games extremely easy to do, as you will discover when we cover the following topics in this very chapter:

- The basics of 3D graphics rendering—projection, clipping, lighting, and so on
- Creating and rendering a simple 3D model entirely in code
- Exporting 3D model data from a modeling package
- Loading exported 3D models into memory and rendering them

A quick 3D graphics primer

Before we get our hands dirty with rendering code, let's just touch on some of the basics of how 3D rendering can be achieved. If you already have a good handle of 3D rendering techniques then feel free to skip this section.

Describing a 3D model

In computer graphics a 3D representation of an object is often referred to as a **model**. When we build a model in three dimensions for use in a video game, we create a group of triangles that define the shape of the model. We can also use quadrilaterals to make the modeling process easier, but these ultimately get converted into two triangles when it comes to rendering time.

The simplest representation of a 3D model is therefore little more than a big list of vertices which define the triangles required to render the model, but we often specify a host of extra information so we can control exactly how the model should appear on screen.

Specifying a model's vertex stream

Every 3D model has a **pivot point**, also called its **origin**, which is the point around which the model will rotate and scale. In a 3D modeling package this point can be positioned wherever you want it to be, but to make the mathematics easier in a game we would normally treat the point (0, 0, 0) as the pivot point.

Each triangle in the model is defined by three vertices, and each vertex consists of an x, y, and z component which declares the position of the vertex in what is called **model space** (sometimes also referred to as **object space**). This just means that the components of each vertex are relative to the model's pivot point.

The following diagram shows an example of a cube. The pivot point is positioned at the very centre of the cube and is hence the origin of model space. The corner points use both positive and negative values, but each component has an absolute value of **100**, which yields a cube with edges of length 200 units. For clarity, the three front faces of the cube also show how they have been built from two triangles.

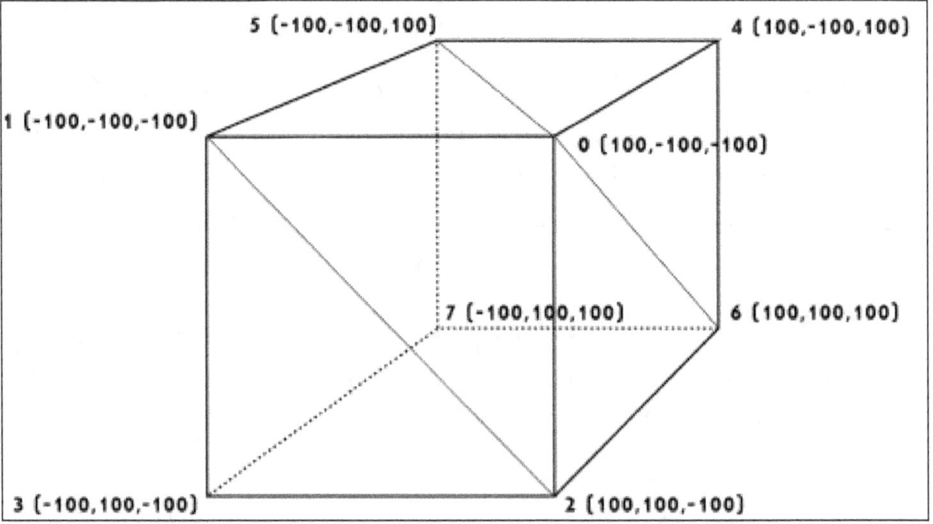

In order to provide Marmalade with the vertices of the cube, we simply use Marmalade's three-component floating pointer vector class `CIwFVec3` to provide an array of vertices. As with the 2D rendering, we've already seen this is called a vertex stream, except that this time the stream consists of three component vectors.

Specifying a model's index stream

You will notice that the corners of the cube in the previous diagram have been labeled with a number as well as their model space coordinates. If we cast our minds back to our work with 2D graphics, we will remember that Marmalade renders polygons by accepting a stream of vertices as input and also a stream of indices that defines the order in which those vertices should be processed.

The same approach applies when rendering 3D graphics. We specify the index stream as an array of unsigned 16-bit integers (`uint16`) and this dictates the order in which the vertices will be read out of the stream for rendering.

One advantage of using an index stream is that we can potentially refer to the same point several times without having to duplicate it in the vertex stream, thus saving us some memory. Since the index stream is just telling the GPU which order it has to process the data contained in the vertex, color, UV, and normal streams, it can be as long or as short as we want it to be. The index stream doesn't even need to reference every single element of the other streams, meaning we could potentially create one set of streams that can be referenced by multiple different index streams.

Another advantage of index streams is that we can use them to speed up rendering. You will recall that we used the function call `IwGxDrawPrims` to render a 2D polygon. To render 3D polygons, we use the exact same call. Each call to this function results in the rendering engine having to perform some initialization, so if we can find a way to minimize the number of draw calls we have to make, we can render the game world more quickly.

We can use the index stream to achieve this by inserting degenerate polygons into the polygon render list. A **degenerate polygon** is one that does not modify any pixels when it is drawn and this is achieved by ensuring that all the vertices that make up the polygon will lie on the same line. Most graphics hardware are clever enough to recognize a degenerate polygon and will not waste time trying to render it.

As an example, let's assume we are rendering some triangle strips. We could render them by calling `IwGxDrawPrims` twice, or we could join the two strips with some degenerate polygons and render them both with a single call to `IwGxDrawPrims`. We can continue to do this to join together as many triangle strips as we want.

How do we specify the degenerate triangle? The easiest way, shown in the following diagram, is to duplicate the last point of the first strip and the first point of the second strip. This yields four degenerate triangles (A3A4A4, A4A4B0, A4B0B0, B0B0B1) but is preferable to making several draw calls. The dotted line in the following diagram shows the extra degenerate triangles (which collapse to form a line!) that join the strips together:

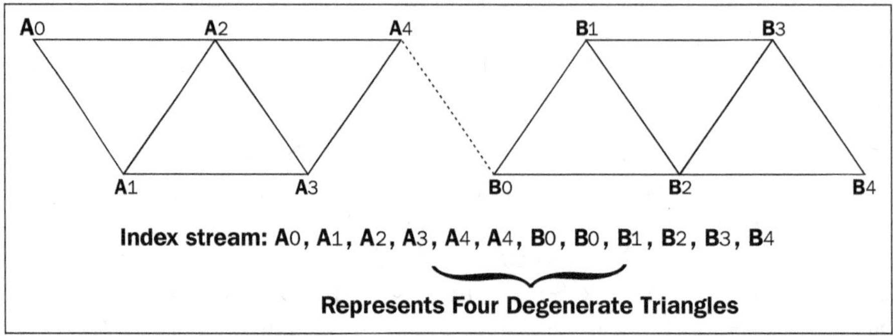

Specifying a model's color, UV, and normal streams

Just as with 2D rendering, there are a number of other stream types we can supply to make the polygons we render look more interesting. We can provide both color and texture UV streams in exactly the same way we did when rendering in two dimensions, but we can also specify a third stream type called a **normal stream**.

In 3D mathematics, a **normal vector** is defined as the vector which is perpendicular to two other non-parallel vectors, or in other words a vector that points in the direction in which the polygon is facing. The following diagram shows an example illustrating this:

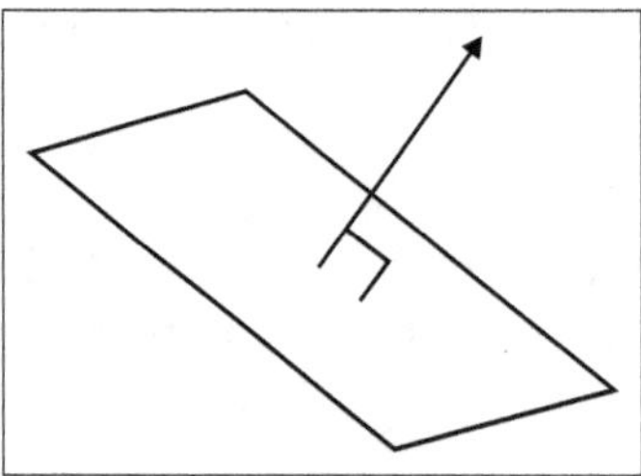

Why is the normal stream useful? Well, it allows us to simulate the effects of lights on our 3D model. By providing each vertex of our model with a **unit normal** (that is, a vector that points in the direction of the polygon's normal and which has a length of one unit), we can calculate the amount of light reflected from that vertex and adjust the color it is rendered with accordingly.

Real time lighting of a 3D model can be a time-intensive task, so when writing a game we try to avoid doing so when possible in order to speed up rendering. If we do not want to light a 3D model, there is no need to specify a normal stream; so, by not lighting a model we save memory too.

There are a couple of points to bear in mind when specifying these additional streams.

Firstly, Marmalade expects the number of colors, UVs, and normals provided to match the number of vertices provided. While you can specify streams of different lengths, this will normally cause an assert to be fired and obviously it could yield unexpected results when rendering.

Secondly, and perhaps most importantly, these additional streams may require us to add extra copies of our vertices into the vertex stream since we can only provide a single index stream.

Take the example of a cube where each vertex is a corner point of three different faces of the cube. Since each face points in a different direction, we will need to duplicate each vertex three times so it can be referenced in the index stream along with the three different normal vectors.

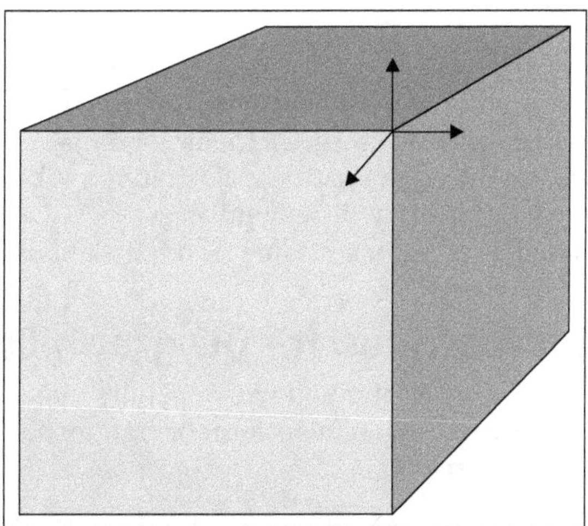

We can also run into the same problem when the UV or color at a vertex varies across each polygon that it forms a part of.

For each different combination of color, UV, and normal we encounter, we need to provide an additional copy of each vertex, and therefore also an additional color, UV, and normal value so that all the streams are the same length.

Performing 3D to 2D projection

When rendering our 3D world to the display, we have to somehow convert our 3D model vertex data into 2D screen coordinates before we can draw anything. This process is called **projection** and is normally carried out using matrix mathematics to convert vertices between coordinate systems until we end up with screen coordinates that allow the triangles that make up a 3D model to be rendered on screen.

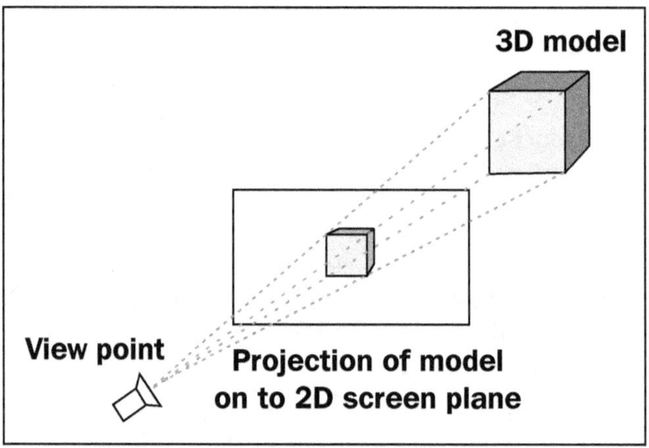

The following sections provide an overview of the steps involved in projecting a point on to the screen to make sure you are familiar with the key concepts involved. A thorough explanation of the mathematics of 3D graphics is beyond the scope of this book, so it is expected that you will be familiar with what a matrix is, and with geometric operations such as rotations, scaling, and translations.

Understanding matrices for 3D graphics

Think back to school math lessons and you will hopefully remember matrices being described as a useful tool when trying to perform operations such as rotations, translations, and scaling on vectors.

My personal recollection about learning matrices was that they seemed slightly magical at the time. Here was a grid of numbers that could be used to perform a range of really useful geometric operations and, what's more, you could combine several matrices by multiplying them together to perform several operations in one go. The concept itself made sense, but there were so many numbers involved that it seemed a bit bewildering.

In 3D geometry we generally use a 4 x 4 matrix, with the top left 3 x 3 grid of numbers representing the rotation and scaling part of the matrix, and the first three numbers of the bottom row representing the required translation.

While the translation part made perfect sense to me, the 3 x 3 rotation and scaling part of the matrix was something I never really had a good handle on until the day I found out that what this part of the matrix actually represents is the size and direction of the x, y, and z axes.

Take a look at the following image that shows the **identity matrix** for a 4 x 4 matrix. All this means is that every element in the matrix is `0` except for those in the top-left to bottom-right diagonal, which are all `1`:

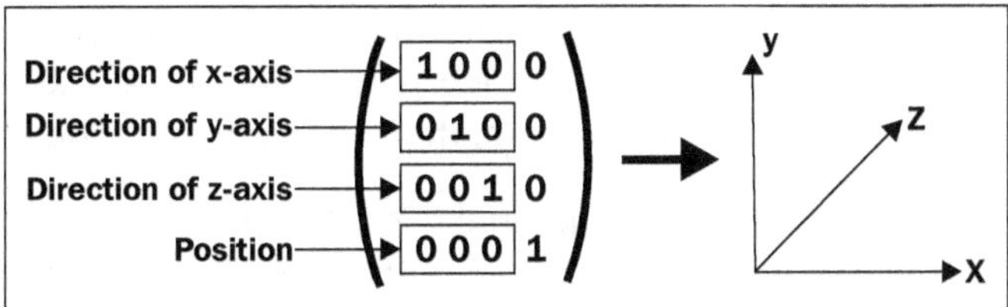

Notice that the first three numbers on the top row are (1, 0, 0), which just so happens to be a unit vector along the x axis. Similarly, the second row is (0, 1, 0), which represents a unit vector along the y axis and the third row (0, 0, 1) is a unit vector along the z axis.

Once I realized this, it became much more obvious how to create matrices to perform different kinds of geometric operations.

Want a rotation around the y axis? Just work out vectors for the directions in which the x axis and z axis would need to lie for the desired rotation, and slot these into the relevant parts of the matrix. Similarly, a scale operation just means that we provide a non-unit-sized vector for each axis we want to scale along.

Some of you may be reading this and thinking "that's obvious", but if this helps just one person to get a better understanding of how to understand matrix mathematics, my work is done!

Converting between coordinate systems

When we looked at how a 3D model is represented in terms of data, we talked about the vertices of the model being in model space. In order to use these vertices for rendering, we therefore have to convert our model space vertices into screen coordinates.

The first step in this process is to use a **model matrix** to convert the vertices from model space into **world space**. Each vertex in the model is multiplied by the model matrix, which will first rotate and scale the vertices so that the model is orientated correctly, then translate each point so that the model's pivot point is now at the translation provided in the matrix.

Now that all our vertices are positioned correctly in our virtual world, the next step is to convert them into **view space**, which is the coordinate system defined by the position and orientation of our viewpoint, which for obvious reasons is normally referred to as our camera. We do this by providing another matrix called the **view matrix** (or **camera matrix** if you prefer), which will rotate, scale, and translate the world space vertices so that they are now relative to our camera view.

With the vertices now in view space, the final operation is to convert the vertices into 2D screen coordinates. We have two ways of doing this, these being an **orthographic projection** or a **perspective projection**.

An orthographic projection takes the view space coordinates and just scales and translates the x and y components of each vertex to put them onto the screen. The z component of the vertex plays no part in calculating the actual screen coordinates but it is used for working out the drawing order of polygons since it is used as a depth value.

However, in most cases we use a perspective projection. Again the x and y components of each view space vertex are used to generate the x and y screen coordinates, but this time they are divided by the z component of the vertex, which has the effect of making objects that are further away appear smaller.

The components are also multiplied by a constant value called the **perspective multiplier**. This value is actually the distance at which the **view plane** lies from the camera. The view plane is the plane which contains the rectangular area of the screen display.

Normally, when we think about a camera view it is more convenient to think about the **field of view**, which is the horizontal angle of our viewing cone. The following diagram shows how we can convert this angle into the correct perspective multiplier value:

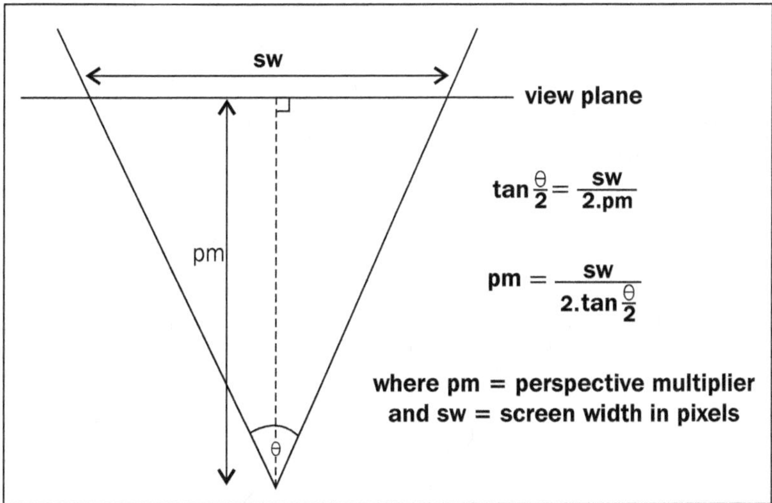

The next part of perspective projection is to translate the projected point. Normally we want a point that is directly in front of the camera to be in the center of the screen, so we would add an offset of half the screen width to the x component and half the screen height to the y-component. It is possible to specify a different offset position, which is particularly useful if we ever want to display a 3D model as part of a game's user interface. Let's say you wanted to draw a 3D model of a collectable object that the player has just picked up at the top right of the screen. Specifying the offset to be this screen position is much easier than trying to calculate a position in 3D space relative to the camera position that equates to the required area of the screen.

Clipping planes

We've already discussed the view plane as being the plane which contains the final screen display, but there are some further planes which are used to help speed up rendering and also avoid some strange graphical glitches from occurring.

First we have the **far clip plane** and the **near clip plane**, which lie parallel to the view plane. We tell Marmalade where we want these planes to reside by supplying the perpendicular distance of these planes from the camera view point.

The far clip plane prevents polygons that are too far away from the camera from being rendered, while the near clip plane, unsurprisingly, prevents polygons that are too close to the camera from being rendered. The near clip plane is particularly important because if we were not to use it we would start to see models that lie behind the camera being rendered on screen.

You should generally try to keep the far and near clip planes as close together as possible, as these values are also used for calculating depth buffer values. If the planes are too far apart, you can start to encounter render issues that are sometimes called **shimmering** or **Z-fighting**. These can occur when there is not enough resolution in the depth buffer values, which results in far distance polygons rendering with jagged edges or worse still, randomly poke through each other as they or the camera are moved. The following image shows another example of Z-fighting that can occur when trying to render two overlapping co-planar polygons:

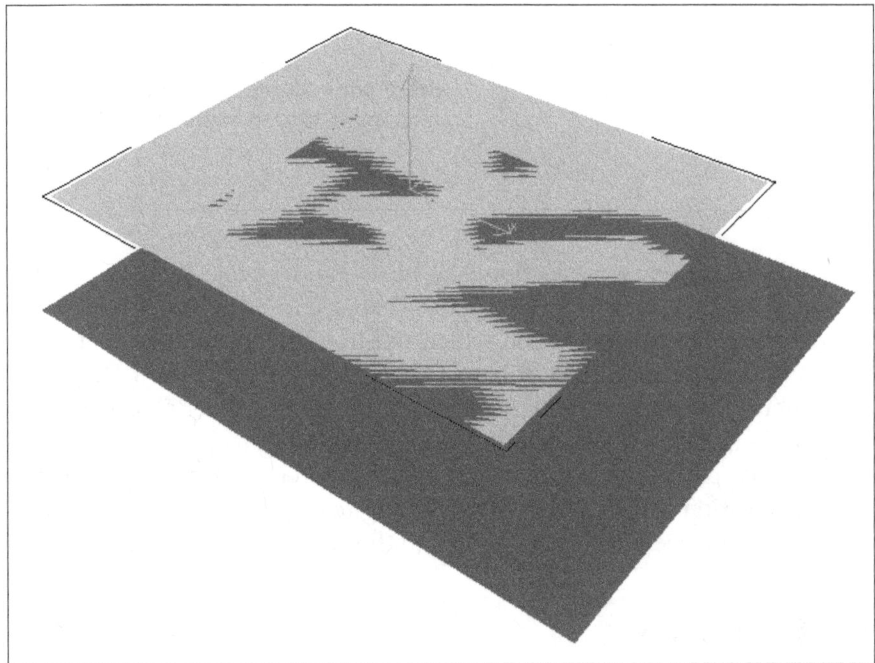

There are also four more clipping planes named left, right, top, and bottom. These are planes which pass through the camera position and one of the left, right, top, or bottom borders of the screen display area on the view plane. Together they form a pyramid-shaped volume that emanates from the camera and defines the part of 3D space that is visible and could therefore appear on screen.

The clipping planes are managed automatically for us by Marmalade, and they are very useful as they allow us to quickly reject an entire model from being submitted for rendering if it is completely off screen. The off-screen check is performed using a bounding sphere for the model we are rendering, which is simply a sphere centered at the model's pivot point that encompasses all the vertices of the model. The bounding sphere can be quickly tested against all six clip planes and the model can be skipped if the bounding sphere is completely outside the clipping volume.

Lighting

To finish up our 3D primer, let's take a quick look at how real-time lighting is achieved. We won't dwell on the mathematics of it all, since Marmalade mostly takes care of this for us, so instead we'll just explain the different types of lighting we can take advantage of.

Each of the lighting types we are about to discuss can be enabled or disabled whenever you want. Disabling different lighting types can yield faster render times.

Emissive lighting

The simplest type of lighting Marmalade provides is **emissive lighting**, which is little more than the amount of color that a rendered polygon will naturally have. The emissive lighting color is provided by the `CIwMaterial` instance that is set when rendering the polygon.

Emissive lighting is useful if you want to draw polygons in a single flat color, but normally we want a bit more flexibility than that, so we might set a color stream instead, or use one of the other forms of lighting.

Ambient lighting

Ambient lighting provides the background level of light in our scene, such as the light which might be provided by the Sun.

Without ambient lighting, any polygon that is not facing a light source directly would have very little light applied to it and so would appear black. Normally this is not very desirable, so we can use ambient lighting to provide a base level of color and brightness to our polygons.

In Marmalade, we set a global ambient lighting term as an RGB color. The `CIwMaterial` instance used when rendering also has an ambient light value that is combined with the global ambient light. If the material ambient light is set to bright white, the polygon will be rendered with the full amount of the global ambient light.

If the global ambient lighting is disabled, the material ambient color is used directly to control the color of the rendered polygons. This provides an easy way of brightening or darkening a model at rendering time.

Diffuse lighting

In order to use **diffuse lighting** our model data must provide a normal stream. A diffuse light comprises of both a color and a direction in which the light is pointing. The light's direction vector is combined with the normal vector for each vertex in the model using the dot product operation.

The result of the dot product operation is multiplied by the global diffuse lighting color and the current `CIwMaterial` diffuse color or the RGB value from the color stream, if one has been provided. This will yield the final color value that is used when rendering the polygon to the screen.

Specular lighting

As with diffuse lighting, **specular lighting** can only work if we have provided a normal stream. It also needs a diffuse light to be specified as it relies on the direction of the diffuse light.

This type of lighting allows us to make a model appear shinier by causing it to briefly become brighter when it is facing the direction of the diffuse light.

We can specify both a global and a specular light color specific to `CIwMaterial`, and additionally the material also provides a setting for the **specular power**. This value allows us to narrow down the response of the specular lighting. A higher number means that the vertex normal must be almost parallel to the lighting direction before the specular lighting will take effect.

Using IwGx to render 3D graphics

Remember when we were looking at 2D graphics rendering in *Chapter 2, Resource Management and 2D Graphics Rendering*, I said we would be using IwGx because it would make the transition to rendering 3D graphics that much easier. Now's the time to see if my claim was true!

In this section, we shall look at how we can implement the 3D equivalent of the "Hello World" program—a spinning cube.

Preparing IwGx for 3D rendering

As with 2D rendering, the very first thing we need to do is initialize the IwGx API by calling `IwGxInit`, and of course we should call `IwGxTerminate` at the end of our program.

With IwGx ready to go we next need to set up our projection. We're going to be using a perspective projection, so we need to be able to specify the perspective multiplier value that we want to use. The code to do this is as follows:

```
IwGxSetPerspMul((float) IwGxGetScreenWidth() * 0.5f);
```

This line of code sets the perspective multiplier up, to provide a 90 degree field of view. See the section *Converting Between Coordinate Systems* earlier in this chapter for more information on how to calculate the required perspective multiplier value.

Next we have to set the far and near clipping planes' distances. For our demo purposes we'll choose a value of `10` for the near plane and `1000` for the far plane; these values are set as follows:

```
IwGxSetFarZNearZ(1000.0f, 10.0f);
```

These values are in view space units and can be set to any value greater than zero (the far value should be greater than the near value too!) that works well for the needs of our game. Normally it is the far clip distance that is most important, as it needs to be set far enough out that our world is rendered satisfactorily, but not so far that the frame rate suffers because we are rendering too much.

You may be wondering why these numbers have been written as `10.0f` and not just 10 or 10.0? The reason is to ensure that the compiler treats these values as a single precision `float` value. The latter two forms will both be interpreted as a `double` and this can lead to a time consuming conversion from `double` to `float`.

Setting lighting information

In order to make our spinning cube look a little more attention grabbing, we'll set up some lights so that as the cube spins its faces change color accordingly. The lighting support provided by Marmalade may look a little limited, but is generally adequate for most mobile games' needs.

Marmalade only allows us to define a single ambient light and a single diffuse light. Let's start by setting the global ambient lighting value.

The first function we call is `IwGxSetLightType`, which takes an ID number to identify the light we wish to modify and a definition describing the type of light we are specifying. Presumably this API has been chosen so that Marmalade can easily be made to support more lights in the future, but for now the ID number can only be zero or one, and the light type must be one of `IW_GX_LIGHT_AMBIENT`, `IW_GX_LIGHT_DIFFUSE`, or `IW_GX_LIGHT_UNUSED`. The latter value can be used to disable the light.

With the type of light taken care of, we set the color of light using the function call `IwGxSetLightCol`. There are two versions of this function. Both take the ID of the light we wish to modify, but the RGB color of the light can either be specified as three `uint8` values for red, green, and blue, or a pointer to a `CIwColour` instance can be supplied instead.

The following code sets the light with ID zero to be an ambient light with a mid-grey color:

```
IwGxSetLightType(0, IW_GX_LIGHT_AMBIENT);
IwGxSetLightCol(0, 128, 128, 128);
```

Now let's create a diffuse light with a specular highlight. We'll need two additional functions to do this, `IwGxSetLightSpecularCol` to set the color of the specular highlight, and `IwGxSetLightDirn` to set the direction in which the light is pointing. The direction is specified as a unit vector in terms of world space coordinates. Here's some code to illustrate this:

```
CIwFVec3 lLightDir(1000.0f, 0.0f, 1000.0f);
lLightDir.Normalise();

IwGxSetLightType(1, IW_GX_LIGHT_DIFFUSE);
IwGxSetLightCol(1, 128, 128, 128);
IwGxSetLightSpecularCol(1, 200, 200, 200, 255);
IwGxSetLightDirn(1, &lLightDir);
```

This code snippet sets up the light ID one to be a diffuse light with mid-grey intensity and a brighter grey specular highlight. The light is pointing at a 45 degree angle between the x and z axes of the world.

Our lights have now been initialized, so all that is left to do is let Marmalade know we want to switch them on! There are a number of functions available to allow us to do this. We can either use `IwGxLightingOn` and `IwGxLightingOff` to enable or disable all the initialized light sources, or we can enable each part of the lighting model independently. The following example code disables emissive lighting but enables ambient, diffuse, and specular lighting:

```
IwGxLightingAmbient(true);
IwGxLightingDiffuse(true);
IwGxLightingEmissive(false);
IwGxLightingSpecular(true);
```

Since we are using specular lighting, there is one more thing to do. The material that is used to render our polygons must have a specular color and power specified. The material's specular color is used to modulate the global specular color, while the power value indicates how close the vertex normal must be to the light direction for the specular highlight to kick in. The power value is a `uint8` value and only very low values (that is, less than 8) produce notable differences in the rendered effect. Here is the code to illustrate this:

```
CIwMaterial* lpMaterial = new CIwMaterial;
lpMaterial->SetColSpecular(255, 255, 255);
lpMaterial->SetSpecularPower(3);
```

The previous examples are just making use of Marmalade's built-in lighting model since it is easy to use and works well enough for most needs. However, there is absolutely no reason we have to use this lighting model, as there is nothing stopping us from generating our own color stream using whatever lighting algorithm we want to use. Alternatively we could employ OpenGL ES 2.0 shaders, although discussion of this particular topic is beyond the scope of this book.

Model data for the cube

We're going to render a lit cube with a different color on each face, so we need to provide some data streams for the vertices, colors, and normals, and an index stream to show how this data should be interpreted by the rendering engine. Since we are not using textures in this example, there is no need to provide a UV stream.

We also want to be as efficient as possible in our drawing, so our aim is to draw the entire cube with just a single call to `IwGxDrawPrims`. To do so we'll need to have three copies of each vertex (one for each face that the vertex is part of) so we can assign different colors and normals to it, and we'll also need to specify some degenerate triangles in our index stream to join all the faces together into one big triangle strip.

Let's start with the vertex stream. We allocate an array of `CIwFVec3` and initialize it with the vertex data. The cube pivot point will be dead center, so all the vertex coordinates will have the same magnitude.

```
const uint32 lVertexCount = 24;
CIwFVec3* v = new CIwFVec3[lVertexCount];
v[0].x = 100.0f;    v[0].y = -100.0f;  v[0].z = -100.0f;
v[1].x = -100.0f;   v[1].y = -100.0f;  v[1].z = -100.0f;
v[2].x = 100.0f;    v[2].y = 100.0f;   v[2].z = -100.0f;
v[3].x = -100.0f;   v[3].y = 100.0f;   v[3].z = -100.0f;
```

```
v[4].x = 100.0f;     v[4].y = -100.0f;   v[4].z = 100.0f;
v[5].x = 100.0f;     v[5].y = -100.0f;   v[5].z = -100.0f;
v[6].x = 100.0f;     v[6].y = 100.0f;    v[6].z = 100.0f;
v[7].x = 100.0f;     v[7].y = 100.0f;    v[7].z = -100.0f;
v[8].x = 100.0f;     v[8].y = -100.0f;   v[8].z = 100.0f;
v[9].x = 100.0f;     v[9].y = 100.0f;    v[9].z = 100.0f;
v[10].x = -100.0f;   v[10].y = -100.0f;  v[10].z = 100.0f;
v[11].x = -100.0f;   v[11].y = 100.0f;   v[11].z = 100.0f;
v[12].x = -100.0f;   v[12].y = -100.0f;  v[12].z = 100.0f;
v[13].x = -100.0f;   v[13].y = 100.0f;   v[13].z = 100.0f;
v[14].x = -100.0f;   v[14].y = -100.0f;  v[14].z = -100.0f;
v[15].x = -100.0f;   v[15].y = 100.0f;   v[15].z = -100.0f;
v[16].x = -100.0f;   v[16].y = 100.0f;   v[16].z = -100.0f;
v[17].x = -100.0f;   v[17].y = 100.0f;   v[17].z = 100.0f;
v[18].x = 100.0f;    v[18].y = 100.0f;   v[18].z = -100.0f;
v[19].x = 100.0f;    v[19].y = 100.0f;   v[19].z = 100.0f;
v[20].x = -100.0f;   v[20].y = -100.0f;  v[20].z = -100.0f;
v[21].x = -100.0f;   v[21].y = -100.0f;  v[21].z = 100.0f;
v[22].x = 100.0f;    v[22].y = -100.0f;  v[22].z = -100.0f;
v[23].x = 100.0f;    v[23].y = -100.0f;  v[23].z = 100.0f;
```

The vertices have been ordered a face at a time, so the first four vertices form the front of the cube, the next four the right hand face, and so on. You are free to specify the order however you see fit, since ultimately it will be the index stream that determines how the individual triangles will be rendered.

Now we'll create the normal stream. Normals in Marmalade are also specified as instances of `CIwFVec3`, and they are expected to have unit length. This means that the magnitude of the vector should be one. Here's a code snippet that will do the job:

```
CIwFVec3* n = new CIwFVec3[lVertexCount];
n[0].x = 0.0f;       n[0].y = 0.0f;      n[0].z = -1.0f;
n[1].x = 0.0f;       n[1].y = 0.0f;      n[1].z = -1.0f;
n[2].x = 0.0f;       n[2].y = 0.0f;      n[2].z = -1.0f;
n[3].x = 0.0f;       n[3].y = 0.0f;      n[3].z = -1.0f;
n[4].x = 1.0f;       n[4].y = 0.0f;      n[4].z = 0.0f;
n[5].x = 1.0f;       n[5].y = 0.0f;      n[5].z = 0.0f;
n[6].x = 1.0f;       n[6].y = 0.0f;      n[6].z = 0.0f;
n[7].x = 1.0f;       n[7].y = 0.0f;      n[7].z = 0.0f;
n[8].x = 0.0f;       n[8].y = 0.0f;      n[8].z = 1.0f;
n[9].x = 0.0f;       n[9].y = 0.0f;      n[9].z = 1.0f;
n[10].x = 0.0f;      n[10].y = 0.0f;     n[10].z = 1.0f;
n[11].x = 0.0f;      n[11].y = 0.0f;     n[11].z = 1.0f;
n[12].x = -1.0f;     n[12].y = 0.0f;     n[12].z = 0.0f;
```

```
n[13].x = -1.0f;      n[13].y = 0.0f;       n[13].z = 0.0f;
n[14].x = -1.0f;      n[14].y = 0.0f;       n[14].z = 0.0f;
n[15].x = -1.0f;      n[15].y = 0.0f;       n[15].z = 0.0f;
n[16].x = 0.0f;       n[16].y = 1.0f;       n[16].z = 0.0f;
n[17].x = 0.0f;       n[17].y = 1.0f;       n[17].z = 0.0f;
n[18].x = 0.0f;       n[18].y = 1.0f;       n[18].z = 0.0f;
n[19].x = 0.0f;       n[19].y = 1.0f;       n[19].z = 0.0f;
n[20].x = 0.0f;       n[20].y = -1.0f;      n[20].z = 0.0f;
n[21].x = 0.0f;       n[21].y = -1.0f;      n[21].z = 0.0f;
n[22].x = 0.0f;       n[22].y = -1.0f;      n[22].z = 0.0f;
n[23].x = 0.0f;       n[23].y = -1.0f;      n[23].z = 0.0f;
```

Now we need a color stream. Just as with 2D rendering, this requires an array of `CIwColour` instances. Here comes the code snippet!

```
CIwColour* c = new CIwColour[lVertexCount];
c[0].Set(255, 0, 0, 255);
c[1].Set(255, 0, 0, 255);
c[2].Set(255, 0, 0, 255);
c[3].Set(255, 0, 0, 255);
c[4].Set(255, 255, 0, 255);
c[5].Set(255, 255, 0, 255);
c[6].Set(255, 255, 0, 255);
c[7].Set(255, 255, 0, 255);
c[8].Set(0, 255, 0, 255);
c[9].Set(0, 255, 0, 255);
c[10].Set(0, 255, 0, 255);
c[11].Set(0, 255, 0, 255);
c[12].Set(0, 0, 255, 255);
c[13].Set(0, 0, 255, 255);
c[14].Set(0, 0, 255, 255);
c[15].Set(0, 0, 255, 255);
c[16].Set(0, 255, 255, 255);
c[17].Set(0, 255, 255, 255);
c[18].Set(0, 255, 255, 255);
c[19].Set(0, 255, 255, 255);
c[20].Set(255, 128, 0, 255);
c[21].Set(255, 128, 0, 255);
c[22].Set(255, 128, 0, 255);
c[23].Set(255, 128, 0, 255);
```

Finally, it's time for the index stream to be created. Again, as with 2D rendering, this is just an array of `uint16` values which indicate the order in which elements of the streams should be accessed. Here's the code:

```
const uint32 lIndexCount = 34;
uint16* i = new uint16[lIndexCount];

// Front face (red)
i[0] = 0;  i[1] = 1;  i[2] = 2;  i[3] = 3;
// Degenerate
i[4] = 3;  i[5] = 7;
// Right face (yellow)
i[6] = 7;  i[7] = 6;  i[8] = 5;  i[9] = 4;
// Degenerate
i[10] = 4;  i[11] = 9;
// Back face (green)
i[12] = 9;  i[13] = 11;  i[14] = 8;  i[15] = 10;
// Degenerate
i[16] = 10;  i[17] = 12;
// Left face (blue)
i[18] = 12;  i[19] = 13;  i[20] = 14;  i[21] = 15;
// Degenerate
i[22] = 15;  i[23] = 16;
// Bottom face (cyan)
i[24] = 16;  i[25] = 17;  i[26] = 18;  i[27] = 19;
// Degenerate
i[28] = 19;  i[29] = 23;
// Top face (orange)
i[30] = 23;  i[31] = 21;  i[32] = 22;  i[33] = 20;
```

Note than the first four values in the stream define the first full face of the cube. The next two values form a degenerate triangle that allows us to link the first face to the second face without actually rendering anything. As we saw earlier in this chapter, the easiest way to link two triangle strips is to repeat the last index of the first strip and start the next strip with two copies of its first index. This pattern continues until we've drawn the last face of the cube.

The order in which the vertices are specified is the most important consideration, as we must ensure we get this correct for the culling mode we'll be using. For back-face culling (so faces that are away from the camera are not rendered) we need the vertex order to be in anti-clockwise order for the first triangle specified.

As we are using triangle strips, the order of the vertices actually alternates between anti-clockwise and clockwise. Normally we don't have to worry about this too much since the natural order of the vertices in the strip takes care of it, but it can cause problems when you try to join together triangle strips that contain an odd number of vertices.

> The general rule for joining triangle strips with degenerate triangles is that a strip with an odd number of points will require the order of the points in the next strip to be reversed. For example, if your first triangle strip contains an odd number of points, the first triangle of the next strip will need to be specified in clockwise rather than anti-clockwise order; otherwise it will not be culled correctly.

The view matrix

When rendering 3D graphics, we need to be able to provide a position and direction that we want to view our game world from. We do this by supplying a view or camera matrix; in Marmalade this can be done using an instance of the `CIwFMat` class.

The `CIwFMat` class represents a 4 x 4 matrix using a 3 x 3 array of `float` for the rotation part, and `CIwFVec3` for the translation part. The remaining elements of the 4 x 4 matrix (that is, the right-most column of numbers) are fixed to be the same as the identity matrix (0, 0, 0, and 1 from top to bottom of the column). These values never have any influence on normal 3D transformations; so by leaving them out we save memory, and also the matrix multiplication code can be made slightly more efficient by not having to perform multiplications for these parts of the matrix.

Time to create a suitable view matrix. For the purposes of our spinning cube, it would be good if we could specify a position for the camera and then calculate the correct rotation for the matrix to view our cube. Luckily the matrix classes have a method called `LookAt` that makes this easy to do:

```
CIwFMat vm;
vm.t.x = 0.0f;   vm.t.y = 0.0f;   vm.t.z = -400.0f;
vm.LookAt(vm.t, CIwFVec3::g_Zero, CIwFVec3::g_AxisY);
```

The previous code declares a new `CIwMat` instance and sets its translation to (0, 0, -400). We then call the `LookAt` method, which is passed the position we want the camera to be placed at, the point in space we want it to be orientated towards, and a unit vector in the vertically up direction.

Marmalade's default coordinate system when rendering in 3D has the x axis positive direction running from left to right across the screen, while the z axis positive direction runs into the screen. However, the positive y axis runs in a direction from the top of the screen to the bottom, which may not be what you initially expect. We are used to thinking about the height above the ground as a positive number, but in Marmalade it would be negative.

Once we have a view matrix, we can call the function `IwGxSetViewMatrix` with a `const` pointer to the matrix.

The model matrix

The model matrix is used to position our 3D model in the world and allow it to be rotated or scaled as desired. As with the view matrix, the model matrix can be specified using a `CIwFMat` instance.

For our spinning cube we will create a matrix that spins the cube around the x and y axes. We do this by creating two matrices, one for x axis rotation and another for y axis rotation, which we then multiply together. We will be positioning our cube at the world origin.

```
CIwFMat lModelMatrix;
lModelMatrix.SetRotY(lRotationY);
CIwFMat lRotX;
lRotX.SetRotX(lRotationX);
lModelMatrix.PreMult(lRotX);
```

The code shown declares two instances of `CIwFMat` and uses the methods `SetRotY` and `SetRotX` to generate the rotation matrices around the y and x axes respectively. The rotation angles are provided by two variables `lRotationY` and `lRotationX`, which are both of the type `float` and represent an angle (in radians) to rotate by. If we increase the values of these two variables with each iteration of the main game loop, it will change the orientation of the cube and make it appear to rotate when rendered.

> Be careful when using the `SetRotX`, `SetRotY`, and `SetRotZ` methods of the matrix classes. These methods take two further `bool` parameters that allow the translation part of the matrix and any elements of the 3 x 3 rotation part of the matrix that are not used in the rotation to be zeroed. Both of these parameters default to `true`; so, in particular, if you set up a translation in the matrix before calling one of these methods, it will get lost unless you specify `false` as the second parameter.

Once we have our two rotation matrices, we multiply them together to generate the final model matrix using the `PreMult` method. The order in which matrices are multiplied together is very important as the end rotation will vary depending on the order used. Marmalade provides us with `PreMult` and `PostMult` methods to allow us to determine whether the calling matrix is the first matrix or the second in the multiplication.

When we have our model matrix ready, we just call `IwGxSetModelMatrix` to use it for rendering.

Rendering the model

All the hard work is now done and we can finally submit our cube for rendering. The following code will submit all our streams and our cube will be rendered. Hopefully you'll see just how close it is to the code we used for rendering in 2D:

```
IwGxSetColClear(128, 190, 220, 255);
IwGxClear();

IwGxSetMaterial(lpMaterial);
IwGxSetVertStreamModelSpace(v, lVertexCount);
IwGxSetNormStream(n, lVertexCount);
IwGxSetColStream(c);
IwGxDrawPrims(IW_GX_TRI_STRIP, i, lIndexCount)

IwGxFlush();
IwGxSwapBuffers();
```

Using a 3D modeling package to create model data

We've seen how to create the streams of data for a cube in code, and to be honest it's not pretty! Even a simple shape such as a cube requires so much data that it becomes very difficult for us to keep track of it all and almost impossible to create a more complex 3D shape.

Luckily there is an easier way. We can use a 3D modeling package to create, color, and texture a 3D model and export all the required data in a format that Marmalade can then load and use.

The Marmalade 3D exporter plugins

Marmalade comes with exporter plugins for the two modeling packages used in most professional game development studios—Maya and 3DS Max. The details in the following sections apply equally to the exporters for both of these modeling packages.

Installing the plugins

The exporter plugins are installed to your computer when you install the main SDK, but they are not automatically installed into the modeling package for use. In order to use the exporters, we must use the **Marmalade Launch Pad** program to set them up, as shown in the following steps:

1. Start the **Marmalade LaunchPad** program. On Windows it can be found inside the **Marmalade** folder in the **Start** menu. You should see a window appear, containing a tabbed view.
2. Click on the tab labeled **Install Exporters**. The following screen shown should appear:

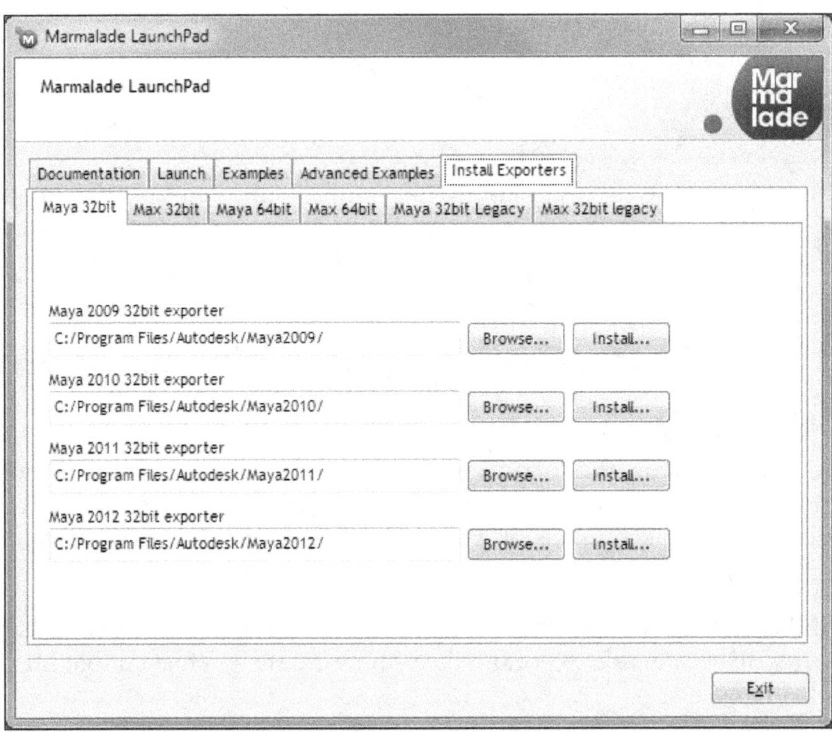

3. Use the tabs on this screen to select the version of the 3D modeling package you want to install. You must choose both the correct version of your package and whether it is a 32-bit or 64-bit installation. Maya 7.0 and 3DS Max 8.0 are the oldest supported versions. The older versions of the exporters are contained in the tabs labeled **Maya 32bit Legacy** and **Max 32bit legacy**.
4. Click on the **Install...** button next to the required version of your modeling package and the exporter will be installed. Windows User Account Control will probably pop up a request first to ensure you want to proceed, so just click the **Yes** button in this dialog.

Exporting a model

With the plugin installed, start up your 3D modeling package and create or load a model that you wish to export. Since this is a coding book, we won't be going into any details about how to create a 3D model.

If you are a programmer by trade and have no idea how to use a 3D modeling package, don't feel bad. I have seen some truly terrible "programmer art" over the years; so think of this lack of knowledge as a good thing and get a real artist involved in making the artwork for your game. You'll be glad you did!

Assuming you have a 3D model ready to export, let's get the Marmalade exporter plugin going. The exporter window itself is shown in the following figure:

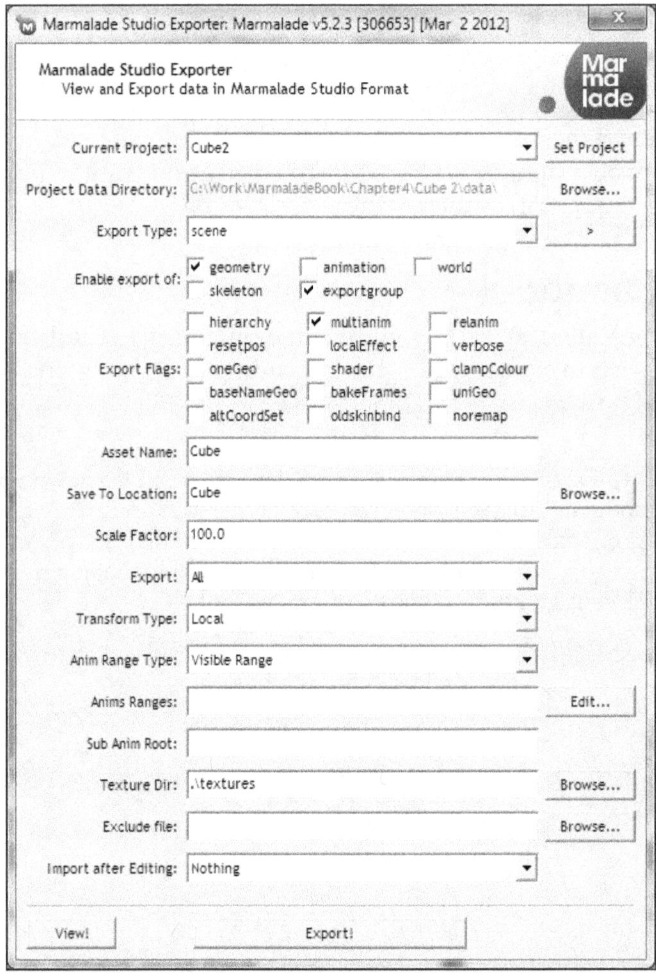

The manner in which the exporter window will be displayed depends on the modeling package you are using.

- In Maya you can access the exporter by using the menu option **Marmalade Tools | Marmalade Studio: Maya Exporter** or from the icon in the **Marmalade Studio** tab.
- In 3DS Max, the exporter can be opened by clicking on the **Utilities** tab, then clicking on the **Marmalade Studio Exporter** button to open the rollout section. Within the rollout, there is another button labeled **Marmalade Studio Exporter**, which will display the exporter window.

The exporter window should now be on screen, and as you can see there are a great many options available. We can do without most of them for now, so we'll only cover the ones we need in order to export a non-animated 3D model.

The first thing we need to set is the **Current Project** field. The exporter maintains a list of projects that, at its simplest level, is just a quick way of choosing a directory where the exported model files will be created.

Since we've not yet created an exporter project, let's do so by clicking on the button labeled **Set Project**. The following dialog will appear:

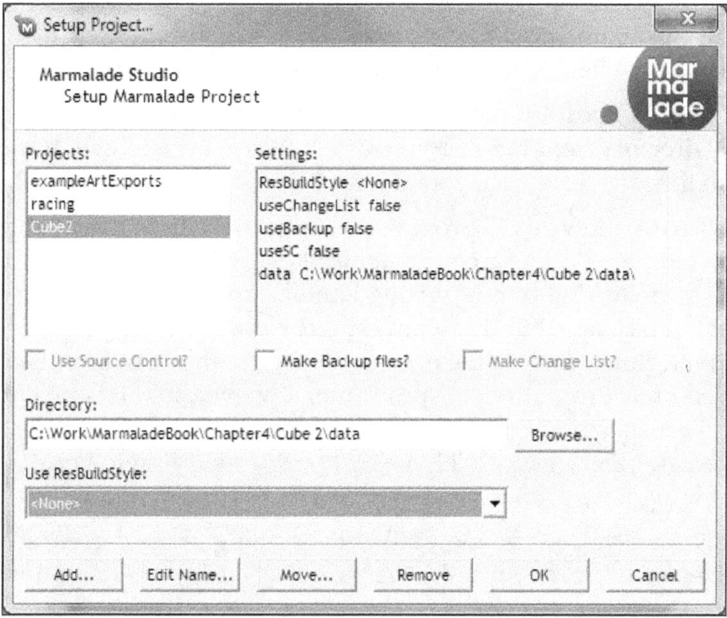

To create a new project click on the **Add...** button at the bottom of the dialog and you will be prompted to enter a name for the project. Once you've accepted the name, the project will appear in the **Projects:** list.

Click on the **Browse...** button and locate the `data` directory in our code project. All resource files need to reside with our code project's `data` directory; this will make exporting model files to the correct place much easier.

For now we will ignore the other settings in this dialog as they are beyond the scope of this chapter; so click the **OK** button to return to the main exporter window, which should now have our newly created project selected in the **Current Project** drop-down list and the `data` directory we set above in the **Project Data Directory** field.

With the project set, we can now follow these steps to export the model:

1. First locate the **Export Type** field. Next to this field is a button with a greater-than symbol. Click this button and choose **model** from the pop-up menu that appears. The **Export Type** field should change to **scene (model)**.
2. Now look at the first set of checkboxes labeled **Enable export of**. We only need the **geometry** and **exportgroup** options to be ticked to export the correct set of files.
3. The next set of checkboxes is labeled **Export Flags**. We don't need to have any of these settings checked.
4. Now we reach the **Asset Name** field. This specifies the base filename that will be used when the exporter generates the various output files.
5. The **Save To Location** field allows a directory path relative to the **Project Data Directory** field to be provided. All files generated will be created within this directory, which will itself be created if it does not already exist.
6. **Scale Factor** allows us to provide a numeric scaling factor that will be applied to the x, y, and z components of every exported vertex. This allows artists to create their models using familiar units such as meters in the modeling package, but then convert those units into a different scale for use in the game, such as the ever popular "number that is a power of 2" so beloved of us programmer types. Note, however, that it is vital to ensure that all artists working on a project use the same units and scale factors as each other, otherwise you'll have real problems trying to get all these models to work together properly in the game!
7. Next we can choose to export either everything in the current scene, just the selected objects, or just the visible objects using the drop-down list labeled **Export**.
8. The **Transform Type** drop-down box lets us choose whether the exported vertices should be in model space or world space. In most cases, when exporting individual models we would choose the **local** option (another way of saying model space!).
9. The final setting we may be interested in is the **Texture Dir** field. This allows a directory to be specified, from which any textures to be used on the model will be exported. It can be either an absolute path or relative to the **Project Data Directory**.
10. That completes all the fields we currently need to be concerned with. All that is left to do is click on the **Export!** button, which will generate the necessary files and then display a window listing all the files that were created during the export process.

The Blender plugin

There's no doubt that both Maya and 3DS Max are superb products, but it's also true that they carry a fairly hefty price tag. Unfortunately, Marmalade does kind of rely on using one of these two heavyweight packages.

Admittedly, Marmalade does also ship with a converter for **Collada**, a file format that was created to enable the interchange of 3D models between different packages. I hesitate to recommend this approach however, as at the time of writing, the Collada converter that ships with Marmalade is known to be a little buggy, particularly when it comes to exporting animations.

Luckily there is a cheaper alternative. There is a 3D modeling package by the name of Blender, which is free to download and use; however, the Blender team is always happy to accept donations to continuously improve the product, so if you find it useful do consider helping them out.

The Marmalade SDK does not come with support for Blender, but thankfully due to the efforts of Benoit Muller there is a rather groovy exporter plugin that does a great job of replacing the 3DS Max and Maya exporters.

Installing Blender and the exporter plugin

If you do not already have Blender installed, head over to the Blender website and download a copy. The URL is as follows:

`http://www.blender.org/`

Installing Blender is just a case of executing the downloaded installer and following the on-screen instructions.

With Blender installed, we now need to get hold of the exporter plugin, which can be found at the following URL:

`http://wiki.blender.org/index.php/Extensions:2.6/Py/Scripts/Import-Export/Marmalade_Exporter`

The plugin is a Python script that can be installed into Blender using the following steps:

1. Copy the downloaded plugin file `io_export_marmalade.py` into the Blender plugins directory. On Windows this will normally be something like `C:\Program Files\Blender Foundation\Blender\2.63\scripts\addons`.
2. Start Blender and go to **File** | **User Preferences...**.

3. Click on the **Addons** tab at the top of the preferences window.
4. In the **Categories** list on the left-hand side of the window, click on **Import-Export**. You should see a screen that looks something like the one shown in the following figure:

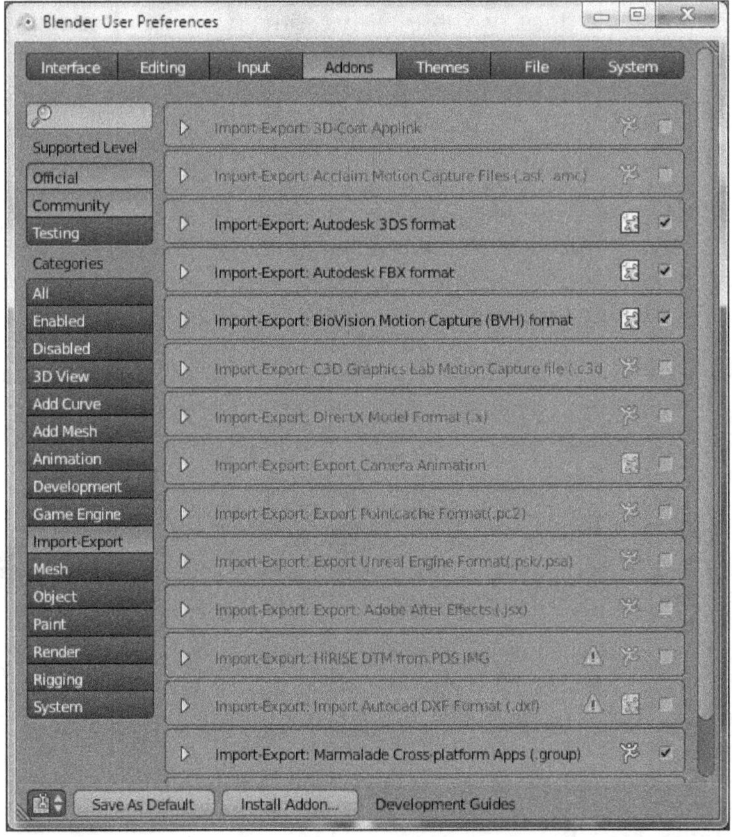

5. Find the **Import-Export: Marmalade Cross-platform Apps (.group)** entry and click the checkbox on the right-hand side of it to enable the plugin.

Exporting a model

To export a 3D model using the Blender exporter, follow these steps:

1. Create or load the model you wish to export into Blender.
2. Go to **File | Export | Marmalade cross-platform Apps (.group)**. The main 3D view will be replaced with a filename requester. The bottom-left corner of the window should contain the exporter options and look like the following image:

3. First choose the location you want to export the datafiles to, using the file requester. There are two text edit boxes at the top of the screen; the topmost is the directory to save to and the bottom specifies the filename we want to use for exporting. This filename should be a GROUP file, so its extension should always be `.group`.
4. In the exporter settings, first use the **Export** drop-down list to select whether you want just the selected models to be exported or all models in the current scene.
5. The **Merge** option controls what happens when there are several models in the scene to be exported. The default option, **None**, exports each model individually with its coordinates in model space, and is the option we require for now. The other two options allow multiple models to be merged as either a single big mesh of polygons or as a number of separate meshes, with all vertices specified in world space coordinates.
6. The **Scale Percent** value allows model vertices to be scaled up or down so that the artist can build the models using the most convenient measurement units in Blender, yet still allow the exported model to have vertices scaled to a set of units that may be more useful in the game.

7. The **Flip Normals** checkbox will reverse the direction of all exported normals. Normally this can be left unchecked, but it can be useful to fix models that have been lit incorrectly and have their normals pointing in the wrong direction.
8. The **Apply Modifiers** checkbox will cause any mesh modifiers applied to the model in Blender to be evaluated before the export data is created. This defaults to being switched off.
9. If vertex colors have been applied to the model, they will only be exported if the **Export Vertices Colors** checkbox is selected.
10. The next checkbox, **Export Material Colors**, determines whether materials created during the export process will be exported with their defined colors.
11. The **Export Textures and UVs** checkbox should be checked if you have texture-mapped polygons in your model.
12. Since Marmalade will need access to any images used in texturing the model, the **Copy Textures Files** checkbox can be selected to ensure image files are also copied across to the export directory.
13. The remaining settings are mostly concerned with exporting animations, so we can ignore them for now; however, it is worth mentioning the **Verbose** checkbox which logs information about the export process to Blender's console window. This may help you solve problems with your models when the export process doesn't work exactly as expected.
14. When all settings have been made, click on the **Export Marmalade** button, which is at the top right of the Blender window. Alternatively, if you wish to cancel the export process, there is a **Cancel** button underneath the export button.

The Marmalade 3D model datafile formats

We've now seen how we can export 3D model data from a modeling package, but we haven't yet looked at the files themselves that are generated as part of the export process.

While we shouldn't need to make manual changes to these files, it is useful to know a little about them as it can help to discover why a model hasn't been exported quite as expected to.

Let's take a look at the files that would be generated for a cube model similar to the one we created in code earlier in this chapter.

The GROUP file

The first file generated is a GROUP file that will be created in the directory specified in the exporter settings. The GROUP file contains a list of the individual model files (called **GEO files**) that were exported. Here's what the GROUP file for the example cube model would look like:

```
// Source file: C:/Work/MarmaladeBook/Maya/Cube.mb
// Exported By: Sean on 05/30/12 16:30:55

CIwResGroup
{
  name "Cube"
  "./models/Cube.geo"
}
```

The exporter helpfully includes the name of the source modeling package file that was used to do the export, details about when the export was made, and by whom.

It then just declares a new `CIwResGroup` instance, named based on the asset name specified at export time. The resource group is populated by a list of the GEO files that need to be loaded.

The MTL file

We've already created an MTL file by hand when working with 2D graphics, so it should already look familiar. Here is what the file might look like for the cube:

```
// Source file: C:/Work/MarmaladeBook/Maya/Cube.mb
CIwMaterial
{
  name "Cube/phong1"
  colAmbient {127,127,127}
  colDiffuse {127,127,127}
  colSpecular {255,255,255}
  specularPower 3
}
```

Again the exporter includes the name of the source modeling package file used to generate the MTL file. The `CIwMaterial` instances defined in this file are all generated from the materials used in the modeling package, so it's easy for an artist to change colors and other material attributes in the comfort of their favorite modeling tool.

The exporter creates a sub-directory called `models` in the specified export directory and the MTL files are written into this directory.

The GEO file

The most important file type to be exported is the GEO file, as this is the file that actually contains all the data to describe our 3D model. In common with all Marmalade resources, this file is yet another use of the ITX file format.

GEO files are processed by way of a resource handler class called `CIwResHandlerGEO`. This class takes care of loading all the data from the GEO file and submitting it to a singleton class called `CIwModelBuilder`. This class processes the model data and generates an optimized version of the data for fast rendering, which is then serialized to a file.

The `CIwModelBuilder` class is only available in debug builds, so you can only load model data in a release build by loading the serialized version of the GROUP file that references the GEO file.

The exporter will write the GEO files into the model's sub-directory in the same way as it does with MTL files.

You may have noticed that the GROUP file shown earlier only references the GEO files, not the MTL files. The GEO resource handler takes care of loading the MTL files automatically by checking to see if an MTL file exists with the same base filename as the GEO file.

Let's look at the innards of the GEO file for our cube model.

```
// Source file: C:/Work/MarmaladeBook/Maya/Cube.mb
CIwModel
{
  name "Cube"
  CMesh
  {
    name "Cube"
    scale 100.0
    CVerts
    {
      numVerts 8
      v {-100,-100,100}
      v {100,-100,100}
      v {-100,100,100}
      v {100,100,100}
      v {-100,100,-100}
      v {100,100,-100}
      v {-100,-100,-100}
```

```
        v {100,-100,-100}
      }
      CVertNorms
      {
        numVertNorms 6
        vn {0,0,1}
        vn {0,1,0}
        vn {0,0,-1}
        vn {0,-1,0}
        vn {1,0,0}
        vn {-1,0,0}
      }
      CVertCols
      {
        numVertCols 6
        col {1,0,0,1}
        col {0,1,1,1}
        col {0,0,1,1}
        col {1,1,0,1}
        col {1,0.50000,0,1}
        col {0,1,0,1}
      }
      CSurface
      {
        material "phong1"
        CQuads
        {
          numQuads 6
          q {2,0,-1,-1,0} {3,0,-1,-1,0} {1,0,-1,-1,0}
{0,0,-1,-1,0}
          q {4,1,-1,-1,4} {5,1,-1,-1,4} {3,1,-1,-1,4}
{2,1,-1,-1,4}
          q {6,2,-1,-1,5} {7,2,-1,-1,5} {5,2,-1,-1,5}
{4,2,-1,-1,5}
          q {0,3,-1,-1,1} {1,3,-1,-1,1} {7,3,-1,-1,1}
{6,3,-1,-1,1}
          q {3,4,-1,-1,3} {5,4,-1,-1,3} {7,4,-1,-1,3}
{1,4,-1,-1,3}
          q {4,5,-1,-1,2} {2,5,-1,-1,2} {0,5,-1,-1,2}
{6,5,-1,-1,2}
        }
      }
    }
}
```

Yet again the exporter will include a comment referencing the source modeling package file before beginning to define an instance of `CIwModel`, which is the class used by Marmalade to represent a complete collection of 3D model data.

The `CIwModel` instance is first given a name. This name actually comes from the name given to the model in the modeling package and is the name used to access the model in our code, so it is important for the artist to name things sensibly.

A `CMesh` instance is declared next, which is a class that groups together all the various bits of model data. This class, and all the other classes we are about to see that are contained within it, are only ever used internally to the model builder. Once the model has been processed these classes will no longer exist in memory, so we can't use them in our code to access the raw model data.

The `scale` value used to export the vertex data is listed first in the `CMesh` instance, and this is followed by classes which declare the various types of model data. In the cube example we can see `CVerts`, `CVertNorms`, and `CVertCols`, which are little more than big lists of vertex, normal, and color data respectively. A similar class called `CUVs` also exists to provide texture information.

Next we see a class called `CSurface`. This class provides polygon information for the model, and an instance will exist for every material used in the model. The material used is specified first, and then comes the polygon information. A `CQuads` instance is used to provide a list of all the quadrilateral polygons using the material, and a `CTris` instance lists the triangular polygons.

A polygon is defined by supplying a collection of data for each vertex in the polygon. The polygon is supplied as a group of five numbers enclosed in curly braces. These numbers are indices into the blocks of data specified earlier in the file and occur in the following order:

```
{Vertex index, Normal index, UV 0 index, UV 1 index, Color index}
```

There are two UV values as it is possible for a material to specify two textures that will be blended together at render time, and each of these textures can have its own UV stream.

Once all this data has been loaded, the model builder class will analyze it and create a version of the data that is far more optimal for real-time rendering purposes.

Loading and rendering an exported 3D model

OK, so now we've got the model data exported, how do we go about loading it into our program and rendering it? It's actually surprisingly easy, as these next sections will show.

Adding the IwGraphics API to a project

Marmalade's 3D model rendering code is part of the IwGraphics API, so before we can draw anything we need to add this library to our project. This is done by adding `iwgraphics` to the `subprojects` section of the MKB file.

We then need to add a call to `IwGraphicsInit` at the start of our program, and `IwGraphicsTerminate` at the end. This API relies on both IwGx and IwResManager, so we must call the initialization functions for both of these APIs before calling the IwGraphics one.

Loading and accessing an exported 3D model

You've probably already guessed that this is almost trivially easy. The exporter generated a GROUP file, so all we have to do is load it into memory and then dig the model out of the resource group. Here's a block of code which does just that:

```
CIwResGroup* lpCubeGroup = IwGetResManager()->
LoadGroup("Cube/Cube.group");
CIwModel* lpCube = static_cast<CIwModel*>(lpCubeGroup->
GetResNamed("Cube", "CIwModel"));
```

Or alternatively you could do the following if you don't want to be bothered with retaining a pointer to the resource group instance:

```
CIwModel* lpCube = static_cast<CIwModel*>(IwGetResManager()->
GetResNamed("Cube", "CIwModel"));
```

That's it. The model is now loaded into memory and ready to render.

Rendering an exported 3D model

It is time to render the model on the screen and this too is incredibly easy. All we have to do is set our view and model matrices using `IwGxSetViewMatrix` and `IwGxSetModelMatrix`, then execute the following:

```
lpCube->Render();
```

The variable `lpCube` is the pointer to the `CIwModel` instance that we retrieved from the resource manager in the previous section.

In actual fact the `Render` method can take two optional parameters. The first parameter is a `bool` value that tells Marmalade to check a bounding sphere for the model against the clipping planes to see if it actually needs to be rendered. This parameter defaults to `true`, so the check is done by default. The bounding sphere is generated automatically for us by the model builder code.

The second parameter is a flags field. Aside from one flag that is supposed to have something to do with a 2D screen rotation (I say "supposed" because I can't say it did very much when I tried it), the other flags are only relevant when dealing with animated 3D models that contain normal data, so we will not worry over these for now.

Releasing 3D model data

Since our 3D model data has been loaded into memory using the resource group system, we can make use of the same mechanism of destroying groups to release model data from memory that we no longer need. As a recap, we just do the following if we have a pointer to the `CIwResGroup` containing the 3D data:

```
IwGetResManager()->DestroyGroup(lpCubeGroup);
```

Alternatively we can release a group from memory by destroying it by name, like this:

```
IwGetResManager()->DestroyGroup("Cube");
```

Example code

Here are some details about the example projects that accompany this chapter.

The Cube project

This is a complete example of the first spinning cube project discussed in this chapter, where we generate the model data in code and submit it to IwGx for rendering using `IwGxDrawPrims`. See the following screenshot:

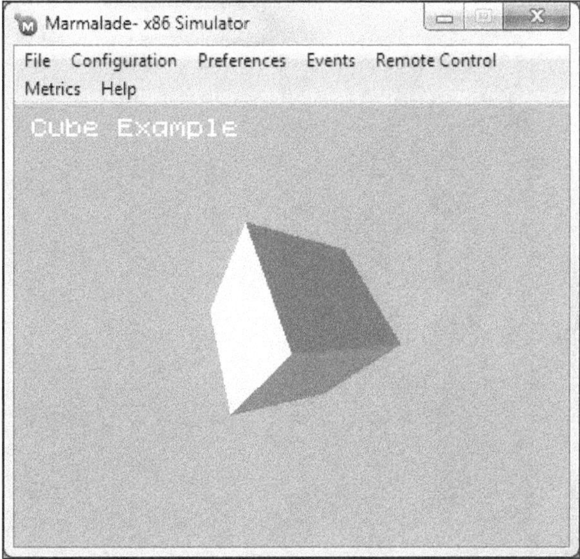

The Cube2 project

This project is almost identical to the previous project, except that the model data for the cube has been exported as a GEO file from a 3D modeling package.

The Skiing project

For this chapter the Skiing game waves goodbye to its old bitmapped graphics and instead says hello to some new 3D models instead. A screenshot of the game with its new 3D skin can be seen in the following figure:

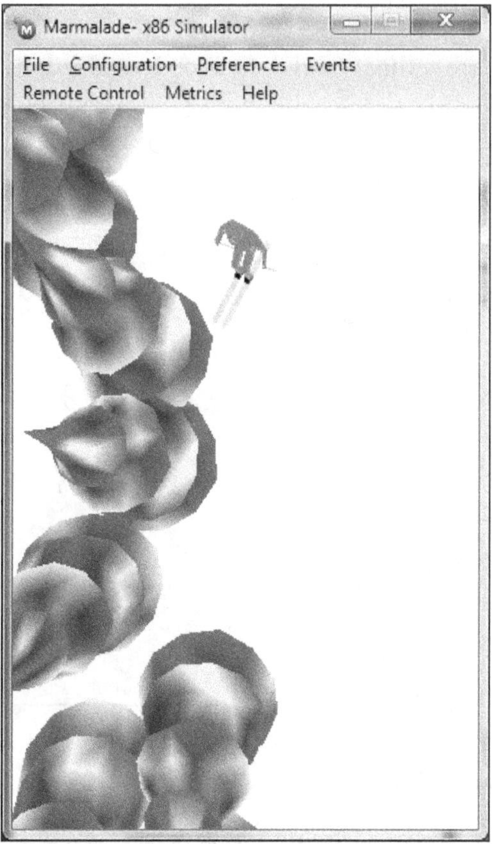

The following sections describe some of the other more interesting changes to the game code for this chapter.

Migration to 3D

The first step was to change all position and velocity information from being 2D vectors to 3D vectors, which meant changing `CIwVec2` instances to `CIwFVec3` and making sure that the extra component in the vector was initialized.

Since we tend to think about the y axis being the height above the ground, the y component was used for height in the game too. However, since the skier and trees are stuck to the floor, this means the y component of all position vectors is always zero.

The game therefore scrolls the trees along the z axis and the camera is placed high in the air and orientated to look at the skier. This still provides the effect of the trees moving up the screen.

The second step was to get rid of all the old 2D textures and replace them with 3D models. Since the `GameObject` class dealt with all the rendering, all that had to be done was to change this class to use `CIwModel` instances instead of `CIwMaterial` instances. The child classes then just provided a pointer to a model instead of a pointer to the material.

The `GameObject` class also had a y axis rotation added to it. This is used to rotate the skier model, which leads to a far smoother motion than we had previously.

The trees also use the rotation feature. The game features only one tree model, but by rotating it at random angles it makes the game look far more interesting without having to add more game resources.

Addition of a collision detection system

The code now features a very simple collision detection system. The `GameObject` class now allows a collision radius to be set, which is then used to perform sphere intersection tests.

The `ModeGame::Update` method now steps through every game object (currently just trees, of course) in the game world and finds out how far away it is from the skier. If the distance is less than the combined collision radius of the skier and the other game object, a collision has occurred.

So, to act on these collisions, a virtual method called `OnCollide` has been added to the `GameObject` class. Child objects can override this class and then react accordingly whenever they collide with another object. The `Skier` class implements this method so that whenever the skier collides with a tree, the game is over.

Summary

We now know how to render 3D graphics that have either been generated in code or have been exported from a 3D modeling package. Which method we eventually use depends on what we are trying to do.

If rendering in game characters or scenery, the exported model route is definitely the best way to go; but creating our own polygon data in code is a much better and more efficient way of creating effects such as particle systems, since it is much easier to batch a large number of individual polygons into a single draw call.

We've also learnt how to export 3D model data from three different modeling packages—Maya, 3DS Max, and Blender—and load this exported data into our program and render it.

We'll be sticking with 3D rendering for a little while longer as the next chapter is all about making our models animated.

5
Animating 3D Graphics

We've now seen how to create a 3D model and display it on the screen, but we're currently limited to non-animated models. Sure, we can rotate or scale to our heart's content, but that really doesn't cut it when you want to animate something more complex than a cube, say for example a human figure.

In this chapter we will be looking at the following topics:

- A quick overview of the concepts involved in 3D animation
- Exporting animations from a 3D modeling package
- Loading and rendering an exported 3D animation in a Marmalade project

A quick 3D animation primer

Let's start by looking at the ways in which animation of 3D models can be achieved.

Animating with model matrices

By far the simplest and most obvious way of animating a 3D model is to alter its position, orientation, and size. All three of these properties can be specified using the model matrix set at the time of rendering the model.

We could store a matrix in our game class, and for each frame multiply it by a second matrix representing the change in position, rotation, and scale; but this approach is generally not reliable. Over time the matrix starts to degrade due to the cumulative effect of precision errors in the multiplications and additions involved. The matrix will often end up becoming non-orthogonal (that is, its three axes are no longer at right angles to each other), which yields a shearing effect on the 3D model. The scale can also be affected by these precision errors, causing the 3D model to gradually shrink in size!

A far more reliable way is to store the translation, rotation, and scale separately, and calculate a fresh matrix for every frame. How this can be achieved is described in the following sections.

Animating by translation

Our game class simply needs to maintain a position vector containing the current world position of the object. We can move an in-game object around the world by adding a velocity vector that indicates how far the game object has moved in this frame and in what direction, with reference to the stored position vector.

To generate the final model matrix all we need to do is copy the position vector into the translation part of the matrix. We normally do this as the last step, as the act of multiplying matrices together when generating the rotation and scale will affect the translation of the matrix.

```
// lTimeStep is the time elapsed since the last frame (here we're
// setting it to the time interval required to run at 30 frames
// per second).
float lTimeStep = 1.0f / 30.0f;

// Calculate how far we've moved this frame and update position
CIwFVec3 lVelocityStep = mVelocity * lTimeStep;
mPosition += lVelocityStep;

// Copy the position into the matrix used to render the model
mModelMatrix.t = mPosition;
```

Animating by rotation

The top left 3 x 3 section of the model matrix specifies the rotation at which we want the model to be drawn. Our game object stores the required rotation and updates it on a frame-by-frame basis. When it is time to render, we just use the stored rotation to calculate the rotation matrix.

There are a number of ways in which the rotation of the object might be stored. Three of the most common ways are shown in the following section.

Rotation using Euler angles

Euler angles consist of the required angle of rotation in the x, y, and z axes, which we would normally store using a vector. If rotation is not desired around every axis, you may choose to store only those rotation values that you require.

Euler angles are quite easy to both visualize and implement, which is why they are used so often. To convert a set of Euler angles into a rotation matrix, all we need to do is generate three matrices for the rotations around each of the axes and then multiply them together.

However, this is where the problem with Euler angles lies. Matrix multiplication yields different results depending on the order in which you multiply the matrices; so when using Euler angles, it is vital that you choose the order of multiplication carefully, depending on what you are trying to achieve. The following diagram shows an example to illustrate this:

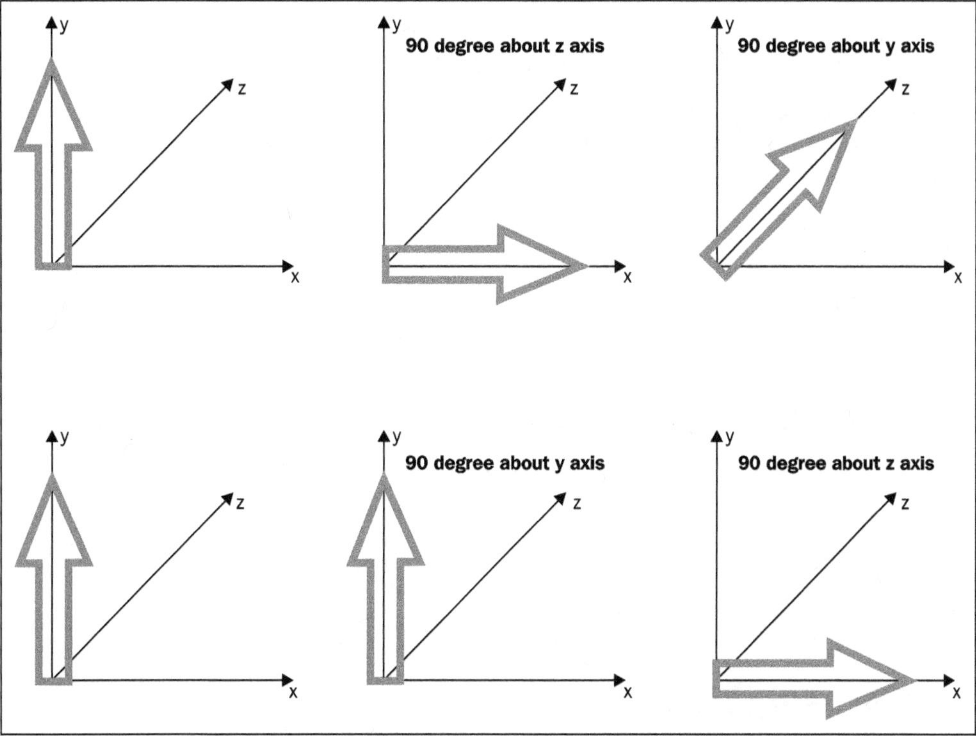

In the diagram, we are rotating an arrow that points straight along the positive y axis. In the first row we rotate by 90 degrees around the z axis and then by 90 degrees around the y axis. The arrow ends up pointing along the z axis.

In the second row of the diagram, we take the same original arrow but apply the rotations in the opposite order. As you can see, this time the arrow finishes in the direction of the x axis.

The following code snippet shows how you can build up a complete rotation matrix for Euler angles applied in the order XYZ:

```
CIwFMat lMatXYZ;
lMatXYZ.SetRotX(xAngle);
lMatXYZ.PostRotateY(yAngle);
lMatXYZ.PostRotateZ(zAngle);
```

All angles used in Marmalade are specified in radians, not degrees.

Rotation using axis-angle pairs

The **axis-angle** method of representing a rotation requires a direction vector and an angle of rotation to be stored. The vector represents the direction in which we want an object to be orientated, while the angle allows the object to be rotated around that axis.

We might find this way of specifying a rotation useful when dealing with player characters. For example, to orient a human character we might specify the direction vector as being the positive y axis, which then allows the angle of rotation to be used to change the heading of the character.

Marmalade allows us to convert an axis-angle pair into a matrix for rendering, as follows:

```
CIwFVec3 lDir(0.0f, 1.0f, 0.0f);
float lAngle = PI / 2.0f;
CIwFMat lMat;
lMat.SetAxisAngle(lDir, lAngle);
```

Rotation using quaternions

A **quaternion** is yet another method of representing three-dimensional rotations, and is a concept that, when you first come across it, seems a little mind-blowing. Instead of going on about four dimensional hyperspheres and making parts of your brain melt, I'm just going to provide a quick guide to what you need to know in order to use quaternions. If you want to learn more about them, I suggest you search for "quaternions" on Google!

A quaternion consists of four components: x, y, z, and w. A 3D rotation is represented as a **unit quaternion**, which, in a similar manner to vectors, just means that the magnitude of the sum of the squares of all four components is one.

Multiplying two unit quaternions is similar to multiplying two rotation matrices together. The result represents the first orientation rotated by the second, and the result is different depending on the order in which you perform the multiplication.

The big problem with quaternions is that they are almost impossible to visualize. If given a set of Euler angles or an axis-angle pair, most people can form an image in their mind of what that rotation would look like, but the same can't be said of quaternions.

Quaternions can however be created fairly easily from both a rotation matrix (and therefore Euler angles) and an axis-angle pair. The following diagram shows the relationship between the axis-angle pairs and quaternions:

For rotation θ around unit vector (x, y, z)

$$Q_x = x.\sin\left(\frac{\theta}{2}\right)$$

$$Q_y = y.\sin\left(\frac{\theta}{2}\right) \qquad Q_w = \cos\left(\frac{\theta}{2}\right)$$

$$Q_z = z.\sin\left(\frac{\theta}{2}\right)$$

Quaternions really come into their own for 3D animation of boned characters, a topic we will be coming to later in this chapter. This is a technique that requires an awful lot of rotations to be calculated every time you want to update the animation frame, and luckily quaternions make this far more efficient in terms of both memory usage and execution speed.

While the theory behind quaternions may be a little scary for us mere mortals, there is really little need to worry about the math, as Marmalade provides us with a quaternion class, `CIwFQuat`, that we can use. As an example, creating a quaternion from an axis-angle pair and then producing a rotation matrix from it can be done as follows:

```
CIwFQuat lQuat;
lQuat.SetAxisAngle(1.0f, 0.0f, 0.0f, PI / 2.0f);
CIwFMat lMat(lQuat);
```

Animating by scaling

The scaling factor is normally stored either as a vector containing the required size in the x, y, and z axes, or alternatively as a single scale value which is applied equally to each axis. Often the latter is sufficient, as models tend to look odd when they are not scaled uniformly in each axis.

A scaling matrix is very simple to create, as all you have to do is place the scaling factors required for the x, y, and z axes in the diagonal going from the top left to the bottom right of the 3 x 3 rotation part of the matrix. All the other cells are left as zero.

Since creating a scaling matrix is so simple, the `CIwFMat` class does not include any methods for creating a general scaling matrix. It does however provide some shortcut methods that make it easy to scale a matrix by the same scaling factor on each axis. The following code snippet provides an example:

```
CIwFMat lMat;
lMat.SetRotX(PI / 2.0f);
lMat.ScaleRot(2.0f);
```

This code will create a rotation matrix of 90 degrees around the x axis and then scale up just the rotation part of the matrix by a factor of two. You can also choose to scale up just the translation part of the matrix or both the rotation and translation by using the `ScaleTrans` and `Scale` methods respectively.

3D model animation

Model matrix animation is, of course, extremely important, as without it we would be unable to orient and move our 3D models in the game world; but on its own it doesn't make for the most exciting looking game.

Most games require more than this. For example, we might want a human or animal character to walk, run, jump, or perform some other type of motion. Ideally, we need a way of making the overall shape of our 3D model change over time.

The following sections explain how we can achieve this.

Using morph targets

A simple approach to 3D model animation is to use **morph targets**. For this we alter the vertex positions of our 3D model to yield **key frames** of the animation. A key frame is just a particular set of vertex positions for the model that are an important part of the overall animation, such as the various positions a character's legs move through as they walk. The key frame also has a time associated with it.

The following diagram shows a very simple example of a stick man raising his arm. **Key Frame 1** at time index **0** seconds has the arm in a lowered position, while **Key Frame 2** at time index **2** seconds has it raised. Each of these key frames can be thought of as an individually exported 3D model.

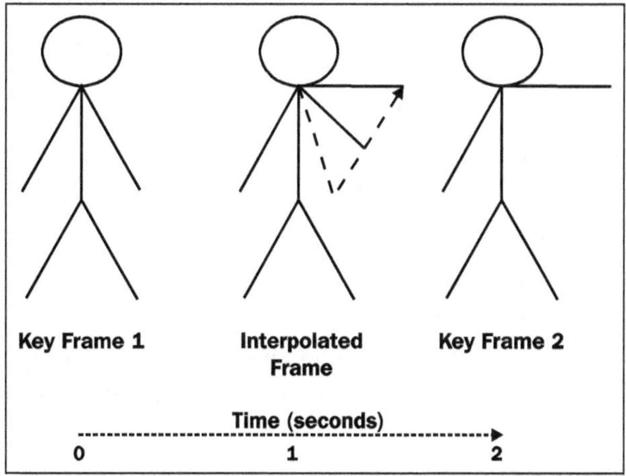

If we want to play back this animation, we could just draw the relevant 3D model at the correct time, but this would yield very jerky results akin to 2D bitmap animation. Instead, we can calculate an **Interpolated Frame** for any time index between **0** and **2** seconds to give a much smoother result.

Calculating the interpolated frame is simple enough. We work out a **delta vector** from each vertex in the first key frame to the corresponding vertex in the second key frame. We then scale the delta vector by the ratio of the time index we want to calculate for, divided by the total time between the two key frames, and add the scaled result on to the position of the vertex in the first key frame.

In the diagram, we want to calculate an interpolated frame at time index **1** second, so we would scale the delta vectors by a factor of half. The end result will be the frame shown where the arm is half raised.

This approach may be easy to implement, but ultimately we find that there are a few problems with it, as follows:

- Accuracy of resultant animation: Take a good look at the interpolated frame of the stick man in the previous diagram and you will see that the stick man's arm has actually shrunk. This is because we are interpolating the vertex positions in a straight line, whereas we really need the end vertices to be rotated around the shoulder point.
- Number of key frames required: In order to produce a good quality animation we need to store a good number of key frames. In the example of our stick man animation, we could provide additional key frames that would then minimize the arm shortening effect. However, since we need to store the position of every vertex in the model, whether it has moved or not, this soon becomes a large amount of data.

- The need to ensure that the vertex order does not change between key frames: The only way we can reliably implement morph target animation is if every vertex in the model is in the same position in the vertex stream for every key frame. When exporting a 3D model from a modeling package, the vertex stream order can end up changing between frames, which would then cause our animation to behave incorrectly as vertices interpolate between completely wrong positions.

For the reasons listed, Marmalade does not support morph target animations, though it is fairly trivial to implement such an approach if you so wish. Morph targets can still be extremely useful for tasks such as facial animation, which, with the increasing power of mobile devices, may soon be a more common feature in mobile games.

Using boned animations

Most 3D video games will implement the animation of 3D models using a boned animation system. This method works by allowing an animator to set up a skeleton of virtual bones, which can then be used to deform the vertices of a 3D model. The 3D model itself often gets referred to as the **skin** for purposes of animation.

To set up a boned animation, the first step is to use a 3D modeling package to create the 3D model you want to animate in its **bind pose**. The bind pose is normally chosen to be a position in which it is easy to access every polygon in the model for texturing and coloring purposes, as well as for laying out the skeleton. For a human character this often means a pose where the arms are held outstretched horizontally from the body and the feet are spaced a short distance apart.

With the bind pose created, the animator then starts the **rigging** process. This involves adding the skeleton to the model by placing bones in relevant places. The bones are linked together to form a **hierarchy**; so whenever a bone is moved, all the bones which are linked to it as children will move too. Ultimately there will be one top-level parent bone in the hierarchy and this is called the **root bone**.

For performance reasons it is good to keep the number of bones to a minimum, but this must be balanced against having enough to allow good quality animation. The following diagram shows what the 3D skier character used in our example game project looks like after being rigged:

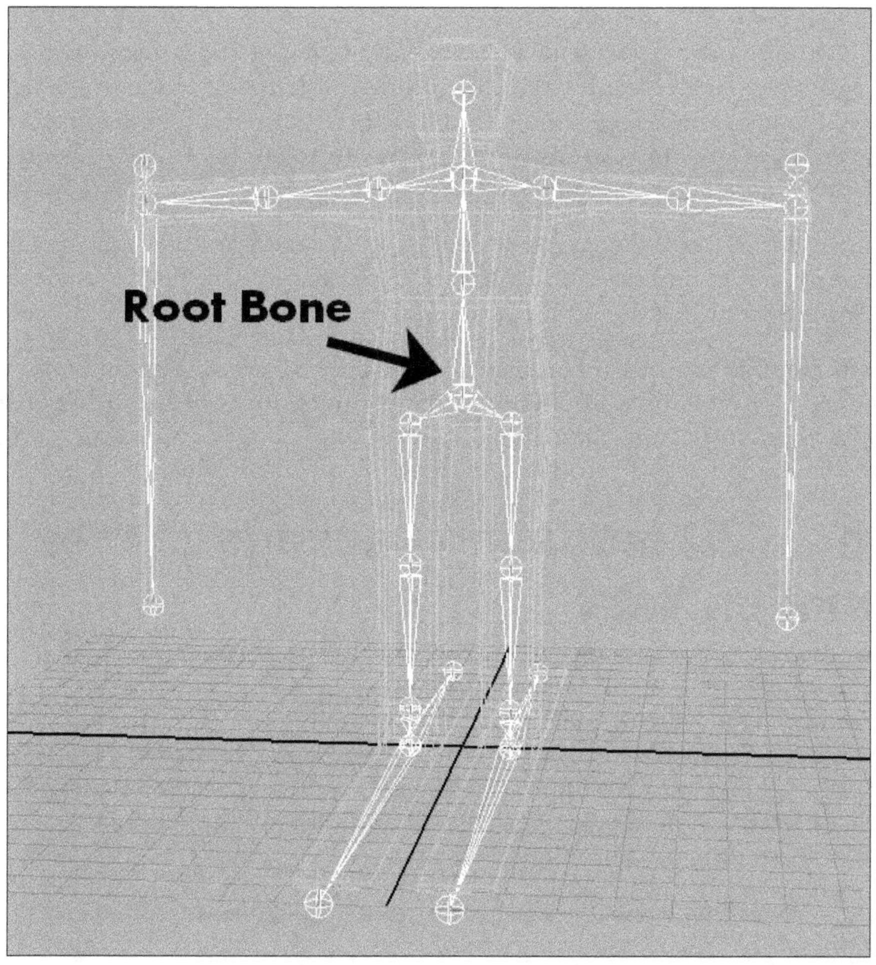

Once the bones have been laid out, the next step is to bind the skin (in other words, the mesh of polygons) to the skeleton. This is done by allowing each vertex of the 3D model to be modified by one or more bones.

If a vertex is mapped to more than one bone, a weight is also defined for each bone that determines how much of an effect it will have on the vertex. Weights range from zero to one and the sum of all the weights for a particular vertex should add up to one.

Most 3D modeling packages will have a good first attempt at doing the binding process automatically, but normally the animator will need to make some adjustments to the binding so that the skin animates correctly when the bones of the skeleton are moved.

With all that done, the animator can then make the character do whatever they want simply by rotating and moving the bones around to define the required key frame positions, just like with morph targets. The boned system will produce much better quality in the final animation, and the amount of memory required to store the key frames is normally not too large, since all that needs to be stored is the orientation and position of each bone.

The Marmalade SDK comes complete with a boned animation system, which we will be learning about in the rest of this chapter. The system is very flexible and there are very few limitations to it.

The main things to be aware of are that you can only have a single root bone, a maximum of 256 bones in total, and each vertex can only be affected by a maximum of four bones. In most cases these limitations are unlikely to cause you any problems.

Using a 3D modeling package to create animation data

Entire books have been written explaining how best to create a 3D animated character; so, unsurprisingly, we won't be looking at how to actually produce an animated 3D model here. Indeed, my warning in the previous chapter about "programmer art" probably goes double for "programmer animation". For evidence to back this statement up, look no further than the graphics accompanying the example programs of this book, which are all examples of "programmer art" made by yours truly. I really should heed my own advice.

Anyway, with that tip hopefully now rammed home, let's see how we can export animation data from a 3D modeling package.

Exporting an animation requires a number of new file types to be exported. These will be discussed in detail later, but in short they are files that represent the skeleton, the skin, and the actual animations themselves. The following sections will show how to export this data.

Exporting animations using the Marmalade 3D exporter plugins

If you are using 3DS Max or Maya to create your animations, the required animation files are exported using the Marmalade exporter plugin. To refresh your memory, the exporter plugin window is shown in the following screenshot:

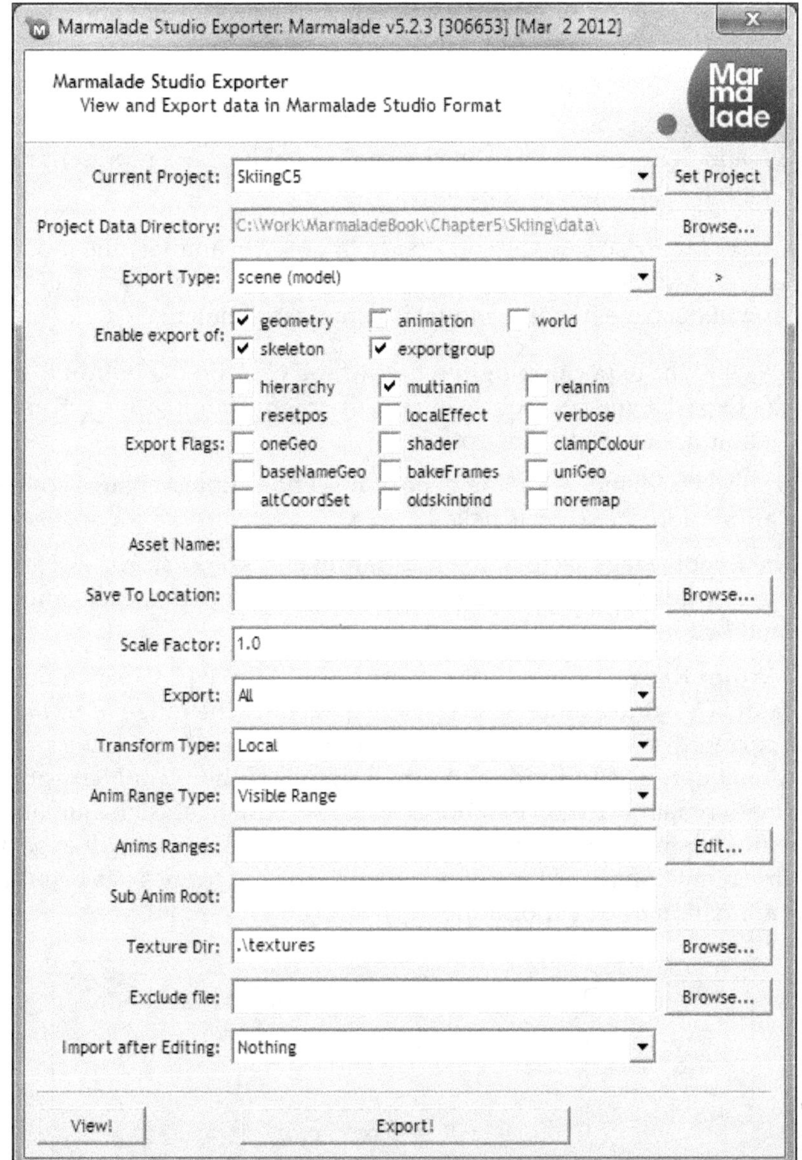

To export an animation, just load it into your modeling package and follow these steps:

1. Set up the export options in the same way as we did for exporting a static model. Please look at the steps listed in *Chapter 4, 3D Graphics Rendering*, if you've forgotten what the various options are for. We'll now take a look at the additional animation-specific options.

2. Ensure that just the **geometry**, **skeleton**, and **exportgroup** checkboxes are ticked in the group labeled **Enable export of**.
3. You can now click on the **Export!** button to write out the GEO, MTL, and GROUP files for the model. Two new file types will also be exported, the SKEL and SKIN files, which as you can probably guess represent the skeleton and skin information for the model.

The files exported in these steps are necessary in order to animate the model, but they don't actually contain any animation data as such. Here's how we get hold of the data that will describe how the model is actually animated:

1. Go back to the exporter plugin window and click on the button to the right of the **Export Type** combobox. A pop-up menu should appear from which you should select the **anim** option.
2. The checkboxes in the **Enable export of** section should change so that only the **animation** checkbox is ticked.
3. In the **Export Flags** section, the **multianim** checkbox can be selected if you have several animations in the scene to export. Note that each animation should be for the same 3D model.
4. The **Anim Range Type** option can take one of three possible values. The default is **Visible Range**, which will export only the range of frames that are currently visible on the animation track bar in the modeling package. The next option is **Individual Anim Range**, which will only export animation data between the first and last key frame of each animation. The final option, **Full Range**, is only available in Maya. It will export the entire animation regardless of whether a range of frames has been set on the animation track bar or not.

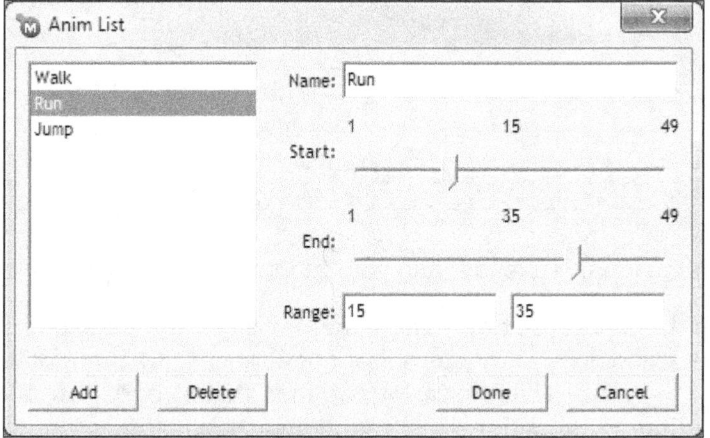

5. The **Anims Ranges** option allows you to split one big animation sequence up into several smaller animations. If you click on the **Edit...** button, the dialog box just seen will be displayed. Use the **Add** button to create a new animation range, use the **Name** textbox to name the animation, and then drag the sliders to set the **Start** and **End** frames for the animation. Use the **Delete** button to delete an animation range from the list. The **Done** button will close the dialog and accept any changes made, while the **Cancel** button will discard any changes made before closing the dialog.
6. The final option that affects animation export is the **Sub Anim Root** textbox. You can enter the name of one of the bones in the skeleton and the animation data will only be exported for that bone and its children. We'll learn more about sub-animations later in this chapter.
7. With all the animation-related options in the exporter now set up, just click on the **Export!** button to output one or more ANIM files. The number of files exported depends on how many animations were in the scene, the status of the **multianim** checkbox, and whether the **Anims Ranges** option was used.

Exporting animations using the Blender plugin

You can also export animations using the Blender plugin. The terminology used in Blender for animations is a little unusual, as Blender calls the skeleton an **armature**, but aside from that the approach to animation is the same.

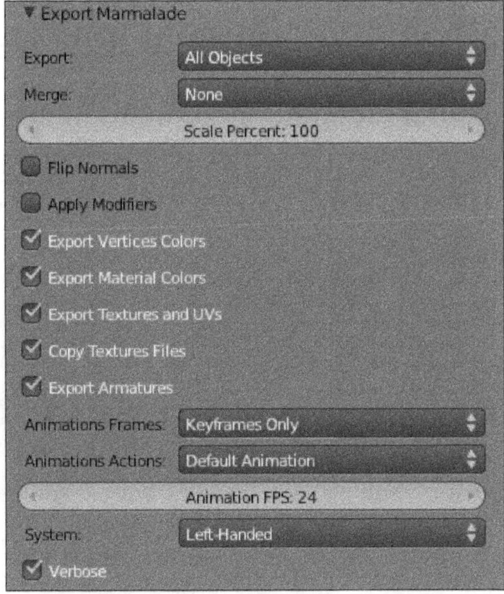

Here are the steps you should follow to export an animated model from Blender:

1. Load the animation you wish to export into Blender and then go to **File | Export | Marmalade Cross-platform Apps (.group)** to display the export options screen. As a reminder, the export options are shown in the previous screenshot, but please refer to the steps listed in *Chapter 4, 3D Graphics Rendering*, for more information about the standard model export settings.
2. To tell the exporter to write out all the different animation file types, ensure that the **Export Armatures** checkbox is selected.
3. The **Animations Frames** combobox contains three options. **None** will export no animation data, **Keyframes Only** will export just the data for the key frames of the animation (this is the option you would normally want to select), and **Full Animation** will export data for every frame regardless of whether it is a key frame or not (this is often referred to as "baking" the animation and means you get the exact animation seen in the modeling package at the expense of an increase in animation memory footprint).
4. The **Animations Actions** combobox contains two settings. **Default Animation** will export only the animation that has been selected as the default for the armature. The other option is **All Animations**, which will export all the animations currently defined for the armature.
5. The final setting is the **Animation FPS** value. This dictates the playback speed in frames per second for the animation, so it is possible to speed up or slow down an animation by changing this value without the need to alter all the key frame timings.
6. To export the data, ensure that you have a file location and name entered in the boxes at the top of the screen and then click on the **Export Marmalade** button.

The Marmalade 3D animation file formats

We can now export the animation data from the 3D modeling package of our choice, but before we actually make use of them, let's take a quick look at the new file types that we've just generated.

The SKEL file

A **SKEL file** contains all the information pertaining to the skeleton of our animation. The file first defines an instance of a `CIwAnimSkel` class, which is a wrapper for a number of `CIwAnimBone` instances.

The `CIwAnimSkel` instance is derived from the `CIwResource` class and therefore has a name associated with it so that it can be looked up in the resource manager. The name of the instance is taken from the filename of a SKEL file, which in turn comes from the name of the root bone of the skeleton.

Each of the `CIwAnimBone` instances have a name, position, and rotation associated with it, which defines the bind pose of the animation. The position is just a vector in model space, while the rotation is stored as a quaternion. Except for the first bone, which is the root bone, each bone will also list its parent bone, thus building up the skeletal hierarchy.

The SKEL file gets exported into the `models` sub-directory alongside the GEO and MTL files. An example of a SKEL file is as follows:

```
CIwAnimSkel
{
  numBones 12
  CIwAnimBone
  {
    name "FlagPoleBase"
    pos {-0.38309,-1.27709,0}
    rot {0.70711,0,0,0.70711}
  }
  CIwAnimBone
  {
    name "PoleA"
    parent "FlagPoleBase"
    pos {258.20248,0.00000,0}
    rot {1,0,0,0}
  }
  CIwAnimBone
  {
    name "PoleB"
    parent "PoleA"
    pos {255.88675,0.00000,0}
    rot {1.00000,0,0,-0.00200}
  }
  CIwAnimBone
  {
    name "PoleC"
    parent "PoleB"
    pos {257.60138,-0.00000,0}
    rot {0.00000,0.99998,0.00615,0.00000}
  }
```

```
CIwAnimBone
{
  name "PoleD"
  parent "PoleC"
  pos {255.08751,-0.00000,-0.00000}
  rot {0.00000,0.99998,0.00621,0.00000}
}
CIwAnimBone
{
  name "PoleE"
  parent "PoleD"
  pos {257.19775,0.00000,-0.00000}
  rot {1.00000,0,0,0.00206}
}
CIwAnimBone
{
  name "FlagStart"
  parent "PoleE"
  pos {152.41219,0.00000,-0.00000}
  rot {0.61894,0,0,-0.78544}
}
CIwAnimBone
{
  name "FlagA"
  parent "FlagStart"
  pos {85.99931,-0.00000,-0.00000}
  rot {0.99505,0,0,0.09934}
}
CIwAnimBone
{
  name "FlagB"
  parent "FlagA"
  pos {57.19376,0.00000,-0.00000}
  rot {1.00000,0,0,0.00128}
}
CIwAnimBone
{
  name "FlagC"
  parent "FlagB"
  pos {61.42473,0.00000,-0.00000}
  rot {0.99996,0,0,0.00846}
}
CIwAnimBone
```

```
    {
      name "FlagD"
      parent "FlagC"
      pos {60.33911,0,-0.00000}
      rot {0.99996,0,0,-0.00877}
    }
    CIwAnimBone
    {
      name "FlagE"
      parent "FlagD"
      pos {60.36695,-0.00000,-0.00000}
      rot {0.99985,0,0,0.01754}
    }
}
```

The SKIN file

The **SKIN file** is the bridge between the skeleton and the vertices of the 3D model in its bind pose. It contains all the data representing which vertices are influenced by which bones.

The file starts by defining an instance of the `CIwAnimSkin` class. This instance contains references to the `CIwAnimSkel` instance that defines the bones of the required skeleton, and also the `CIwModel` instance that will be used for rendering the model once the new vertex positions have been calculated. As with the SKEL file, the name given to the `CIwAnimSkin` instance is derived from the filename of the SKIN file.

The file then contains a number of instances of the `CIwAnimSkinSet` class, which indicates which vertices are modified by which bones. This is achieved by first listing the bones, up to a maximum of four, then the number of vertices in the set. The bone weights are then specified for each vertex by providing the index of the vertex in the model vertex stream, followed by a weight value for each bone. The sum of the weight values for each vertex must total to one.

The SKIN file is also exported to the `models` subdirectory and the following code provides a partial example of one. These files tend to be quite large due to the sheer amount of data required for even a simple animation, so an extract should provide enough of a flavor of what these files look like.

```
CIwAnimSkin
{
  skeleton "FlagPoleBase"
  model "Flag"
  CIwAnimSkinSet
```

```
{
  useBones { FlagPoleBase }
  numVerts 16
  vertWeights {0,1}
  vertWeights {1,1}
  vertWeights {2,1}
  vertWeights {3,1}
  vertWeights {4,1}
  vertWeights {35,1}
  vertWeights {58,1}
  vertWeights {60,1}
  vertWeights {62,1}
  vertWeights {64,1}
  vertWeights {65,1}
  vertWeights {90,1}
  vertWeights {91,1}
  vertWeights {92,1}
  vertWeights {93,1}
  vertWeights {94,1}
}
CIwAnimSkinSet
{
  useBones { FlagPoleBase PoleA }
  numVerts 10
  vertWeights {5,0.50170,0.49830}
  vertWeights {6,0.50251,0.49749}
  vertWeights {7,0.50177,0.49823}
  vertWeights {8,0.50116,0.49884}
  vertWeights {9,0.50114,0.49886}
  vertWeights {57,0.50251,0.49749}
  vertWeights {59,0.50177,0.49823}
  vertWeights {61,0.50116,0.49884}
  vertWeights {63,0.50114,0.49886}
  vertWeights {66,0.50170,0.49830}
}

// Several more CIwAnimSkinSet instances would have been
// defined here but they have been left out to avoid
// filling the book with boring numbers!

CIwAnimSkinSet
{
  useBones { FlagA FlagB FlagC FlagD }
```

```
        numVerts 8
        vertWeights {39,0.15992,0.33285,0.33292,0.17431}
        vertWeights {44,0.15632,0.33444,0.33462,0.17462}
        vertWeights {49,0.17817,0.32895,0.32812,0.16476}
        vertWeights {54,0.18163,0.32749,0.32638,0.16450}
        vertWeights {106,0.15632,0.33444,0.33462,0.17462}
        vertWeights {112,0.17817,0.32895,0.32812,0.16476}
        vertWeights {120,0.18163,0.32749,0.32638,0.16450}
        vertWeights {121,0.15992,0.33285,0.33292,0.17431}
    }
    CIwAnimSkinSet
    {
        useBones { FlagB FlagC FlagD FlagE }
        numVerts 20
        vertWeights {40,0.14751,0.34532,0.34603,0.16114}
        vertWeights {41,0.02763,0.13480,0.41879,0.41879}
        vertWeights {45,0.14368,0.34743,0.34842,0.16046}
        vertWeights {46,0.02625,0.13072,0.42151,0.42151}
        vertWeights {50,0.16232,0.34459,0.34444,0.14865}
        vertWeights {51,0.03730,0.16777,0.39776,0.39717}
        vertWeights {55,0.16581,0.34255,0.34229,0.14936}
        vertWeights {56,0.03875,0.17110,0.39544,0.39471}
        vertWeights {102,0.02763,0.13480,0.41879,0.41879}
        vertWeights {103,0.02625,0.13072,0.42151,0.42151}
        vertWeights {107,0.14368,0.34743,0.34842,0.16046}
        vertWeights {108,0.02625,0.13072,0.42151,0.42151}
        vertWeights {109,0.03730,0.16777,0.39776,0.39717}
        vertWeights {113,0.16232,0.34459,0.34444,0.14865}
        vertWeights {114,0.03730,0.16777,0.39776,0.39717}
        vertWeights {115,0.03875,0.17110,0.39544,0.39471}
        vertWeights {122,0.16581,0.34255,0.34229,0.14936}
        vertWeights {123,0.14751,0.34532,0.34603,0.16114}
        vertWeights {124,0.03875,0.17110,0.39544,0.39471}
        vertWeights {125,0.02763,0.13480,0.41879,0.41879}
    }
}
```

The ANIM file

The final file type we need to consider is the **ANIM file**, which as its name suggests is the file that actually defines a particular animation.

The file first declares an instance of the `CIwAnim` class, which, as with the other animation class types, will be given a resource name derived from the filename.

The skeleton that this animation will be applied to is the first thing that the `CIwAnim` instance will specify. This is then followed by a number of `CIwAnimKeyFrame` declarations that detail the positions and orientations of each affected bone at a particular time index.

Key frames do not need to list the orientation and position of each bone in the skeleton. If a bone has not moved relative to its parent, its position will remain as it was at the previous key frame.

The exporters will create an `anims` sub-directory to hold all the ANIM files. An example of an ANIM file is provided in the following code; but as with the SKIN file, this is just a partial example so as to not fill the pages of this book with lots of numbers:

```
CIwAnim
{
  skeleton "FlagPoleBase"
  // Keyframe# 1
  CIwAnimKeyFrame
  {
    time 0
    bone "FlagPoleBase"
    pos {-0.38309,-1.27709,0}
    rot {0.70711,0,0,0.70711}

    bone "PoleA"
    pos {258.20248,0.00000,0}
    rot {1,0,0,0}

    bone "PoleB"
    pos {255.88675,0.00000,0}
    rot {1.00000,0,0,-0.00200}

    bone "PoleC"
    pos {257.60138,-0.00000,0}
    rot {0.00000,0.99998,0.00615,0.00000}

    bone "PoleD"
    pos {255.08751,-0.00000,-0.00000}
    rot {0.00000,0.99998,0.00621,0.00000}

    bone "PoleE"
    pos {257.19775,0.00000,-0.00000}
    rot {1.00000,0,0,0.00206}

    bone "FlagStart"
```

```
    pos {152.41219,0.00000,-0.00000}
    rot {0.61894,0,0,-0.78544}

    bone "FlagA"
    pos {85.99931,-0.00000,-0.00000}
    rot {0.99505,0,0,0.09934}

    bone "FlagB"
    pos {57.19376,0.00000,-0.00000}
    rot {1.00000,0,0,0.00128}

    bone "FlagC"
    pos {61.42473,0.00000,-0.00000}
    rot {0.99996,0,0,0.00846}

    bone "FlagD"
    pos {60.33911,0,-0.00000}
    rot {0.99996,0,0,-0.00877}

    bone "FlagE"
    pos {60.36695,-0.00000,-0.00000}
    rot {0.99985,0,0,0.01754}

}
// Keyframe# 5
CIwAnimKeyFrame
{
    time 0.16667
    bone "FlagPoleBase"
    pos {-0.38309,-1.27709,0}
    rot {0.73026,0,0,0.68317}

    bone "PoleA"
    pos {258.20248,0.00000,0}
    rot {0.99889,0,0,-0.04716}

    bone "PoleB"
    pos {255.88675,0.00000,0}
    rot {0.99864,0,0,-0.05222}

    bone "PoleC"
    pos {257.60138,-0.00000,0}
    rot {0.00000,0.99857,-0.05338,0.00000}
```

```
    bone "PoleD"
    pos {255.08751,-0.00000,-0.00000}
    rot {0.00000,0.99624,0.08662,-0.00000}

    bone "PoleE"
    pos {257.19775,0.00000,-0.00000}
    rot {0.99483,0,0,-0.10158}

  }
  // Keyframe# 15
  CIwAnimKeyFrame
  {
    time 0.58333
    bone "FlagPoleBase"
    pos {-0.38309,-1.27709,0}
    rot {0.70668,0,0,0.70754}

    bone "PoleA"
    pos {258.20248,0.00000,0}
    rot {0.99873,0,0,0.05033}

    bone "PoleB"
    pos {255.88675,0.00000,0}
    rot {0.99775,0,0,0.06711}

    bone "PoleC"
    pos {257.60138,-0.00000,0}
    rot {0.00000,0.99951,0.03144,-0.00000}

    bone "PoleD"
    pos {255.08751,-0.00000,-0.00000}
    rot {0.00000,0.99996,0.00868,0.00000}

    bone "PoleE"
    pos {257.19775,0.00000,-0.00000}
    rot {0.99853,0,0,0.05420}

  }
  // Further key frames follow to define the remainder of the
  // animation but these have been removed to avoid including
  // large amounts of datafile in the pages of this book
}
```

Loading and rendering an exported 3D animation

We're now in a position to start rendering a 3D animation, and as with rendering a static 3D model it's also surprisingly easy to do.

Adding the IwAnim API to a project

Before we can use Marmalade's animation functionality, we first need to add the IwAnim API to our project. This API builds on top of the IwGraphics API required for rendering static 3D models.

As with all such Marmalade APIs, we add support for IwAnim to a project by listing `iwanim` in the `subprojects` section of the MKB file. We must then call `IwAnimInit` after `IwGraphicsInit` has been called, and at shutdown time we need to call `IwAnimTerminate`.

Loading and accessing a 3D animation

The GROUP file format comes to our rescue once again in order to get animation data loaded into memory. The export process will have created a GROUP file for us already that will include the GEO, MTL, SKEL, and SKIN files, so we just need to add entries for the ANIM files that we want to use.

With everything referenced in the GROUP file, we just need to load it into memory using the resource manager, and then access the resources in the same way as we do for any other resource.

The following code snippet illustrates how we might load a GROUP file and then access the resources needed for rendering an animated 3D model:

```
CIwResGroup* lpFlagGroup = IwGetResManager()->
  LoadGroup("Flag/Flag.group");
CIwModel* lpFlag = static_cast<CIwModel*>(lpFlagGroup->
  GetResNamed("Flag", "CIwModel"));
CIwAnimSkel* lpSkel = static_cast<CIwAnimSkel*>(lpFlagGroup->
  GetResNamed("FlagPoleBase", "CIwAnimSkel"));
CIwAnimSkin* lpSkin = static_cast<CIwAnimSkin*>(lpFlagGroup->
  GetResNamed("Flag", "CIwAnimSkin"));
CIwAnim* lpFlagWobble = static_cast<CIwAnim*>(lpFlagGroup->
  GetResNamed("FlagWobble", "CIwAnim"));
```

Right, now that we have the resources in memory, we need to do something with them.

Playing back a 3D animation

In order to play back an animation, we need to let Marmalade know which animation we want to play, how fast it should be played back, and whether we want it to be a one shot or looping animation. All this and more is provided by the `CIwAnimPlayer` class.

After creating a new instance of `CIwAnimPlayer`, we must provide it with a pointer to the skeleton instance for animation. This is done as follows:

```
CIwAnimPlayer* lpAnimPlayer = new CIwAnimPlayer;
lpAnimPlayer->SetSkel(lpSkel);
```

The player object is now ready to start animating, so we just need to pass it details about the animation we want to play. This can be done with just a single line of code:

```
lpAnimPlayer->PlayAnim(lpFlagWobble, 1.0f,
                       CIwAnimBlendSource::LOOPING_F, 0.0f);
```

The `PlayAnim` method first takes a pointer to the `CIwAnim` instance we wish to play. It then expects to see a playback speed, some control flags, and a blending interval.

The playback speed is specified so that a value of `1` yields the normal exported animation speed. Doubling this value will play the animation back at twice the speed, and so on.

The function's third parameter is a set of control flags that are primarily used to indicate whether the animation should loop when it reaches the last key frame. If looping is desired, the flag `CIwAnimBlendSource::LOOPING_F` should be used.

There are a number of other values defined by `CIwAnimBlendSource`, but most of these are intended for read-only status flags and the `CIwAnimPlayer` class provides other methods that should be used to determine the current status. Therefore, the only other flag that will be used in this method is `CIwAnimBlendSource::RESET_IF_SAME_F`, which will force the animation player to restart the specified animation if it is already the current animation. If an animation that is already being played is passed in to the `PlayAnim` method, the request will be ignored unless this flag is used.

The animation player is now initialized, so the final thing that must be done is instruct it to calculate the required animation frame. This is done by calling the `Update` method of the `CIwAnimPlayer` instance on every iteration of the main game loop, as shown in the following code:

```
lpAnimPlayer->Update(lTimeStep);
```

The `lTimeStep` parameter is a `float` value indicating the amount of time (in seconds) by which the current animation state should be advanced. When this call completes, a copy of the skeleton will have been created with all the bones positioned and rotated correctly in order to render the current frame of animation.

Rendering a 3D animation

With the animation player now merrily updating away, the final step is to render the animated model. This is possibly the easiest part of the entire process, as the following code demonstrates:

```
IwGxSetViewMatrix(&lViewMatrix);
IwGxSetModelMatrix(&lModelMatrix);

IwAnimSetSkelContext(lpAnim->GetSkel());
IwAnimSetSkinContext(lpSkin);

lpFlag->Render();

IwAnimSetSkelContext(NULL);
IwAnimSetSkinContext(NULL);
```

Hopefully most of this already looks familiar to you. The first step is to set the view and model matrices we want to use for rendering. We then need to provide some information about the frame of animation, namely the animated skeleton and the skin data.

The skeleton information is maintained by the `CIwAnimPlayer` instance and can be retrieved using the `GetSkel` method. The skin is just the `CIwAnimSkin` instance as loaded by the resource manager. We use the `IwAnimSetSkelContext` and `IwAnimSetSkinContext` functions to provide this data to the rendering engine.

To render the animated model to the screen, all we have to do is call the `Render` method on `lpFlag`, which is a pointer to a `CIwModel` instance, just as we would if we were rendering the model without any animation.

After rendering, we clear the skin and skeleton contexts so that future model rendering calls won't try and use incorrect data during rendering. This is a good habit to get into as determining why an unanimated model has suddenly started deforming wildly could be a tricky bug to track down.

Exploring 3D animation further

Congratulations! You're now able to render fully animated 3D models! While this is a pretty cool achievement, the functionality we've seen so far has only scratched the surface of what the IwAnim API allows us to do. The following sections describe some of the other features that we have at our disposal.

Playing an animation backwards

There are some occasions when it is useful to be able to play an animation backwards. As an example, imagine a character kneeling down to examine an object. Rather than create a whole new animation to enable them to stand up again, we could just play the kneeling animation backwards instead.

Playing an animation backwards is achieved simply by passing a negative animation speed into the call to `PlayAnim`, so a value of `-1` will play the animation backwards at normal speed.

Blending between animations

When transitioning between two animations, we often don't want to just snap straight to the beginning of the new sequence, as this can result in a noticeable jump between the current frame of animation and the first frame of the new animation. We can solve this problem by blending between animations.

We touched on how to achieve this earlier, when we first introduced the `PlayAnim` method. The final parameter in this method is the blending time, which is specified as a value in seconds using a floating point number.

By specifying a non-zero blending interval, the animation player will calculate the frames of animation required for both the old and new animations, then generate a third transition frame by interpolating between these two frames over the specified time. The transition frame is what is then used to draw the 3D model. Once the blend interval is over, the original animation will stop being calculated as it is no longer required.

Detecting animation playback events

Being able to detect when an animation has looped or has finished playing is important because we can start to link animations together or prevent the user from performing a task until an animation has completed. For instance, imagine a player has to reload a weapon and an animation is played to show this happening. We need to know when the animation has completed so we can allow the player to start attacking again.

The CIwAnimPlayer class allows us to detect when a one shot animation has completed, by calling the IsCurrentAnimComplete method that will return true when the animation has finished.

There is also the IsCurrentBlendComplete method that will return true when the animation player has finished blending between two animations.

Detecting when an animation has looped is also possible, although CIwAnimPlayer does not provide us with a quick shortcut way of detecting this event. Instead, we have to do a little manual flag testing.

At any time, the animation player can be updating two main animations: current animation (defined as the animation that was last specified using the PlayAnim method) and the previous animation (the one that was playing at the time PlayAnim was last called with a blending interval).

The current status of these two animations are stored in instances of the CIwAnimBlendSource class, which we can access using the CIwAnimPlayer class' methods named GetSourceCurr and GetSourcePrev. The CIwAnimBlendSource class has a method called GetFlags that returns playback status information as a bitmask. To detect if the animation has looped, we just need to see if the flag CIwAnimBlendSource::LOOPED_F is set. The following source code shows this in action:

```
if (lpAnimPlayer->GetSourceCurr()->GetFlags() &
                        CIwAnimBlendSource::LOOPED_F)
{
  // Animation has looped!
}
```

If you prefer this approach, you can also use the flag CIwAnimBlendSource::COMPLETE_F to detect when a single shot animation has finished.

Optimizing animation playback

Do you remember that we calculated the current animation frame by calling the Update method of CIwAnimPlayer? This method has to do quite a lot of work, some of which we might not actually need to do on a frame-by-frame basis. For example, if an in-game character is currently not visible on the screen, we might want to ensure that we still step through its animation; but calculating the bone positions for the current frame of animation is a waste of processor time as we won't be rendering the animation.

The `Update` method is actually implemented by calling three other methods of `CIwAnimPlayer`, which we can call independently if we so wish.

The first method is `UpdateParameters`, which takes the time increment we need to update the animation by as its sole parameter. This method will update the current time indexes of all the animations currently in use by the animation player and set flags to indicate whether those animations have completed or looped.

The `UpdateSources` method takes no parameters and is used to work out the current bone orientations for each animation, applying any blending between animations as required.

Finally there is the `UpdateMatrices` method, which again takes no parameters. This performs the final step of converting all the positions and orientations of each bone into a matrix that will be used to update the vertex stream of the 3D model during rendering.

These methods need to be called in the order presented previously, but there is no need to call all three methods in every frame if we do not need the results of that method to be calculated.

Playing sub-animations

Sub-animations allow us to animate only a part of the entire skeleton, which can be useful when we want an in-game character to be able to perform two different actions at once. For example, a character might be able to wield several different weapons while moving around the game world. The main animation applied to the character would be an animation for walking, running, or just standing still. Sub-animations can then be overlaid on top of the main animation to show the player holding, firing, or reloading the different weapon types.

In order to export a sub-animation, all we need to do is specify the name of the bone that is the root of the sub-animation in the **Sub Anim Root** field of the Marmalade exporter plugin. In the example situation given previously, you might choose to export the sub-animation starting at a bone that has the two arm bones as children.

The Blender plugin does not currently support this feature unfortunately, though you could potentially export the entire animation and then delete by hand any references to bones higher in the hierarchy than the sub-animation root bone in the ANIM file.

With the sub-animation exported, all we have to do to play it back is call the `PlaySubAnim` method of `CIwAnimPlayer`. An example of how to use this function is as follows:

```
lpAnimPlayer->PlaySubAnim(0, lpFlagWave, 1.0f,
CIwAnimBlendSource::LOOPING_F, 0.0f);
```

As you can see, it is almost identical in structure to the `PlayAnim` method. The only difference is an extra initial parameter, which is the sub-animation index number. The animation player can support two different sub-animations at the same time and the index number should be `0` or `1` to indicate which sub-animation you wish to change.

To detect the current playback status of a sub-animation, we can get hold of the `CIwAnimBlendSource` instance using the `GetSourceSub` method of `CIwAnimPlayer`. This method takes a single parameter, which is the index number of the sub-animation required.

Offset animations

When dealing with animations that cause a game character to move, such as walking, running, or making an attacking move, it is desirable to update the position of the character with respect to the animation being played so that the character's feet do not appear to slip on the ground.

Marmalade provides a method of doing this by way of an **offset animation**, which is an animation that consists of a single bone whose position and rotation can be used to move an object around the game world. Offset animations are exported using the same export process as any other animation.

To use an offset animation, we use the `PlayOfsAnim` method of `CIwAnimPlayer`, as shown in the following code:

```
lpAnimPlayer->PlayOfsAnim(lpMovementAnim, 1.0f, 0);
```

The parameters of this function are pointers to the offset animation instance, the speed of playback (again a value of `1` will play back at normal speed), and the required animation flags; so it is possible to play back offset animations as one shot or looped.

To find the current status of the offset animation, we can use the `GetSourceOfs` method on `CIwAnimPlayer` to retrieve the `CIwAnimBlendSource` instance that maintains it.

We can also find out position and rotation information for the start, end, and current offsets using the methods `GetMatOfsInitial`, `GetMatOfsFinal`, and `GetMatOfs` of `CIwAnimPlayer`. Each of these methods allows access to a `CIwFMat` object representing the current orientation of the offset. We can then use this information to allow us to update the position of a game character accordingly, so that other game functions such as collision detection continue to work correctly.

Obtaining bone positions and rotations

When discussing sub-animations earlier, we presented the example of a character being able to hold a variety of different weapons. Sub-animations will, of course, only provide half the solution to this problem, as they will move the character's arms to the correct pose; but, because the weapon is not part of the source 3D model, the character will just appear to be clutching at thin air.

We need some way of drawing a further model depicting the weapon, but how can we get it positioned in the correct place?

The answer is to ask the animation player to provide us with the current orientation and position of a bone that is located at the point where the weapon model would need to be drawn. We can do this by calling the `GetBoneNamed` method of `CIwAnimPlayer`, which will return a pointer to a `CIwAnimBone` instance representing the current orientation of the requested bone.

The position and rotation of the bone can be found using the `GetPos` and `GetRot` methods of `CIwAnimBone`, which allow us to generate a matrix in model space, or alternatively the `GetMat` method will return a model space matrix representing both the position and rotation of the bone if it has been calculated during the update of the `CIwAnimPlayer` instance.

Using the bone information, we can easily calculate a model matrix for rendering the weapon model in the correct place. First we use the bone information to generate a matrix in model space, we then multiply this by any rotation matrix needed to orient the character in the game world. Finally, add the world position of the character and the weapon model can be rendered in the character's hand.

Example code

The following sections give an overview of the sample projects accompanying this chapter.

The Flag project

This example demonstrates playing back both a main and sub-animation. A flag is rendered waving in a virtual breeze. Every few seconds the flagpole will wobble around but the flag on the end of the pole will continue to flap around. A screen grab can be seen in the following figure:

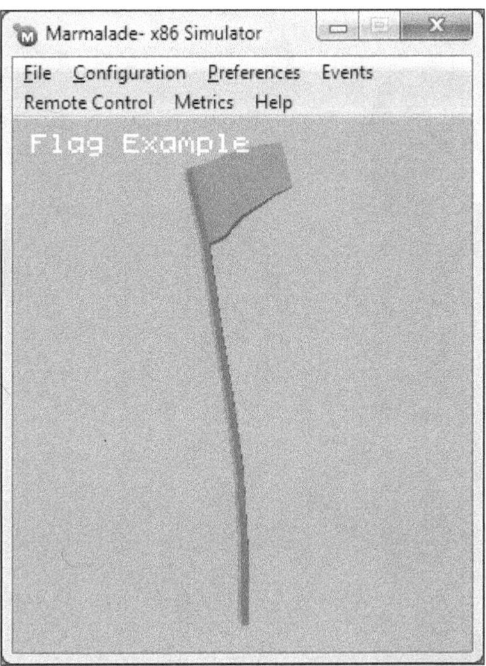

The animation of the flag waving is achieved as a looping sub-animation, while the flagpole wobble is the main animation, which is started every five seconds as a one-shot animation.

One of the problems with this approach is that the sub-animation will only play if there is a main animation currently in progress. Rather than create a one frame animation of the flagpole standing still, a cunning trick has been employed.

The flagpole wobble animation is actually playing continuously, but at zero speed. Since the first frame of the wobble animation is of the pole in an upright position, we have achieved our aim of a static animation frame.

Every five seconds the wobble animation is then restarted as a one-shot animation. When the wobble animation has completed, we return to playing it at zero speed to hold the flagpole steady again.

The Skiing project

The changes to the Skiing project for this chapter really make it seem like much more of a game. The following screenshot and the following sections highlight the new bits and pieces that have been added:

New gameplay features

Previously, there was not a great deal of actual gameplay to be had in the game. We could steer the little skier left and right, but aside from crashing into a tree there wasn't actually an awful lot to do.

To combat this, gates consisting of a couple of flags have been added. The player must steer the skier through these in order to increase their score, which is now displayed at the bottom of the screen.

To implement the gates, a new class called `Flag` has been created. The `ModeGame` class picks a random position across the course and spawns a flag a short distance left and right of that position. The flags scroll up the screen, and when they scroll off the top a new random position is chosen for them at the bottom of the game world.

The `ModeGame` class maintains pointers to the two instances of `Flag` so that it can be detected when they have scrolled offscreen and need repositioning, plus we can also use these pointers to work out when the player has moved between them.

Randomly placed rocks have also been introduced, which must be avoided because colliding with them ends the game, just like steering into the trees does. These are represented by another new class called `Rock`. This class is very similar to the existing `Tree` class, the main difference being that when the rock scrolls off the top of the screen it is replaced at the bottom with a new horizontal position.

Animations added

Given the subject matter of this chapter, it's fairly obvious that adding animations to the game would be one of the changes made.

Our little skier character has been given a looping animation, so the little chap now pushes himself along using his skiing poles. If the player collides with a tree or rock, the poor little fellow will also now take a tumble and end up in a heap on the ground. Ouch!

The other animation added to the game has been for the flag. It is the same animation structure demonstrated in this chapter's other example project. A sub-animation plays to make the flag wave in the wind, while the main animation is of the flagpole wobbling about.

Rather than wobbling at set time intervals, the animation is instead triggered when the player skis too close to the flag.

Summary

We've covered the topic of 3D animation quite extensively in this chapter. We can now move, rotate, and scale our 3D models in the game world, and we can make the actual shape of the model change using boned animations to make characters walk, run, jump, dance, or whatever we require them to do.

We've also looked at some more advanced topics, such as blending between animations, applying sub-animations on top of a main animation, and retrieving bone position and orientation information from an in-progress animation to allow us to find the location of a particular part of a model.

In the next chapter we'll return to just two dimensions, as we look at how we can make the user interface of our games look a little prettier than just using badly laid out debug fonts.

6

Implementing Fonts, User Interfaces, and Localization

Now that we have the knowledge to create 3D worlds populated with animated characters, we really need to start thinking about how to improve the look of the user interface we present to the player.

In this chapter we'll be covering the following:

- Creating fonts that can be used in a Marmalade project
- Drawing and formatting of text
- Discussing ways of implementing your game's user interface
- Localizing your game into multiple languages

Implementing fonts

The first step toward improving the look of our game is to say goodbye to the debug font and replace it with something a little more stylish. The Marmalade SDK comes complete with an API called IwGxFont dedicated to font rendering, so let's put it to good use.

Adding the IwGxFont API to a project

By now I'm sure you must be able to hazard a guess as to how this is done. That's right, just add `iwgxfont` to the subprojects section in the MKB file, and then make a call to `IwGxFontInit` to initialize the API, and `IwGxFontTerminate` to free it at shutdown time.

As the name of this API suggests, it requires IwGx in order to work. We also need IwResManager so we can load the font data into memory, so the initialization call for IwGxFont must occur after these two modules have been initialized, as shown in the following code snippet:

```
IwGxInit();
IwResManagerInit();
IwGxFontInit();
```

Creating a font resource

The first thing we need to do is create a `CIwGxFont` resource describing the font that we want to use. This is easily done thanks to the **Marmalade Studio - Font Builder** utility that is installed as part of the Marmalade SDK. The following image shows a screenshot of this program in action:

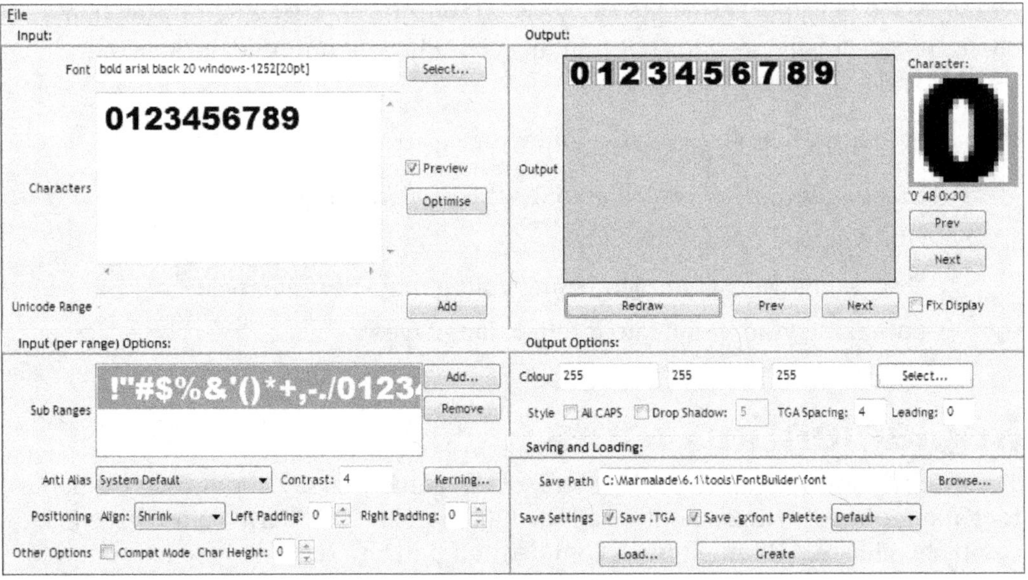

The IwGxFont API renders text by drawing each character individually by using sections of a large bitmap that contains an image of all the characters we need to render. Generating the bitmap itself is fairly trivial and could be done with any art package, but we need to somehow be able to specify which part of the bitmap represents which character. This is where IwGxFont and the font builder utility come to our aid.

Here are the basic steps needed to generate a font resource:

1. Start the **Marmalade Studio - Font Builder** utility. You can find a Windows Start button menu shortcut for it under **Marmalade** | **x.x** | **Tools**, where **x.x** represents the version number of the Marmalade SDK you have installed.
2. In the top-left panel labeled **Input**, first click on the **Select...** button to display a font selection dialog. Choose the font, size, and style you require and click on **OK**. You can choose any installed Windows font, whether it be a scalable TrueType font or a fixed-size bitmapped font.
3. The **Characters** textbox allows you to specify a list of the characters you require in your font. A default selection covering most European languages is present, but you can add or remove as many characters as you want. Fewer characters is obviously better though, as it will reduce the size of the bitmap that gets generated and thus take up less memory. It is also possible to populate this textbox by loading a text file using **File** | **Load Character Map**. The **Characters** textbox will then contain every unique character present in the text file, minus formatting characters such as tabs or newlines.
4. Moving on to the section labeled **Output Options**, you can choose a color for the font using the numeric entry boxes or by clicking on the **Select...** button to display a color selection dialog. It is recommended that you keep the color set to the default of bright white as the text color can then easily be set at runtime.
5. There are also some other settings here that allow you to adjust the look of the font. There are checkboxes to force all characters to be in capitals and to enable the addition of a drop shadow to the font. If this checkbox is ticked, a textbox allows the pixel offset of the drop shadow to be specified.
6. Next, look at the top right panel labeled **Output**. Here we can see a preview of what the generated font characters will look like. Just click on the **Redraw** button and after a short delay the characters will appear in the view area. You can then use the two sets of **Prev** and **Next** buttons to cycle through each character.
7. We're nearly ready to export the font; but before we can, we need to specify where we want the font files to be created, which is done in the **Saving and Loading** panel. Click on the **Browse...** button to display a file requester to choose the required directory or enter it directly into the **Save Path** textbox. The last part of this filename is the base filename that will be used to export the font data.
8. To create the font files, ensure that the two checkboxes labeled **Save .TGA** and **Save .gxfont** are checked, then click on the **Create** button.

There are a number of options we haven't explored in this run-through, as most of the time you won't need to worry about them. In particular, we skipped the panel labeled **Input (per range) Options** entirely.

This panel provides control over font features such as kerning, which is the offset between the characters of a font. Kerning can sometimes be useful for bringing certain character combinations closer together. For example, consider the capital letters A and V. The shapes of these characters mean you may want to draw them slightly closer to provide a more natural looking result when they are displayed next to each other.

You can also declare subranges of characters, which allow you to apply different global settings to certain ranges of characters. You can use this facility to use completely different sizes of characters or even completely different source fonts, for different character ranges. This can be particularly useful if we want to create a font that contains characters from the standard ASCII set and characters from another language. The font we use for the ASCII characters may not contain the characters for the other language, so we can create a sub range that allows us to pick a completely different font for those characters.

The GXFONT file format

The font builder utility creates two types of files to define a font resource. The first of these is the actual font bitmap, which is exported in the Targa file format, an image file format usually identified by the file extension `.tga`.

The second file exported is a **GXFONT file**, which acts as both a way of allowing the font to be reloaded into the font builder for further editing, and a way of loading the font into our own programs.

The following is an example GXFONT file for a font containing only numeric characters drawn using the standard Windows font Arial Black at 20 points:

```
//Temp file created by AS Font Builder (User: Sean At: 06/29/12
18:00:06)
//Command Line:
//: -fontdesc "0;-27;0;0;0;900;0;0;0;0;3;2;1;34;Arial Black" 0 4 0
-pad 0 0
//: -col #FFFFFF -shadow 0 -spacing 4 -force16 0

CIwGxFont
{
  utf8 1
  image numbers.tga
  charmap "0123456789"
}
```

As you can see, it's fairly self-explanatory. The comments at the start of the file are primarily used by the font builder utility to know what settings were used to create the font, so you should leave these values well alone if you want to edit the font later.

We can edit a font in the font builder utility at a later date by using **File | Load Font** or by pressing the **Load...** button. A file requester will appear allowing us to choose the GXFONT file we wish to edit.

The part of the GXFONT file we're really interested in is the definition of the `CIwGxFont` instance. The three parameters we see here indicate that the character encoding to be used with this font should be UTF-8, the bitmap image to use is called `numbers.tga`, and the characters present in the font are the numerals zero through nine.

By default, UTF-8 character encoding is chosen, as this format often provides the most compact memory representation of text strings, at least as far as European languages are concerned.

If we've specified any other font settings in the font builder utility, such as character subranges or kerning information, this will also be represented in both the comments at the top of the file and the `CIwGxFont` structure. We won't cover this here though, since the font builder takes care of all the hard work for us.

Loading and accessing font resources

As with all the resource types we've seen, we load a font resource into our program by adding a reference to it into a GROUP file, loading the GROUP file using the resource manager, and then searching for the font resource.

For completeness, here is a code snippet showing how to do this:

```
CIwResGroup* lpResGroup = IwGetResManager()->
LoadGroup("fonts/fonts.group");
CIwGxFont* lpSmallFont = static_cast<CIwGxFont*>(IwGetResManager()->
GetResNamed("small", "CIwGxFont"));
```

Drawing text using a font resource

With a font resource loaded and a pointer to it obtained, we can start to draw some text on screen with it. First we'll look at the basics of drawing a string of text, then we'll take a look at how we can justify the text, change its size, and how we can make drawing it a little more optimized.

Drawing text on screen

When we were looking at how to create a font resource, it was mentioned that a color could be chosen for the font. It is recommended to choose white so we can change the color of our text at runtime to any color we want. We change the color of the font by modulating the font bitmap with our chosen color, so if the font bitmap is not white this will not produce the desired color change.

We'll be seeing how to change the font color in a moment, but in order for font coloring to work there is one quirk of IwGxFont that must be mentioned first.

> When attempting to recolor a font at runtime, we must ensure that emissive lighting is enabled using the function call `IwGxLightingEmissive(true)`. IwGxFont affects the color of a font by using the emissive lighting component, which will not be applied if it is disabled.

With the note about lighting out of the way, the first step in rendering text is to indicate which font we want to use to draw it. This is done by passing a pointer to the relevant `CIwGxFont` instance into the function `IwGxFontSetFont`.

Next, we can set the color we want to use with `IwGxFontSetCol`. There are two versions of this function, one that takes a reference to a `const CIwColour` instance, and another that takes the color value as a uint32 value. When using the latter, bear in mind that the color is specified as ABGR—that is, alpha in the most significant byte, then blue, green, and red in the least significant byte.

We now need to indicate where on the screen we want the text to appear, which we do by defining a rectangular area in which the text should appear. This is specified by using a `CIwRect` instance that contains x and y values for the top left of the rectangle, plus a width and height value. The function call we use is `IwGxFontSetRect`.

Drawing the text is now possible using the `IwGxFontDrawText` function. The first parameter is the string of text to print and is specified as a `const CIwChar` pointer. `CIwChar` is just a `typedef` type for the standard C `char` type.

The default encoding for text is UTF-8. For text comprising of characters from the ASCII set, this means we don't have to do anything to the text data at all.

The function also takes a second parameter, which is the length of the text to be drawn. This has a default parameter value of `-1`, which indicates the entire string should be drawn. Any other value will draw the specified number of characters. This is handy if you want to implement a system common in many games where text appears on screen one character at a time.

Putting this all together, here's an example that draws "Hello World" on the screen in yellow:

```
IwGxLightingEmissve(true);
IwGxFontSetFont(lpSmallFont);
IwGxFontSetCol(0xFF00FFFF);
IwGxFontSetRect(CIwRect(0, 0,IwGxGetScreenWidth(), 100));
IwGxFontDrawText("Hello World");
```

Text wrapping and justification

Wondering why we specified a rectangular area for our text rather than just a screen position? The reason is so that IwGxFont can wrap and justify our text for us.

While Marmalade does allow us to include the line feed character in our code to force a new line in our text, it does not provide support for other formatting characters such as tabs or backspace. It is far better to allow Marmalade to word wrap text for us than to insert line feeds in our text by hand, because if we change the font size or the dimension of the rectangular draw area we won't have to change the text itself in any way.

The default behavior when rendering text is to word wrap whenever a line of text exceeds the bounds of the rectangular area set with `IwGxFontSetRect`. We can alter this behavior using the `IwGxFontSetFlags` function, which can take a combination of the following values OR'ed together:

Value	Definition
IW_GX_FONT_DEFAULT_F	Uses default font settings.
IW_GX_FONT_NOWRAP_F	Does not wrap text at the edge of the rectangle's boundary.
IW_GX_FONT_NOWORDWRAP_F	Does not perform full word wrapping on text.
IW_GX_FONT_ONELINE_F	Only renders a single line of text. Rendering stops when a newline character (`'\n'`) is reached.
IW_GX_FONT_NUMBER_ALIGN_F	Forces all numbers to be displayed with the same width.
IW_GX_FONT_UNDERLINE_F	Draws the text with underlining.
IW_GX_FONT_ITALIC_F	Draws the text in italics.

Value	Definition
IW_GX_FONT_RIGHTTOLEFT_F	Draws characters from right to left. Useful for drawing languages such as Arabic.
IW_GX_FONT_NOWORDSPLIT_F	Wraps text at the end of words. A word can overlap the end of the rectangle boundary, but the next word will start on the next line.

Flags can be cleared again using `IwGxFontClearFlags`.

We can also specify whether text is drawn left aligned, right aligned, or centered in the rectangular bounding area using the function `IwGxFontSetAlignmentHor`, which takes one of the following values:

Value	Definition
IW_GX_FONT_ALIGN_LEFT	Aligns text to the left of the bounding box.
IW_GX_FONT_ALIGN_CENTRE	Centres text horizontally in the bounding box.
IW_GX_FONT_ALIGN_RIGHT	Aligns text to the right edge of the bounding box.
IW_GX_FONT_ALIGN_PARAGRAPH	Performs left or right alignment, as defined by the device's localization settings.

We can do similar alignments vertically as well using `IwGxFontSelAlignmentVer` with one of these values:

Value	Definition
IW_GX_FONT_ALIGN_TOP	Text is drawn so that the top line of text touches the top of the bounding box.
IW_GX_FONT_ALIGN_MIDDLE	Text is centered vertically in the bounding box.
IW_GX_FONT_ALIGN_BOTTOM	Text is drawn so the bottom of the last line of text touches the bottom of the bounding box.

Changing font size at runtime

Sometimes it is desirable to be able to animate text by making changes in its size. For example, in a shooting game the score awarded for killing an enemy might appear at the position of the enemy then gradually grow larger and fade out.

The function `IwGxFontSetScale` enables us to do this. It takes two parameters so the font can be scaled by different amounts, both horizontally and vertically. The scaling factors are passed in as fixed point values, with `IW_GEOM_ONE` indicating a scaling factor of `1` and therefore no change in size.

IwGxFont draws text by rendering a rectangular polygon for each character in our text, with the relevant part of the font image mapped on to it. By specifying a scaling factor we can change the size of the polygons used to render the individual characters, though this can yield poor results if we scale up by a large factor (for example, more than double the original size of the font).

Optimizing drawing by preparing text

One of the problems with rendering text is that in order to perform alignment, word wrapping, and the like, it is necessary to format the text by considering it one character at a time to see if the next character crosses the rectangular bounding box area.

If we need to draw a piece of fixed text, such as an instructions screen, we can prevent having to calculate the formatting information in every frame by preparing the text for rendering once and then using some cached data to draw it from then on.

To do this we use the function `IwGxFontPrepareText`. This function takes a reference to a `CIwGxFontPreparedData` class instance, the string of text to prepare, and optionally the number of characters in the string that we want to consider. If this parameter is omitted, the entire string is processed.

With the text prepared we can then draw it using another version of the `IwGxFontDrawText` function. This version takes a reference to the `CIwGxFontPreparedData` instance and two optional parameters that indicate the first character from the prepared data to draw and the number of characters to draw. Here's a code example:

```
CIwGxFontPreparedData lFontData;
IwGxFontSetRect(CIwRect(100, 100, 200, 100));
IwGxFontPrepareText(lFontData, "This is the text to be prepared!");
IwGxFontDrawText(lFontData);
```

Note that the text will be drawn on screen at the position indicated by the formatting rectangle set in the call to `IwGxFontSetRect`.

Implementing user interfaces

Every game will need some kind of user interface, even if it is just a button that can be pressed to start a new game. In this section we will take a look at how a user interface can be implemented for your own game.

The IwUI API

The Marmalade SDK ships with an API called IwUI, which allows us to create user interfaces for our projects consisting of buttons, labels, and other common controls.

This API is very feature-rich and allows interfaces to be created not just for games, but also for more serious applications. Marmalade used to ship with a tool called the Marmalade Studio UI Builder, but this is sadly no longer a supported part of the SDK. However, it is still possible to access this tool by either installing an older version of Marmalade (one of the v5.2.x releases is probably best) or by downloading its source code from `https://github.com/marmalade/UI-Builder`.

It is also possible to use IwUI without using the UI creation tool by constructing ITX files that describe our interface layouts, by hand. These layout files can end up being quite verbose and therefore hard to maintain, so the Marmalade Studio UI Builder made editing layouts a bit more manageable.

The Marmalade documentation states that the reason for dropping the UI Builder from the SDK was to allow a standardized UI markup system to be used that is supported by a number of other third party tools. At the time of writing this book, no further announcement had been made regarding exactly what form this will take.

There seems no doubt that the IwUI API will remain a part of Marmalade for the foreseeable future. However, we won't be delving any deeper into the API itself in this book as it seems likely that a new UI system will be making its way into Marmalade soon. If you are interested in what IwUI can do, take a look at the Marmalade documentation and the plethora of sample code that ships with the SDK.

The IwNUI API

Marmalade provides a second user interface API called IwNUI. The "N" stands for Native, as this API allows you to construct user interfaces using the standard UI controls for the platform that your application runs on.

This may sound like a good idea but the main drawback is that it is only supported on iOS and Android. All other platforms will use a default style implemented using the previously mentioned IwUI API.

At any rate most games tend to implement their own UI that is in keeping with the style of the game, and this normally means we don't want to use standard OS user interface controls, but IwNUI is a good choice if you happen to want to develop a utility or other application type.

Implementing our own user interface solution

Given that we're effectively starting from square one with our user interface implementation, let's consider how we could go about creating our own solution.

The following sections highlight some of the issues to be aware of when developing user interface code. One of the example projects accompanying this chapter implements a user interface library that tries to take most of the following into account.

Using a generic approach

It really is worth taking the time to develop as generic a solution as possible when dealing with user interface code. While implementing the frontend of a game isn't particularly difficult to code, it is far too easy to find yourself writing UI code from scratch for each project.

By investing in a generic approach, you can quickly put together a functional UI for all your projects. Frontend menu systems actually tend to be little more than a collection of buttons and labels; so why write this code multiple times? Implement these types of controls once and you can then spend more time creating customized controls when your game demands it.

It is recommended that you implement your UI code by creating a separate subproject, as this will help ensure that your solution is as generic and self-contained as possible.

Marmalade makes it easy for us to create our own library modules by using the same system the SDK uses for including its component parts. Simply create an MKB file referencing all the source files that are part of the library, but save it with the extension `.mkf` instead of `.mkb`. You can then reference this module by adding the name of the MKF file (minus the extension) to the `subprojects` section of the main project MKB file. Library module directories should be placed in the same place as the main project directory so that they can be located when creating the project from the MKB file.

Making good use of class inheritance

A good class hierarchy can make implementing your UI a much more pleasant experience and it is well worth taking a look at existing systems to see how they have been constructed.

Most modern UI implementations will normally start with a base level class from which all other control types are derived, which for discussion purposes in this chapter we will call an **element**. An element will take care of things such as the positioning of a control and internal naming so that the handling of UI events can be standardized.

When implementing a class representing an element, we should make use of virtual methods that can be overridden by child classes to change default behavior. At the very least this normally means that we should have methods that can be called to update and render the control.

Another extremely useful concept is that of a **frame**, which has the ability to group several elements together so they can be moved, enabled, or hidden at the same time.

When updating or rendering the user interface, the frame is responsible for deciding whether or not to update or render the child elements it contains.

The positioning and sizing of all elements contained within a frame should also be calculated relative to the position and size of the frame itself.

Having implemented classes representing both elements and frames, it is possible to implement most common UI controls very simply. Here are a few examples to illustrate this:

- A **label** control simply displays a line of text on screen. It can be derived from the element class and at its simplest all we need to define are member variables to store the text to be drawn, and some font and color information. We can then override the virtual render method to allow the text to be drawn at the position indicated by the element class.
- A **bitmap** control is very similar to a label but displays an image instead of text. We just need to store a pointer to the image we want to draw (perhaps as a `CIwTexture` or `CIwMaterial` pointer) and then implement the render method to draw it on screen.
- A **button** control can be derived from a frame. Most UI systems allow an image or a text string (or both) to be displayed on the button, so we can implement this just by adding label or bitmap controls to the list of elements contained within the frame.
- A **slider** control could also use the frame as a basis and could include two bitmap controls, one for the backing of the slider and another for the selection knob. A label could also be included if you want to display the current position of the slider as a numeric value.

Hopefully this gives you an idea of how, with a little initial planning, implementing a diverse range of user interface controls actually becomes very easy.

Implementing a data-driven system

With a good class hierarchy in place, the next step is to ensure that your UI can be created easily from a configuration datafile. While it is perfectly possible to create all your controls in code, this is hard to maintain and, most crucially, can then only be edited by a programmer.

Allowing your UI to be constructed from a datafile means that other members of your team can help with designing the UI. Having a datafile format also makes it easier to develop a user interface layout tool if you want to make the process even easier for people to use.

We've already seen how we can use the ITX file format to construct our own custom classes from a file at runtime, so it makes sense to employ this methodology to our UI code (refer back to *Chapter 2, Resource Management and 2D Graphics Rendering*, if you want to refresh your memory on this). No point in writing more code than we have to!

Responding to user input events

The user interface of a game must solve two main issues. The first is relaying information to the player, and we've already discussed how this can be done earlier. The second is responding to user inputs.

As discussed earlier in this book, modern mobile devices allow a great many ways of allowing the player to interact with a game. Which of these you support, depends on the devices you are trying to target, but by far the most popular choice is the touch screen. Pressing on-screen buttons is just a very natural way of interacting with a application, so it is pretty much guaranteed you will end up supporting touch screens for your own UI.

Obviously not all controls need to respond to being touched. For example, a label is unlikely to do anything, so it makes sense to provide some mechanism that allows us to indicate which controls should respond to touches and which shouldn't.

While we could just add some virtual methods to the element class that gets called whenever a touch has been detected within its bounding area, this is probably not the best solution as it starts to make the element class a little cluttered.

We really want to encapsulate this sort of functionality somehow, and a good way of doing this is by using an Event system. Such a system works by having a central event manager whose sole job is to receive event messages from one part of the code and pass those messages on to any class instance that has registered itself with the event manager to be notified of a particular event.

To implement such a system, we can introduce two new base classes. An Event class, which is the base class for all event message types, and an `EventHandler` class, which contains a single virtual method called `Execute` that will be called in order to respond to an Event.

At its most basic level, the Event class will just contain a single member that is used as a unique identifier for a particular type of event, for example, an enumerated type. We can declare our own event types by deriving them from an Event and adding members for any information we might want to pass along with the message. For example, a touch screen event might contain the screen coordinates of where the touch occurred.

Any class that wants to respond to a particular event can then derive from the `EventHandler` class and provide an implementation for the virtual method. When a new instance of a class is constructed, it registers its interest in any event by passing the unique identifier of the event and a pointer to itself (cast as an `EventHandler` pointer) to the event handler.

Now, whenever an event occurs we create an instance of the event type in question, populate its members with information about that event, and pass it to the event manager. The event manager will compare the unique identifier of the event against its list of registered instances and then call the `Execute` method of `EventHandler` for any of registered instance that wanted to be notified about the type of event that has just occurred. The event message will be passed into the `Execute` method of the instance so that its data can then be acted upon accordingly.

Screen resolution and orientation

Chances are that your game could well be executed on a number of different devices that have different screen resolutions and aspect ratios, which can make creating a nice looking user interface a real chore.

It is therefore important to provide a very flexible way in which the position and size of UI controls can be specified.

When specifying screen coordinates, widths, and heights for controls, consider allowing both exact pixel sizes and ratios of the width and height of the containing frame to be used.

It is also good to allow a control to be conformed to a particular aspect ratio when using ratios to define sizes. Being able to ensure that the control has a particular aspect ratio makes it much easier to keep a consistent layout of any child control and is particularly important when drawing bitmapped images that will look strange if they end up stretched. When fixing a control to a particular aspect ratio, you will want to be able to indicate whether the width or the height should change to keep the control in the correct shape.

Being able to lay out controls relative to each other is also a useful thing to be able to do. One way of doing this is by specifying that a control should take in its position by adding an offset to the position of another control.

Another thing that can throw a spanner in the works is when the user rotates the device and the screen changes between portrait and landscape orientations. For most games we will want screen orientation changes to be ignored, since most games are designed to either be played in portrait or landscape and not both.

Ignoring screen orientation changes is made simple by adding the `DispFixRot` setting to the application's ICF file, as follows:

```
[S3E]
DispFixRot=Landscape
```

This setting can take the following values:

Value	Description
`Free`	Screen will rotate when the user rotates the device. This is the default value if `DispFixRot` is not used.
`Portrait`	Screen will always be kept in portrait aspect but can rotate when the device is held in either of the possible portrait orientations. It is easy to miss the fact that there are two possible portrait orientations since the phone could be held upside down!
`Landscape`	Screen will always be kept in landscape aspect but can rotate when the device is held in either of the possible landscape orientations. Again, note that there are two possible landscape orientations depending on which direction you rotate the phone from its normal portrait position.
`FixedPortrait`	Screen will be fixed in the device's default portrait orientation and will not rotate at all.
`FixedLandscape`	Screen will be fixed in the device's default landscape orientation and will not rotate at all.

If we do choose to support screen orientation changes, we need some way of detecting when the orientation has changed. We can do this by setting up a callback function as follows:

```
// This is the callback function
int32 OnOrientationChanged(s3eSurfaceOrientation* apOrientation,
void* apUserData)
{
  if (apOrientation->m_OrientationChanged)
```

```
    {
      if (apOrientation->m_Width > apOrientation->m_Height)
      {
        // Switch to landscape
      }
      else
      {
        // Switch to portrait
      }
    }
    return 0;
  }

  // Call this somewhere in our set up code
  s3eSurfaceRegister(S3E_SURFACE_SCREENSIZE, (s3eCallback)
     OnOrientationChanged, NULL);
```

It is highly recommended, if you are supporting both portrait and landscape in your game, that you define specific layouts of your controls for each orientation and switch between them when the device is rotated. Trying to accommodate both orientations with a single layout is possible but tends to yield uninspiring results in both orientations, so make the most of the available screen space by providing custom layouts for each.

Adding template functionality

Consistency is an important part of the user interface design. We expect controls of a similar type to look the same. If they don't, the design starts to look sloppy and unprofessional. It's therefore useful to be able to provide a way of defining certain aspects of our UI once, and **Template** definitions allow us to do just that.

A relatively easy way of implementing templates is to be able to copy the settings of one UI control into another. We can create a control that will never actually be displayed, but will act as a template for other controls. When creating a new control we can copy all member settings from the template and then proceed to make changes to the settings so that the control displays whatever we need it to.

One way of implementing this is to add a virtual method to the element class, which is given a pointer to the template control. Each class can override this method to set its member variables based on the values contained in the template. By calling the virtual method in the parent class, we can copy all member variable settings from the template right down to the base element class.

Localizing your project

As the progress of technology marches on, the world seems to become a smaller place and your game may well end up being played on devices all across the globe. It's therefore well worth considering localizing your game so that players across the world can experience your game in their own language.

While supporting every language known to man would be impractical, many best-selling games now offer support for at least the **EFIGS** languages (English, French, Italian, German, and Spanish), and you can often add Portuguese, Russian, Polish, Japanese, Korean, and both Simplified and Traditional Chinese to the list as well.

Supporting other languages other than your own native tongue is well worth it, as players would much rather play a game they can read and understand than one they can't.

Whether or not you decide to support other languages, there is still a benefit in implementing your game's text in the manner I am about to describe, since it allows you to remove all the text from your source code and put it all in one place, which makes changing the text a much easier process.

Creating a text spreadsheet

The first step in localizing the text in your game is to use a program such as Microsoft Excel or OpenOffice Calc to create a spreadsheet containing all the text for your game. By using a spreadsheet it is very easy to add or insert new strings of text, and the columns of the spreadsheet can be used to provide translations of the strings for each language you want to support. The following screenshot shows an example of such a spreadsheet:

StringList.xls [Compatibility Mode]

	A	B	C
1		EN	FR
2	MM_STARTGAME	Start Game	Commencez du jeu
3	MM_OPTIONS	Options	Paramètres
4	MM_QUIT	Quit	Arrêter?
5	YES	Yes	Oui
6	NO	No	Non
7	SG_STARTNEWGAME	Do you want to start a new game?	Voulez-vous commencer un nouveau jeu?
8	OP_MUSICON	Music: On	Musique: Oui
9	OP_MUSICOFF	Music: Off	Musique: Non
10	OP_BACK	Back	Revenir
11	Q_QUITGAME	Do you want to quit?	Voulez-vous arrêter?
12			

Sheet1 Sheet2 Sheet3

In this spreadsheet the first column is used as a text identifier field. This is just a string of text that we can use in our source code and datafiles to represent a particular string of text.

The first row is used to indicate which language each column of the spreadsheet represents. In the example, we have used the standard two letter ISO country codes to represent the supported languages, namely English (EN) and French (FR).

The rest of the spreadsheet is then just the actual text that we want to appear in the game.

Getting the text into the game

With the text for our game now in a spreadsheet, how do we access it from inside our game code? The answer is to process the spreadsheet into a format that is easy for us to load and use in game code.

Comma-separated values files

One option would be to export the text as a **Comma-Separated Values** (**CSV**) file from our spreadsheet program. This is a simple text-only format that outputs each row of the database as a separate line in the file, with the contents of each cell listed separated by commas.

The trouble with this approach is it can be error-prone. Having a comma in the text of one of your strings can play havoc with the output since the comma is already used to indicate the end of one string and the beginning of the next. This is often gotten around by enclosing each string in quote marks, but then this can cause further problems if a string needs to include a quote mark too!

Remember also that IwGxFont expects text to be supplied in UTF-8 format by default. If you are supporting languages such as Japanese or Korean, this becomes very important and some spreadsheet programs do not support exporting a CSV File in UTF-8 format.

Processing using a Python script

A much better method of getting the text out of a spreadsheet and into our game is to process the spreadsheet into a simple datafile, which can be easily loaded into our game. To demonstrate this, we'll be making use of the Python scripting language.

Python may have a rather strange approach to code layout (the scoping level of your code is indicated by how much it is indented, rather than using notation such as curly braces to indicate the start and end of a section of code), but there is no denying that it is extremely good at this kind of task.

You can get hold of an installer for Python from the following URL:

`http://www.python.org/download/`

The approach we will be using is to access the data from the text spreadsheet by accessing it directly. If we save the spreadsheet in Excel 97 format (file extension `.xls`, supported by most spreadsheet programs), there is an excellent Python library called `xlrd` that can be downloaded here:

`http://pypi.python.org/pypi/xlrd/`

Install Python first and then install the `xlrd` library. It's a good idea to ensure that the Python executable can be easily found by adding the Python install directory to your path environment variable. An easy way to check if the Python directory is already in your path variable is to open up a command prompt window and enter `path` to display the current list of directories that will be searched.

To illustrate just how simple accessing data from a spreadsheet file is, using Python and xlrd, the following script will open a spreadsheet file and output all the rows and columns it contains:

```
import xlrd

lXLS = xlrd.open_workbook("StringList.xls")
lSheet = lXLS.sheet_by_index(0)
for lRow in range(lSheet.nrows):
  lCells = lSheet.row_values(lRow, 0, lSheet.ncols)
  print lCells
```

Even if you've never set eyes on a Python script before, this should be fairly easy to follow, but here's a brief explanation.

The `import xlrd` line is equivalent to the `#include` directive in C/C++. It's just stating that we want to make use of the `xlrd` library.

Next we open the spreadsheet file by calling the `xlrd.open_workbook` method, passing in the filename of the spreadsheet we want to use. This returns an instance of a Python class defined by `xlrd` that represents the spreadsheet file. Note that Python is a loosely typed language and there is no need to declare what type the variable must be.

We call the `sheet_by_index` method on the spreadsheet object to retrieve the first worksheet from the spreadsheet. This yields another Python object representing the worksheet.

We then enter a `for` loop that causes the `lRow` variable to iterate between `0` and the number of populated rows in the spreadsheet. Within the loop we use the worksheet object to access the spreadsheet cells an entire row at a time using the `row_values` method.

Python has a built-in list type and this is what is being used to access all the cells on the row in one go. The `lCells` variable will contain a list whose elements are each cell in the row.

Finally we use the Python `print` command to display the entire list to standard output. You can use `print` in Python to display just about any type, including lists, in a human-readable form.

The UI example project that accompanies this chapter includes a Python script that will take a spreadsheet as input and convert it into a simple datafile for each language contained in the spreadsheet.

The datafiles list the number of strings in the file followed by a hash value generated from the text identifier field (the first column of the spreadsheet) and the string itself. It is fairly trivial to write C++ code to load this file into memory.

> The use of a hashing function here means it is possible for two strings to end up with the same hash value, causing a collision in the string table that means the wrong string may get returned. In practice a good hashing function will mean this hardly ever happens, but if you start getting the wrong string returned this might be the cause. The easiest way to rectify such a problem is just to rename one of the text identifiers in the collision!

To access a particular text string, we use the identifier field in our code. A hash value is generated from the identifier field and the list of string data is searched for that hash value. If a match is found, the corresponding text string is returned, otherwise an assert can be raised and a default string of text returned. The default text can be something like "Missing String!", which makes it easier to track down problems such as getting the identifier field wrong in code, or the string just not being present in the text datafile when it should be.

Selecting the correct language to use at runtime

We now have the ability to supply our game with strings of text in multiple languages, but how do we decide which of those languages to actually use? One method of course is to implement a language select screen during startup of our game and then load the relevant string table depending on the user's input. However, there is a much nicer way available to us.

The s3eDevice API allows us to find out which language is currently in use on the device we are running on. Simply insert the following line of code during the startup portion of your game code:

```
int32 lLanguage = s3eDeviceGetInt(S3E_DEVICE_LANGUAGE);
```

The return value will be a member of the `s3eDeviceLanguage` enumeration, for example `S3E_DEVICE_LANGUAGE_ENGLISH` or `S3E_DEVICE_LANGUAGE_GERMAN`. A full list of all possible language codes can be found in `s3eDevice.h`.

With the language type determined by this call, we can then load the correct table of strings and the user will magically get to see your game in their own language, assuming you've supported it of course!

Example code

There are three example projects associated with this chapter, which are described in the following sections.

The Font project

The first example project demonstrates the use of the IwGxFont API and can be seen in the following screenshot. This example demonstrates how to use multiple fonts in a project, preparing text for printing, and scaling a font up and down in size:

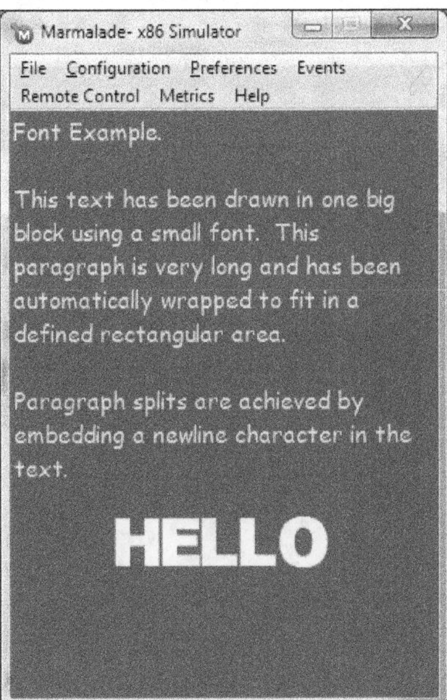

The UI project

The UI example implements a user interface library that adheres to the discussion on how to implement UI code presented earlier in this chapter. It also presents a fully functional localization library, including a Python script that can convert an XLS spreadsheet into separate language datafiles. The script also produces a file for each language detailing all the characters that were used by any of the strings for that language. This can be very useful when generating a font resource to display the text.

The UI and localization library have been implemented as Marmalade subprojects (called GUI and `Localise`), which makes them very easy to re-use in other projects. If you find either of them useful, feel free to make use of them in your own projects.

The text strings are contained in an XLS file contained in the `data/text` directory. English and French strings have been included, though apologies to any French-speaking readers if these strings are not a 100 percent correct, as they were generated using an online translation engine

In the Windows Simulator it is possible to see the program running using both of the supplied language files. With the application running, go to **Configuration** | **Device...**. In the dialog that appears, there is a drop-down box labeled **Reported Device Language**. Choose **ENGLISH** or **FRENCH** in this list and then click on the **OK** button. Quit the program and run it again and the selected language will be used.

A screenshot of this sample in action is as follows:

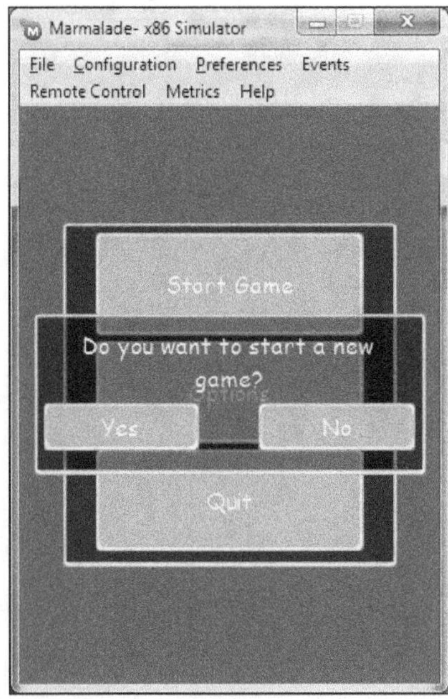

The Skiing project

Finally we come to our evolving **Skiing!** game, which now has a simple yet much nicer looking user interface thanks to the GUI and `Localise` modules created for the UI example. The following screenshot shows the new main menu screen:

Summary

In this chapter we've seen how we can add fonts of any style and size to our projects using the IwGxFont API. We also learnt how to use the Marmalade Studio Font Builder to convert TrueType fonts into bitmapped fonts that can be loaded by IwGxFont.

We also discussed how to implement our own user interface library and how we can localize our game by adding support for more than one language.

In the next chapter we'll be looking at how we can stop our games from being silent affairs with the addition of sound effects and music. We'll also be taking a brief look at how to add a video file playback.

7
Adding Sound and Video

Your game may look stunning, but if it's silent your audience will probably find it a dull experience. Fortunately, Marmalade allows us to remedy this with its support for sound and video playback. In this chapter we will learn about the following:

- Playing back audio files recorded in formats such as MP3
- Adding multiple simultaneous sound effects using sound samples
- Playing back full-motion video clips

Multimedia support in Marmalade

Modern mobile phones and tablet devices are now capable of playing back good quality music and video, so it makes sense that Marmalade should provide ways in which we can harness these abilities.

Marmalade provides three different API layers that apply to multimedia support. These are s3eSound, s3eAudio, and s3eVideo. Unsurprisingly, the latter relates to the playback of video files, but you may be wondering why there are two APIs provided relating to sound.

The difference between s3eSound and s3eAudio is that the former is generally used for sound effects while the latter is normally used for music. The s3eSound API allows us to play several different sound effects at the same time, but by default only provides support for 16-bit mono-PCM sound samples. The s3eAudio API on the other hand allows us to play compressed formats such as MP3, but we are limited (on most devices) to playing a single audio track.

The good news is that most modern devices lets us have the best of both worlds by allowing both s3eSound and s3eAudio to be used at the same time.

In the following sections we'll look at how to make use of all three of these APIs and will also take a look at another module called `SoundEngine`, that makes using the s3eSound API a bit easier.

The s3eAudio API

Let's start with the quickest and easiest way of allowing our games to stop being the strong, silent type.

The s3eAudio API allows us to play compressed music formats such as MP3 and AAC. Some devices may also allow us to play other formats, such as MIDI files. Marmalade makes use of whichever audio codecs a particular device may have built-in rather than decoding the audio itself, so be sure to check that your chosen audio format is supported by all the devices you wish to target.

Due to its ubiquity, it is recommended that you use MP3 as your format of choice. There are very few devices (if any) that can't play an MP3 file and the format itself allows you a wide variety of bit rates so you can trade-off between audio quality and file size.

Let's now take a look at how we can get an audio track playing and what other functionality the s3eAudio API provides for us. There is nothing we need to add to our MKB file in order to allow us to use s3eAudio, as it is one of the low level APIs of Marmalade that is always available for use. All we need to do is include the header file `s3eAudio.h` in any source file that needs access to s3eAudio functions.

Starting audio playback

There are two ways of starting the playback of an audio track. The first allows us to specify the filename of the audio track we want to play and the number of times we would like the track to repeat, and looks like this:

```
s3eAudioPlay("music.mp3", aRepeatCount);
```

The filename is just a standard C, null-terminated string and is relative to the `data` directory when run from Windows or the application install directory on the device. Specifying a number for the repeat count will cause the audio track to play that many times, while setting it to zero will cause the track to loop continuously.

The other method is to play the audio track from an area of memory as follows:

```
s3eAudioPlayFromBuffer(apBuffer, aBufferLength, aRepeatCount);
```

The parameters `apBuffer` and `aBufferLength` provide the memory location where the audio track resides and the length of audio data in bytes. The repeat count is specified in the same manner as with `s3eAudioPlay`.

In most cases we will find that the first method is good enough since it is easy to use and doesn't require us to allocate blocks of memory and fill it with data. You may find that the buffer method provides slightly faster initial playback if you have preloaded the audio data, but on most recent devices the difference is negligible.

If you make a call to either of these functions while an audio track is currently playing, that track will be stopped and the new track will begin playing.

Pausing, resuming, and stopping playback

Once an audio track is playing, we can pause playback by calling the `s3eAudioPause` function. The audio can be started again from the point at which it was paused by calling `s3eAudioResume`. Finally, to stop playback completely just call `s3eAudioStop`.

All three of these functions take no parameters and will return `S3E_RESULT_SUCCESS` when no errors occur. An error is raised if any of these functions are called when it makes no sense to do so, for example calling `s3eAudioPause` when there is no audio playing.

Changing volume

Like most of the low level APIs in Marmalade, s3eAudio features a pair of functions called `s3eAudioGetInt` and `s3eAudioSetInt` that are used to change attributes related to that API. In s3eAudio, one of the things we use these functions for is to change the volume of audio playback.

To set the playback volume we can make the following call:

```
s3eAudioSetInt(S3E_AUDIO_VOLUME, S3E_AUDIO_MAX_VOLUME / 2);
```

In the aforementioned example we set the volume to half of `S3E_AUDIO_MAX_VOLUME`, which is the maximum allowed volume.

To determine the current volume we use this code:

```
int32 lVolume = s3eAudioGetInt(S3E_AUDIO_VOLUME);
```

We can also request the default volume for audio by passing in the value `S3E_AUDIO_VOLUME_DEFAULT`. This is the default volume level for playing audio and has been chosen by the Marmalade SDK so as to provide a fairly consistent volume level across all devices.

Other audio queries

The s3eAudioGetInt function allows us to make several other queries regarding audio playback. The following table shows which properties can be specified:

Property	Description
S3E_AUDIO_STATUS	Returns current audio status—one of S3E_AUDIO_STOPPED, S3E_AUDIO_PLAYING, S3E_AUDIO_PAUSED, or S3E_AUDIO_FAILED.
S3E_AUDIO_POSITION	Returns the current position in the audio track in milliseconds, or 0 if no track is playing. Note that not all platforms support this feature.
S3E_AUDIO_CHANNEL	Returns the currently selected audio channel. This property can also be used in s3eAudioSetInt to select which audio channel the future audio commands will be applied to. See the following property for more on audio channels.
S3E_AUDIO_NUM_CHANNELS	Returns the number of audio channels available. On most platforms this will return 1 since most devices only allow a single audio track to be played at any time. Some devices provide more than one channel, meaning more than one audio track can be played simultaneously.
S3E_AUDIO_MUTES_S3ESOUND	Returns 1 if the hardware is not capable of outputting sound through both s3eAudio and s3eSound at the same time. In this instance playing an audio track will cause s3eSound processing to continue, but without actually producing any output.
S3E_AUDIO_DURATION	Returns the length, in milliseconds, of the track currently playing.
S3E_AUDIO_PLAYBACK_FROM_HTTP_AVAILABLE	Returns 1 if the hardware is able to play an audio track by streaming from a URL.

End of track notification

There are two methods we can use to determine when an audio track has finished. One is to use a polled approach, the other is to make use of a callback.

To poll whether an audio track has completed or not, we can do the following:

```
if (s3eAudioIsPlaying() == S3E_FALSE)
{
  // Audio is not playing!
}
```

This function returns `S3E_TRUE` if the audio is currently playing, or `S3E_FALSE` if it is stopped or paused. This function is actually just a shortcut for calling `s3eAudioGetInt` with the property `S3E_AUDIO_STATUS`.

The callback approach is also very simple to use, as the following code snippet shows:

```
int32 AudioFinished(s3eAudioCallbackData* apAudioData,
void* apUserData)
{
  // apAudioData->m_ChannelID identifies the audio channel that
  // has completed.
  // s3eCallback functions must return a value, but in case of
  // audio callback the value returned does not matter.
  return 0;
}

// Use the following line to set up the audio callback
s3eAudioRegister(S3E_AUDIO_STOP, (s3eCallback) AudioFinished, NULL);

// And this line to remove the callback function
s3eAudioUnRegister(S3E_AUDIO_STOP, (s3eCallback) AudioFinished);
```

The callback function will be called whenever an audio track finishes and will pass the pointer to user data supplied as the last parameter in the `s3eAudioRegister` call by using the `apUserData` argument. It will not be called if we have asked the audio track to be looped unless it is the last repetition. The function will also be called if the audio is stopped due to an error, such as a corrupted track. We can determine whether completion was caused due to error by calling the `s3eAudioGetError` function, which returns an error code of the enumerated type `s3eAudioError`. A complete list of error codes can be found in `s3eAudio.h`.

The decision of whether to use the polling or callback-based approach depends on your application, and indeed quite often in games we don't even really care that much about when an audio track has finished as we often just want the same track to loop forever until a new piece of audio is required. If you are just waiting for a jingle to finish during a splash screen, the polled method is probably adequate, but if you want to join several tracks together one after the other, the callback approach would probably lead to a clean solution.

The s3eSound API

If you want to add spot sound effects to your game, such as laser bolts and explosions, the s3eSound API is what you need to use. This API allows multiple sound samples to be played simultaneously at different volumes and pitch by mixing them together into a single output.

To make use of the s3eSound API, simply include the file `s3eSound.h` in your source code.

The API expects all sound effects to be supplied as uncompressed 16-bit signed PCM. File formats such as WAV are not supported by the API, so you must write your own code to load and extract the sample data from such files.

As you read through this section you may start to think that there's an awful lot to do in order to play some sound effects. While this may appear to be the case, s3eSound is actually a very low-level API and provides enough flexibility to allow you to code your own complex sound routines.

Later in this chapter we will be covering the `SoundEngine` module, which comes with Marmalade to provide a wrapper for the s3eSound API. The `SoundEngine` module takes care of most of the hard work involved in using the s3eSound API for us and also includes the ability to load WAV files directly from a GROUP file.

Starting sound playback

In order to play a sound sample using s3eSound, the first thing we have to do is allocate a free sound channel. The s3eSound API provides a limited number of channels (we'll see later how to determine exactly how many are available) that allow us to specify a sound sample, volume, and playback rate. The sound data for all currently active channels is then mixed together in the inner workings of s3eSound into a single waveform and this is what is played through the device's sound hardware. To allocate a free channel, we make the following function call:

```
int32 lChannel = s3eSoundGetFreeChannel();
```

This will return the ID number of a free channel, or `-1` if no channel is available. Most of the time it is unlikely that a free channel will not be available, but if we are playing a lot of sound effects we might want to consider tagging each of our sound effects with a priority value and maintaining a list of currently active sounds. When we run out of channels, we can check the list of sounds and reclaim the channel being used by the lowest priority sound effect, assuming that it is at a lower priority than the sound we wish to start of course!

Assuming a channel is available we must set up the playback rate of our sample data, which is done like this:

```
s3eSoundChannelSetInt(lChannel, S3E_CHANNEL_RATE, lFrequency);
```

The first parameter is the sound channel ID we just allocated. The second parameter indicates that we want to set the playback rate for that channel, and the third parameter is the actual desired playback rate in Hertz (Hz). The maximum frequency that can be set is specified by the define `S3E_SOUND_MAX_FREQ`.

We should also set the volume that we want the sound to be played at, which is also done using the `s3eSoundChannelSetInt` function:

```
s3eSoundChannelSetInt(lChannel, S3E_CHANNEL_VOLUME, lVolume);
```

The valid values for the `lVolume` parameter are from `0` to the define `S3E_SOUND_MAX_VOLUME`.

It is possible to change the volume and playback rate at any time once the sound has started playing. This makes it possible to implement effects such as volume fades or pitch shifts.

Now we can start playing our sound sample. We do this with the following call:

```
s3eSoundChannelPlay(lChannel, lSampleData, lNumSamples, lRepeatCount,
lLoopIndex);
```

Unsurprisingly, we first pass in the channel ID we are using, followed by the address in memory where the 16-bit PCM sample data can be found in the `lSampleData` parameter. The `lNumSamples` parameter is the number of actual sound samples in our waveform (not the number of bytes), and `lRepeatCount` indicates how often we want the sound to repeat. A value of `0` will play the sound forever. Finally the `lLoopIndex` parameter allows us to specify which sample to start at if the sound repeats. This makes it possible to use sounds that only need to repeat a portion of the sample data.

Pausing, resuming, and stopping playback

Once a sound channel has started playing a sound sample, we might want to temporarily suspend its playback or stop it entirely. To pause a sound channel we use the function `s3eSoundChannelPause`, and we can start playing it again from the paused position using `s3eSoundChannelResume`. To stop a sound channel entirely we call `s3eSoundChannelStop`. Each of these functions takes a single parameter, which is the channel ID we want to affect.

To determine the current playback status of a particular sound channel we can use the `s3eSoundChannelGetInt` function as follows:

```
if (s3eSoundChannelGetInt(lChannel, S3E_CHANNEL_STATUS) == 1)
{
  // Sound channel is currently playing
}

if (s3eSoundChannelGetInt(lChannel, S3E_CHANNEL_PAUSED) == 1)
{
  // Sound channel is currently active, but paused
}
```

Note that this function can also be used with the `S3E_CHANNEL_RATE` and `S3E_CHANNEL_VOLUME` properties to discover the current sample rate and volume for a particular channel.

Finally, it is also possible to affect all currently active sound channels at once using the functions `s3eSoundPauseAllChannels`, `s3eSoundResumeAllChannels`, and `s3eSoundStopAllChannels`. These functions take no inputs and are extremely useful for handling situations like going in and out of pause mode, or when switching from one part of the game to another (for example, when exiting the title screen and entering the main game).

Global sound settings

As well as being able to read and write settings on a per channel basis, we can also make settings that affect sound support globally. To do this we use the `s3eSoundSetInt` and `s3eSoundGetInt` functions as follows:

```
// To read a global sound setting
int32 lValue = s3eSoundGetInt(lProperty);

// To change a global sound setting
s3eSoundSetInt(lProperty, lValue);
```

Here are some of the more useful values for the `lProperty` parameter:

Property	Description
`S3E_SOUND_VOLUME`	Can be used to read or write the current master sound volume. This will scale the volumes of each individual channel appropriately. The maximum value is determined by the define `S3E_SOUND_MAX_VOLUME`.

Property	Description
S3E_SOUND_DEFAULT_FREQ	This is the default frequency that will be used when starting playback on a sound channel. If all our sound waveforms have the same sample rate, it is possible to write to this property once and not have to set the sample rate explicitly when playing each individual sound.
S3E_SOUND_NUM_CHANNELS	A read-only value indicating the maximum number of simultaneous sounds that can be played.
S3E_SOUND_USED_CHANNELS	A read-only value that shows which sound channels are currently in use. This is returned as a bit mask with the least significant bit relating to sound channel 0. This value could be used to determine an available sound channel, but for future compatibility using `s3eSoundGetFreeChannel` to do this is recommended.
S3E_SOUND_AVAILABLE	A read-only value that returns `1` if s3eSound is available on the device.
S3E_SOUND_VOLUME_DEFAULT	A read-only value that is used as the default value for the global sound volume. It can vary from device to device and is intended to allow sound output to be at a similar volume across all devices.

There are other values described in the Marmalade documentation, but we won't cover them here as they are used for purposes such as custom sound stream generation, which are beyond the scope of this book.

Sound notifications

We have already seen how to use a polled method of detecting whether or not a sound channel is currently playing, but sometimes it is useful to know exactly when a sound sample has finished playing, for example, so we can immediately start playing back a new sound effect.

The s3eSound API allows us to set several different callback functions on a per channel basis and we use the functions `s3eSoundChannelRegister` and `s3eSoundChannelUnRegister` to enable and disable them as follows:

```
// To set up a sound channel callback
s3eSoundChannelRegister(lChannel, lCallbackType, (s3eCallback)
              CallbackFunction, lpUserData);

// To disable a sound channel callback
s3eSoundChannelUnRegister(lChannel, lCallbackType);
```

As with all other Marmalade callbacks, we specify the code for the callback function by passing in a pointer to the function itself, and we can also register a block of user data that will be passed into this function when it is triggered. There are four different callback types called `S3E_CHANNEL_END_SAMPLE`, `S3E_CHANNEL_STOP_AUDIO`, `S3E_CHANNEL_GEN_AUDIO`, and `S3E_CHANNEL_GEN_AUDIO_STEREO`. We will only take a look at the first two of them here, as the latter two are concerned with generating custom audio streams and are beyond the scope of this book. For an example of how to use these callback types, take a look at the source code for the `SoundEngine` module, which we'll be covering in the next section.

First let's look at the `S3E_CHANNEL_END_SAMPLE` callback, which allows us to loop sounds and join different sounds together as a sequence. The registered callback function is passed a pointer to an `s3eSoundEndSampleInfo` structure as its first parameter. The structure indicates which sound channel has ended by using its `m_Channel` member.

If we want to start a completely new sound playing on this channel, we can set the `m_NewData` member of the `s3eSoundEndSampleInfo` structure to the start address of the new sample data, and the `m_NumSamples` member to the number of samples in the new waveform.

The structure also contains a member called `m_RepsRemaining`, which allows us to change the number of repetitions of the sample data we want on this sound channel. Note, though, that this callback will still be triggered every time the end of the sample data has been reached.

If we wish the channel to continue playing sample data, be it the original data or a new sample specified using the `m_NewData` and `m_NumSamples` members of the `s3eSoundEndSampleInfo` structure, we must return a non-zero value from the callback function. If zero is returned, the sound channel will stop playing.

The following code example puts the functionality described previosuly into practice:

```
// Simple structure used to indicate the next sound sample to play
typedef struct
{
  void* mSampleData;
  uint32 mSampleCount;
} NewSoundData;

// Sample callback function that will start a new sound effect
// playing if one has been specified when registering the
// callback function
int32 SoundEndCallback(s3eSoundEndSampleInfo* apInfo,
   NewSoundData* apSound)
{
  if (apSound)
  {
     apInfo->m_NewData = apSound->mSampleData;
     apInfo->m_NumSamples = apSound->mSampleCount;
     apInfo->m_RepsRemaining = 1;
  }
  return apInfo->m_RepsRemaining;
}

// Register the callback function to play a new sound when
// current sound completes
s3eSoundChannelRegister(lChannel, S3E_CHANNEL_END_SAMPLE,
   (s3eCallback) SoundEndCallback,
   &lNewSoundDataInstance);
```

The second callback type we'll consider is `S3E_CHANNEL_STOP_AUDIO`. This callback will occur whenever a sound channel finishes playing a sound completely (for example, if we have an `S3E_CHANNEL_END_SAMPLE` callback set and we return zero from it to end all playback). It is passed a pointer to an `s3eSoundEndSampleInfo` structure, but the only valid field is the `m_Channel` member.

The SoundEngine module

As the previous section of this chapter shows, the basics of using s3eSound are actually fairly straightforward. The main issue that we have to deal with as developers is the fact that s3eSound can only support raw uncompressed 16-bit PCM samples, which means it is our responsibility to get the sound data into memory so it can be played.

One of the most common file formats for storing sound samples is the WAV file, so wouldn't it be great if we could use this format to store our sound effects? Wouldn't it also be great if we could load these files into memory using the same resource manager code that we've used for textures and 3D models?

The answer to our prayers is the `SoundEngine` module, which is a layer that sits on top of s3eSound and allows us to easily load and access sound effects using the resource manager.

The `SoundEngine` module doesn't just stop there though. It also wraps up the s3eSound calls we've learnt about in this chapter and it allows us to support a further sound format that can be stored in WAV files—namely the compressed IMA ADPCM type. This is particularly useful given that sound sample data can be quite large in size; so this format helps us claw back some memory space at the expense of a slight drop in sound quality.

The following sections give a brief introduction to using this module, but for full details you should refer to the source and header files to see all the functionality `SoundEngine` has to offer. The sound example project accompanying this chapter also makes use of this module, so take a look at that to learn more.

Adding the SoundEngine module to a project

The `SoundEngine` module actually ships with the Marmalade SDK, but it lives, awkwardly, in the `examples` directory. The easiest way to solve this is to just copy the entire `SoundEngine` directory to the directory where your project resides and then reference it by adding `SoundEngine` to your MKB files subprojects. This is the same approach we used with the GUI and `Localise` modules that were introduced in the sample code for the previous chapter.

> The location of the `SoundEngine` module in the `examples` folder means it isn't really considered part of the main Marmalade SDK. In practice it is highly unlikely that the `SoundEngine` code will suddenly disappear from the SDK, since the s3eSound API is unlikely to change drastically from what it is now; so you shouldn't have any concerns about using it directly in your own projects. If you prefer to write your own code, `SoundEngine` does at least serve the purpose of being a very good example of how to use the s3eSound API.

With the module added to our project, we can include the file `IwSound.h` in our code to make use of it. A call to `IwSoundInit` is needed to set everything up and a call to `IwSoundTerminate` cleans up at the end of our program.

We must also add a custom resource handler to allow WAV files to be loaded by the resource manager. The following code snippet will do the trick:

```
IwGetResManager()->AddHandler(new CIwResHandlerWAV);
```

Finally, there is a manager class that takes care of all sound-related events and we must ensure that we call the `Update` method of this class somewhere within the main game loop. We do this with the following line of code:

```
IwGetSoundManager()->Update();
```

Loading and accessing sound resources

To load a WAV file all we have to do is add a reference to its filename into a GROUP file, though we still need to do a little more in order to be able to play the sound back. What we need to do is declare an instance of the class `CIwSoundSpec`.

This class allows us to reference a particular sound sample by name and lets us set a volume and pitch to play the sound at. We can also specify whether or not we want the sound to loop (note that `SoundEngine` currently provides no way of specifying the number of times to loop the sound; we can only indicate continuous looping). Here's an example definition:

```
CIwSoundSpec
{
  name gun1
  data gun_shot1

  // Play at the default pitch for the sample
  pitch 1.0

  // Play at half volume
  vol 0.5

  // Do we want this sound to loop?
  looping false
}
```

The `pitch` and `vol` (volume) parameters are specified as fractional scales, where `1.0` indicates the default pitch or volume level of a sound. We can also specify a range for both these parameters that allows a random value to be chosen when starting the sound. Specifying a range for the pitch can be quite useful to add a bit of variety to the sound effects in your game without having to add lots of slightly different sound samples.

The example below shows how to specify ranges for the volume and pitch:

```
CIwSoundSpec
{
  name gun2
  data gun_shot2

  // Choose a random pitch when playing this sound
  pitchMin 0.9
  pitchMax 1.1

  // Choose a random volume when playing this sound
  volMin 0.9
  volMax 1.1

  // Do we want this sound to loop?
  looping false
}
```

Another useful class that we have access to is `CIwSoundGroup`. This allows us to collect a number of different sound effects together and pause, resume, stop, or alter the volume or pitch of any that are currently being played all at the same time. Note that a sound group only allows a single volume or pitch value to be specified, not a random range:

```
CIwSoundGroup
{
   name guns

   // Reduce volume of all gun sounds by a half
   vol 0.5

   // Include the gun1 sound in this group
   addSpec gun1
}
```

Sounds can be added to groups using the `addSpec` keyword, or alternatively you can add `CIwSoundSpec` to a group when it is defined by using the `group` keyword followed by the group name, in its definition. We can use either method, but the group or sound must have been declared before we make reference to it.

To access a sound specification or group, we just load the GROUP file and retrieve them using the resource manager in the normal way. Here's an example:

```
IwGetResManager()->LoadGroup("sounds.group");
CIwSoundSpec* lpGunSpec = static_cast<CIwSoundSpec*>(
  IwGetResManager()->GetResNamed("gun1", "CIwSoundSpec"));
CIwSoundGroup* lpGunsGroup = static_cast<CIwSoundGroup*>(
  IwGetResManager()->GetResNamed("guns", "CIwSoundGroup"));
```

Playing, stopping, and altering sound parameters

Once we have hold of a pointer to `CIwSoundSpec` we can start playing it by calling the `Play` method, which will do all the behind-the-scenes stuff of allocating a free channel and setting volume and playback speed. The `Play` method can be passed an optional parameter, which is an instance of the class `CIwSoundParams`, that allows the volume and pitch to be modified when starting the sound.

The `Play` method returns a pointer to a `CIwSoundInst` class, which has methods to allow that single instance of the sound to have its volume or pitch modified, and also provides methods called `Pause`, `Resume`, and `Stop`, which should be self explanatory! If no free sound channel is available, the `Play` method will return `NULL`.

If we have a pointer to `CIwSoundGroup` we can affect all currently playing instances of sounds contained within it. Again there are `Pause`, `Resume`, and `Stop` methods that do what you would expect, plus there are the methods `SetVol` and `SetPitch` that will scale the current volume and pitch of the sounds. These methods use the value `IW_GEOM_ONE` (4096) to indicate a scale of one.

The s3eVideo API

We'll finish our look at Marmalade's multimedia support by having a whirlwind look at support for playing video clips using the s3eVideo API. To make use of the functions it provides, we just need to include the `s3eVideo.h` file into our source code.

Before we begin, there are two things to consider when using video clips in our games. The first is that while it is possible to specify where on the screen the video clip will appear, it will always be drawn on top of all other graphics. The second issue is that due to hardware limitations in many mobile devices, the s3eVideo API cannot be used at the same time as the s3eAudio and s3eSound APIs. In the case of s3eAudio, any currently playing track will be stopped (this also applies the other way around—starting an audio track will stop a currently playing video clip). The s3eSound API will continue processing its events while a video clip is playing, but its sound output will be silenced until the video clip is finished. For most games we would probably decide it is best to explicitly stop all s3eSound playback before starting a video clip, particularly if we are doing anything advanced like joining sound samples together using the callback system.

Starting video playback

The s3eVideo API works in a similar manner to the s3eAudio API. To start playing a video clip we use the `s3eVideoPlay` function, specifying the filename of the video clip, the number of times we want it to loop, a screen position, and the size that we want to display it at, as follows:

```
s3eVideoPlay(lFileName, lRepeatCount, lX, lY, lWidth, lHeight);
```

The video clip will automatically resize to fit the rectangle, but no attempt is made to keep the correct aspect ratio.

Where possible it is usually best to try to make your video clips the same resolution as the rectangular area you want to display them in. This will avoid any unnecessary stretching of the image (which can look quite ugly!) and may lead to slightly better performance, though on most modern devices the resize will be happening in hardware and there will be no appreciable difference.

The actual size of the video file itself is also worth bearing in mind, since we often want to minimize the size of the final install package. Ultimately, we need to use a bit of trial and error until we get a result that ticks all the boxes for acceptable quality, performance, and file size.

Determining video codec support

The s3eVideo API makes use of the device's built-in video decoding, so not all video formats will be playable on all devices. To determine whether support for a particular codec is available, there is a function called `s3eVideoIsCodecSupported` that takes a value from the `s3eVideoCodec` enum. Take a look at the `s3eVideo.h` file or the Marmalade documentation for a complete list of possible values.

Pausing, resuming, and stopping video playback

Again the parallels with the s3eAudio API are apparent when it comes to controlling video playback. The functions `s3eVideoPause`, `s3eVideoResume`, and `s3eVideoStop` all take no parameters and are used to pause, resume, and finish video clip playback respectively.

End of video notification

We have the choice of polling or callbacks once more for detecting the end of video playback. Let's start with the polled method that involves a call to the function `s3eVideoIsPlaying`, which will return `S3E_TRUE` if a video is playing or `S3E_FALSE` if a video is paused or stopped. Quite simple really!

If we want to use the callback approach, the following code snippet illustrates what to do:

```
int32 VideoFinished(void* apSystemData, void* apUserData)
{
  // apSystemData will always be NULL as there is no data associated
  // with this callback.
  // Return value is unimportant.
  return 0;
}

// To set up the callback function
s3eVideoRegister(S3E_VIDEO_STOP, (s3eCallback) VideoFinished, NULL);

// And to cancel it again...
s3eVideoUnRegister(S3E_VIDEO_STOP, (s3eCallback) VideoFinished);
```

The callback will be triggered whenever video playback stops, either because we explicitly call `s3eVideoStop`, an error in playback such as a corrupted video file occurs, or if an audio track is started using `s3eAudioPlay`. Note that the callback is not triggered between repetitions of the video clip if we are looping it.

For most games, video clips will probably only be used during introductory sequences or tutorials, since using video in the game itself is probably not practical. With this in mind, a polled approach for detecting when a video clip is finished is normally sufficient.

Other video queries

The s3eVideo API, like the s3eSound and s3eAudio APIs, also has a pair of functions for reading and writing global video parameters. They are called `s3eVideoGetInt` and `s3eVideoSetInt`. They are called as follows:

```
int32 lValue = s3eVideoGetInt(lProperty);
s3eVideoSetInt(lProperty, lValue);
```

The following table shows the values that can be used for the `lProperty` parameter:

Property	Description
`S3E_VIDEO_VOLUME`	This property is used to find the current volume level for the sound associated with the video clip and also to set a new volume. The maximum volume level is defined by the value `S3E_VIDEO_MAX_VOLUME`.
`S3E_VIDEO_DEFAULT_VOLUME`	This is a read-only property that shows the default volume that will be used for playing back the sound in a video clip. Its value is intended to provide a similar level of volume across all device types.
`S3E_VIDEO_STATUS`	This is a read-only parameter showing the current status of the video playback. It will return one of the following values: `S3E_VIDEO_STOPPED`, `S3E_VIDEO_PLAYING`, `S3E_VIDEO_PAUSED`, or `S3E_VIDEO_FAILED`.
`S3E_VIDEO_POSITION`	This property returns the current playback position of the video in milliseconds, or `0` if no video is playing. This parameter cannot be written to, so it is not possible to jump to a particular point in a video clip.

Example code

This chapter has three example projects associated with it and they are described in the following sections. The sound, audio, and video clips used in these projects were sourced from a couple of great websites that offer a vast variety of stock media for free! Links to these websites are provided here:

`http://www.royalty-free-music-room.com`

`http://www.partnersinrhyme.com`

The Sound project

This project demonstrates use of the s3eAudio API and the `SoundEngine` module (which in turn makes use of s3eSound).

On running the example you'll be presented with three clickable buttons that have been implemented using the GUI module introduced in the last chapter. The first button toggles an MP3 track on and off using s3eAudio, while the other two start some sound effects using `SoundEngine`.

The Video project

This is another simple example showing how to use the s3eVideo API to start and stop a video clip. A button at the bottom of the screen will start and stop a video clip, which is played in a continuous loop.

The Skiing project

Finally we come to the Skiing project once again and it will come as no surprise that it has been enhanced by the addition of some music and sound effects.

The main menu now plays an MP3 audio track while waiting for the player to press a button. On pressing a button, a confirmation sound effect is played.

In the game itself, several sounds have been added. A swooshing sound is produced, by using a looping sample, whenever the skier moves and the pitch of this sample is decreased as the player turns, to make things sound a little more dynamic.

Other sounds that have been added include a selection of celebratory sounds for when the player passes through a gate, a painful-sounding yell for when the player collides with an obstacle, and a springy sound that gets played when the player collides with a flag pole and causes it to wobble.

Summary

As this chapter draws to a close, our look at Marmalade's multimedia support has now given us the ability to play sound effects, music tracks, and also play back video clips.

There are very few games that don't feature sound or music of some sort, and adding a few sound effects can make a world of difference to your game. While not all games need to make use of video, it is nice to know we have it at our disposal should we ever need to use it.

In the next chapter we'll be looking at how Marmalade can make it easier for us to target as wide a range of devices as possible, from entry-level handsets to top-of-the-range ones.

8
Supporting a Wide Range of Devices

It's really great that the Marmalade SDK allows us to target so many different devices and platforms. However, a certain degree of care and awareness is required in order to optimize your application fully for all of these varying device types.

In this chapter we'll be covering the following subjects:

- A general overview of the kinds of things to be wary of when trying to support a wide range of different devices
- A more advanced look at the ICF filesystem we encountered back in the first chapter of this book
- Using Marmalade's built-in systems to allow multiple different data sets to be used and to process those data sets in different ways (for example, allowing the final texture format used on the device to be specified)
- Configuring the deployment system to make different types of builds
- Using the Derbh archiver to reduce the size of our assets in the install package

Accommodating a wide range of device types

Mobile operating systems such as iOS or Android are capable of running on a widely varying range of devices. Before we get on to discussing the ways in which Marmalade makes it easy for us to target multiple device types, we'll first highlight some of the things to keep in mind when developing a game so that it will look and run its best on as many different devices as possible.

Marmalade also ships with a whitepaper that covers some of the things to be careful about when developing a game destined to run on more than one device specification. You can find it in the Marmalade documentation at **Whitepapers | Device Independent Code**.

Dealing with different screen resolutions

Probably the most immediately notable difference between different devices will be the screen resolution. Taking iOS as an example, you may find yourself having to support screen resolutions ranging from 320 x 480 at the low end through the two different iPhone Retina screen resolutions (640 x 960 and 640 x 1136) and iPad at 1024 x 768, right up to the frankly crazy resolution of 2048 x 1536 of the most recent iPad (you'll be hard pressed to find a PC monitor capable of displaying that resolution!).

We've already touched on this subject in *Chapter 6, Implementing Fonts, User Interfaces, and Localization*, when we discussed the best way of implementing a user interface. We should never hardcode our game to work at a fixed screen resolution as it will be much harder to port it across to other screen resolutions later.

Instead, we should query Marmalade for the screen dimensions and then use these values to position and size everything we want to draw, whether that be through using percentages of the screen size, by clamping objects to the edges of the screen, or indeed some other method of your own choosing. We can find the screen width and height as follows:

```
uint32 lScreenWidth = IwGxGetScreenWidth();
uint32 lScreenHeight = IwGxGetScreenHeight();
```

These functions will also automatically take care of device orientation. The returned values will change when the player rotates the device, unless we have disabled this functionality using the `DispFixRot` ICF file setting (more on this setting shortly).

Using different resources for different screen resolutions

Using the screen dimensions to position and size the elements we wish to draw works well, but it does lead to a further problem. We may find that any images used to render items on screen start to look blurry or blocky if they have to be scaled up in size too much.

Similarly, fonts that work well at a low resolution may become impossible to read because they are too small when used on a higher-resolution device. While we could just apply a scale to the font when rendering, a more aesthetically pleasing solution is to use a different version of the font created at a bigger point size.

Luckily, as we'll see later in this chapter, Marmalade has a very easy-to-use solution for this problem that allows us to provide alternate sets of resources that can be used when targeting different sets of screen resolutions.

Checking device capabilities

Another thing to be vigilant of when targeting a large number of different devices is that some devices may not include support for certain Marmalade SDK features.

Some devices may feature a multi-touch display while others only have single touch or indeed no touch screen at all. Some may not feature accelerometer inputs or keypads. It is therefore a good idea to ensure that we call the various Marmalade functions that enquire whether these and other features are available for use and what capabilities are provided, so that we can then provide the user with options tailored to their device.

Configuring your game using ICF file settings

If you cast your mind back to the "Hello World" project in the very first chapter of this book, you will recall that we used the ICF file to display a different welcome message depending on which platform the code was being executed on. Don't worry if you've forgotten how all this works, as we'll be covering it again shortly.

This functionality proves extremely useful when we are trying to target as many different devices as possible, as there are built-in parameters that allow us to apply different settings for a range of things including memory usage, OpenGL ES graphics performance, splash screens, and much more.

Built-in ICF settings

ICF file settings are assigned to a section identifier which is defined by placing the name of the section in square brackets. When specifying a value for an ICF setting you must ensure that it appears after the correct section identifier, otherwise it will not be found at runtime and an assert will be raised. Here's an example:

```
[S3E]
MemSize=10000000
SysAppVersion="1.0.0"
```

There are far too many ICF settings to be able to cover all of them in this book, so instead we'll be taking a look at some of the more immediately useful ones. If you want to see a complete list, take a look in the Marmalade documentation, by going to **Marmalade | Marmalade Development Tools Reference | ICF File Settings**.

The following table shows a few of the settings that control Marmalade at its lowest level. The section identifier for these settings is `[S3E]`:

Setting	Value type	Description
`MemSize`	Integer	The size, in bytes, of the main memory heap available to an application. A Marmalade application can actually have up to ten memory heaps available, so there are also settings called `MemSize0` through `MemSize9`, which allow the sizes of these heaps to be declared. `MemSize0` is actually equivalent to using `MemSize`. For more information on memory heaps take a look at the s3eMemory API in the Marmalade documentation.
`MemSizeDebug`	Integer	The size, in bytes, of the debug memory heap when a Windows debug build is executed. This is a special block of memory that is used for tasks such as processing 3D models and converting textures to different formats during the resource building process.
`SysAppVersion`	String	Allows an application to access its version number. While this value can be set in the ICF file, it can also be set using the MKB deployment's `version` setting.
`SysGlesVersion`	Integer	Identifies whether the application should attempt to initialize an OpenGL ES 1.x or 2.x interface. Only the major version number (that is, 1 or 2) can be specified.
`SysStackSize`	Integer	The size of the stack available to the program, in bytes. It is useful, for example, when an application requires extra stack space (due to heavily recursive algorithms).

Setting	Value type	Description
`SplashScreenFile`	String	The name of an image file that will be displayed while an application is loading. The filename is relative to the `data` directory.
`SplashScreenBkR`, `SplashScreenBkG`, and `SplashScreenBkB`	Byte	A value from `0` through `255` to specify the red, green, and blue component values of the splash screen background color. This is the color that will be used to clear the screen before displaying the specified splash screen image, assuming the image is smaller than the screen size.
`SplashScreenWidth` and `SplashScreenHeight`	Integer	The width and height that the splash screen image should be drawn at. If smaller than the screen size, the image will be centered.
`AudioAllowBackground`	`0` or `1`	When set to `1` this allows any audio track a user may have started (for example, through the iPod application on an iOS device) to continue playing when our application starts.
`DispFixRot`	String	Allows the screen to be locked to a particular orientation, rather than rotating when the user rotates the device. Can be set to one of the following values: `Free`, `Portrait`, `Landscape`, `FixedPortrait`, or `FixedLandscape`. The `Free` setting allows any device orientation, while `FixedPortrait` and `FixedLandscape` keep the screen orientation locked to a default portrait or landscape aspect, which can be very important to prevent unwanted screen rotations when using the accelerometer to control a game!

The following table lists some useful parameters for altering the initialization of OpenGL ES. These settings must occur after the section identifier `[GL]`:

Setting	Value type	Description
`AlphaInFrameBuffer`	`0` or `1`	When set to `1`, this setting indicates that the frame buffer also includes the destination alpha channel.
`EGL_RED_SIZE`, `EGL_GREEN_SIZE`, `EGL_BLUE_SIZE`, `EGL_ALPHA_SIZE`	Integer	Indicates the number of bits to be used to store each of the red, green, blue, and alpha channels in the frame buffer. For best render quality, all of these settings would normally be given the value `8`, yielding an RGBA8888 display. Most hardware can also support formats such as RGBA5551 and RGB565, which will use less video memory and may render faster at the expense of a drop in visual quality.
`EGL_DEPTH_SIZE`	Integer	The number of bits to use for the depth buffer. Valid values are `16`, `24`, and `32`, with the latter giving the most precision and therefore least chance of Z-buffer clashes when rendering, at the expense of slower rendering and more memory usage.

We'll finish off with some settings related to resource management that we'll be looking at in more depth later in this chapter. They have been included here for easy reference. The settings reside in the ICF section `[RESMANAGER]`:

Setting	Value type	Description
`ResBuild`	`0` or `1`	When set to `1`, the Windows debug build will load resources by parsing the original GROUP files and loading the source models, textures, and other resources. Once the data has been processed, it is saved to the `data-ram` directory in a binary format. If this setting is set to `0`, the source assets will not be loaded and any existing binary-formatted data will be loaded directly. This can speed up testing when there have been no changes made to game data.
`ResBuildStyle`	String	Specifies the resource building style to use when the Windows debug build is processing the original source assets. As we will learn later in this chapter, this parameter allows us to provide different sets of resources to cater for devices of varying abilities.

Defining new ICF settings

One of the best things about ICF files is that we are able to make use of them ourselves by creating our own custom settings. To define new settings we just need to add them to the file `app.config.txt`, which is automatically generated for us when creating a new project using an MKB file.

When defining new settings, we can also provide a string of text that explains what this setting is for. While this description isn't actually used or needed by the Marmalade SDK, it's a good way of documenting what a setting is supposed to do!

It is, however, important to add definitions for all our settings to the `app.config.txt` file because it will prevent the application generating lots of asserts when it is executed. In a Windows Debug build, Marmalade checks to see if an ICF setting has been declared both when loading the ICF file at the start of execution and also whenever we try to access a setting from within our own code.

We can also define our own section identifiers in the `app.config.txt` file simply by listing the name of the section in square brackets and following it with the new setting definitions. Here's an example illustrating how to create new section identifiers and settings:

```
[GAME_DEBUG]
SkipToLevel       Skip to a level at game start

[GAME]
FrameRate         The frame rate we want the game to run at
MaximumHealth       Amount of energy the player has at game start
```

Defining our own section identifiers can be extremely useful when creating library modules, such as the GUI and `Localise` modules created in *Chapter 6, Implementing Fonts, User Interfaces, and Localization*. The only difference when creating a module is that the `app.config.txt` file changes to `modulename.config.txt` and it should reside in a subdirectory called `docs` in the module's main directory. As an example, if we were to add our own settings to the GUI module we would create a directory called `GUI\docs`, and the file that lists the settings would be called `GUI.config.txt`.

Accessing ICF settings in code

It's very little use to be able to provide settings in the ICF files without some way of accessing them. This is where the s3eConfig API comes into play and we can use it by just including the `s3eConfig.h` header file.

The first function we will look at is `s3eConfigGetString`, which takes the section identifier and setting name we want to access and also a pointer to an array of `char` that will be used to return the value of the setting when the function completes. Since the `app.icf` file is really little more than an ASCII text file, all this function does is return the string of text following the equals sign for the specified ICF setting.

The `char` array supplied to `s3eConfigGetString` should be at least of length `S3E_CONFIG_STRING_MAX`, as this is the largest string size the function can return. If the requested setting can't be found in the ICF file this buffer will not be changed, which is very useful as it allows us to set up a default value for the parameter in our code.

```
// Set default first level
char lLevelName[S3E_CONFIG_STRING_MAX];
strcpy(lLevelName, "level1");

s3eConfigGetString("GAME_DEBUG", "SkipToLevel", &lLevelName);
// lLevelName will still contain "level1" if the SkipToLevel setting
// could not be found in the ICF file
```

Quite often we will want to specify ICF settings, which just need a numeric value. To make this easier for us, Marmalade provides another function called `s3eConfigGetInt`, which, instead of a pointer to a `char` array, takes a pointer to an `int` variable.

This function will read the setting string from the ICF file and then attempt to convert it into an integer value. If this fails (for example, the string contains non-numeric characters or is out of the range of an `int`) or the setting does not exist in the ICF file, the variable's current value will not be changed, thus allowing default values to be specified in code.

Both functions will return `S3E_RESULT_SUCCESS` if the setting value could be retrieved, or `S3E_RESULT_ERROR` if there was a problem. The function `s3eConfigGetError` will let us discover what the problem was by returning one of the following values:

Value	Description
`S3E_CONFIG_ERR_NONE`	No error occurred.
`S3E_CONFIG_ERR_PARAM`	One of the parameters to `s3eConfigGetInt` or `s3eConfigGetString` was not valid. For example, a `NULL` value passed in.
`S3E_CONFIG_ERR_NOT_FOUND`	The requested ICF setting could not be found.
`S3E_CONFIG_ERR_PARSE`	There was a problem converting the ICF setting value to an integer when using `s3eConfigGetInt`.

Limiting ICF settings by platform and device

When targeting a large number of different devices, it is not uncommon to have a situation where we want to be able to do different things depending on the device the application is running on.

The ICF filesystem makes handling this incredibly easy by allowing us to provide different values for parameters based on both the operating system of the device and even by individual device type.

To begin with, we can provide different settings on a platform-wide basis. The "Hello World" project from *Chapter 1, Getting Started with Marmalade,* has already demonstrated this, but to recap, we limit the settings to a particular operating system using the `OS` conditional. This is best illustrated by an example:

```
[GAME]
FrameRate=20

{OS=BADA}
FrameRate=15

{OS=IPHONE}
FrameRate=30
{}
```

This example sets a default value for the `FrameRate` setting of `20`. It then overrides this value for Bada devices with a value of `15` and for iOS devices with a value of `30`. Note that for legacy reasons the value `IPHONE` refers to all iOS devices (all versions of iPad and iPod touch as well as all iPhones).

The earlier example ends with open and close braces. This returns all settings made after this point to being global settings that apply to all devices and platforms.

It is also possible to make settings that will only apply to a particular subset of devices on a particular platform. This is done using the `ID` conditional that first specifies the platform type and then has a comma-separated list of device identifiers that the setting should apply to. Here's another example:

```
[GAME]
FrameRate=30

{ID=ANDROID "HTC Hero", "T-Mobile G1"}
FrameRate=20
{}
```

Here we set a default value for the `FrameRate` setting of `30`, then limit the value to just `20` if the game is running on either of the listed Android devices. Quote marks are only required on device names that contain spaces.

Wondering how to discover the device name? Often it is the name of the device, but this is not always the case. The easiest way to discover the device name for a particular device is to create a short test program that makes a call to `s3eDeviceGetString`, as follows:

```
const char* lpDeviceID = s3eDeviceGetString(S3E_DEVICE_ID);
```

The `s3eDeviceGetString` function and its sibling `s3eDeviceGetInt` allow us to determine an awful lot of information about the device we're running on, including the operating system, processor type, phone number, current language settings, and much more. Take a look at the `s3eDevice.h` header file or the Marmalade documentation for more details.

Creating multiple resource sets

Since Marmalade allows us to target so many different devices, it seems a shame to limit ourselves to a subset of them just because our graphics are too low or too high resolution for certain devices, or some devices have less memory and therefore can't handle lots of high resolution textures.

Another issue we might face is that different devices support different file formats for audio or video clips. To improve render speed and memory usage we might also consider using hardware texture compression, which of course varies depending on the type of graphics processor a particular device has.

Marmalade provides a couple of solutions to these problems. The first, more global approach is to make use of **build styles**, which allow us to both load different sets of resource files when loading a GROUP file and specify the type of hardware texture compression to apply.

Build styles are then enhanced by the concept of **resource templates**, which allow us to more finely control the configuration of resources. Resource templates can be used to affect the final format of a texture or to modify the way a 3D model is converted for use in the game, among other things.

Using build styles

Marmalade comes with a number of built-in build styles that allow us to build resources for all the common GPU formats used across mobile devices. The build styles available are shown in the following table:

Build style	Description
`sw`	Build resources optimized for use with Marmalade's legacy software renderer. Resources built in this way cannot be rendered using hardware acceleration. This format is now only of use if we are using the `IW_USE_LEGACY_MODULES` define in our MKB file in order to make the software renderer available for use.
`gles1`	Builds resources without any form of texture compression. This is the default if no build style is specified.
`gles1-pvrtc`	Same as `gles1`, but uses the PVRTC format for texture compression on images where this type of compression works well. Typically this just means images with no alpha channel, as PVRTC tends to perform badly on such textures.
`gles-atitc`	Same as `gles1`, but uses the ATITC texture compression format where possible.
`gles1-dxt`	Same as `gles1`, but uses the DXT format for texture compression.
`gles2-etc`	Intended for use on devices that make use of OpenGL ES 2.x and support the ETC texture compression format.

We can also define our own custom build styles should the default ones not suffice. To do this we create a file in the `data` directory called `resbuildstyles.itx`. This file is automatically loaded by the resource manager when it is initialized in the call to `IwResManagerInit` and it contains one or more instances of the `CIwResBuildStyle` class.

To declare a build style instance we must give it a name so that it can be selected for use, an optional list of directories in which resource files can reside, and an indication of the platform this build style is targeting. Note that in the case of build styles, the platform does not refer to any particular operating system; instead it refers to the type of GPU the style targets, which for the most part means the type of hardware texture compression to be used.

Here's an example of a `resbuildstyles.itx` file that will be used for discussion in the following sections:

```
CIwResBuildStyle
{
  name              "default"
  platform          "GLES1"
}
CIwResBuildStyle
{
  name              "pvrtc"
  addReadPrefix     "data-pvrtc"
  platform          "IMG_MBX"
}
CIwResBuildStyle
{
  name              "atitc"
  addReadPrefix     "data-atitc"
  platform          "ATI_IMAGEON"
}
```

Adding extra resource directories

The `addReadPrefix` parameter allows us to add a new search path that will be checked whenever we attempt to load a file of any kind. A directory name is specified; this must be a subdirectory within the project's `data` directory. If you want to add more than one extra search directory, just include further `addReadPrefix` entries.

Whenever we try to open a file, Marmalade will first look in the list of extra directories specified by the build style in the order they were specified. If the requested file is found in one of these directories, it will be loaded from there; otherwise the resource manager will revert to looking in the `data` directory.

Supported build style platforms

The `platform` field of a `CIwResBuildStyle` instance can take one of the following values:

Platform value	Description
SW	Build resources optimized for use with Marmalade's legacy software renderer. Again, we must be using the IW_USE_LEGACY_MODULES define in our MKB in order to use this.
GLES1	This is the default option if none is specified and builds resources that can be rendered efficiently using OpenGL ES.
IMG_MBX	Same as GLES1, but uses the PVRTC format for texture compression on images where this type of compression works well.
IMG_MBX_VGP	Currently the same as IMG_MBX.
ATI_IMAGEON	Same as GLES1, but uses the ATITC format for texture compression where possible.
NVIDIA_GOFORCE	Currently performs the same as GLES1.
ARM_MALI	Currently performs the same as GLES1.

While the platform identifier makes it easy to create resources for different types of GPU, it is also possible to be a little more specific about the type of texture compression to use. This can be done by specifying the platform as GLES1 and adding a textureFormat setting. For example, the atitc entry from the earlier example could be written as follows:

```
CIwResBuildStyle
{
  name              "atitc"
  addReadPrefix     "data-atitc"
  platform          "GLES1"
  textureFormat     "ATITC"
}
```

The following values can be used for the textureFormat parameter:

Value	Description
PVRTC_2	Uses 2-bit PVR texture compression. Not normally recommended, as it tends to produce poor-quality results. Can be used on devices featuring an Imagination-produced chipset, such as iOS devices.
PVRTC_4	Uses 4-bit PVR texture compression. This type generally yields good results for textures with no alpha channel, but can be quite poor when compressing transparent textures. By default Marmalade will not perform this type of compression on any source texture with an alpha component. This type of compression is supported by devices using an Imagination GPU, for example iOS devices.

Value	Description
ATITC	Will compress textures using ATI compression. Automatically uses 4-bit compression on textures with no alpha channel, or 8-bit compression on textures with transparency. Supported on ATI/Qualcomm chipsets typically used in many Android devices.
ETC	Uses 4-bit Ericsson texture compression on textures with no alpha channel. Transparent textures cannot be compressed. Supported on ATI/Qualcomm chipsets and most chipsets that support OpenGL ES 2.x.
DXT1, DXT3, and DXT5	DXT1 compression is a 4-bit format used for non-transparent textures. DXT3 is an 8-bit format that allows transparent textures to be compressed. DXT5 is another 8-bit format that has better support for gradients in the alpha channel. If DXT3 or DXT5 is specified and an opaque texture is encountered, Marmalade will automatically use DXT1 compression instead. Available on NVidia Tegra2 chipset devices.

Specifying which build style to use

With our build styles declared, we now just need to let Marmalade know which of them to use when loading resources. The easiest way of doing this is to use the `ResBuildStyle` ICF setting, which we do by adding the following to our ICF file:

```
[RESMANAGER]
ResBuildStyle=pvrtc
```

We can also switch between build styles at runtime as the resource manager provides methods for us to set and get the current build style. The following code snippets illustrate this:

```
// Discover the currently selected build style
CIwStringL lCurrentStyle = IwGetResManager()->
   GetBuildStyleCurrName();

// To change to a different build style
IwGetResManager()->SetBuildStyle("atitc");
```

Bear in mind, however, that while it is easy to switch between build styles, this behavior is only supported in Windows debug builds. When we create a release build for devices, we will generally only provide the resources required for that device type in order to reduce the size of the installation package. We'll be looking at how to achieve this later in this chapter.

Using resource templates

Build styles allow us to make decisions on how the resources for our game are processed on a global level; but sometimes we want a little more fine-grained control so we can treat different types of resources in different ways.

This is where resource templates come into play. Put simply, all a resource template allows us to do is alter the default settings that are applied when processing textures, materials, 3D models, animations, and GROUP files.

Resource templates can be defined in an ITX file that we parse before attempting to load any resources. Since these are only required in Windows debug builds, we do not need to load this file if we won't be building resources.

Marmalade provides a handy define, `IW_BUILD_RESOURCES`, which is only defined in Windows debug builds. Using this define, we can reduce the size of our compiled code by excluding any resource processing code. For example, if our resource template definitions are contained in a file called `restemplates.itx`, we could use the following code snippet to load the file:

```
#ifdef IW_BUILD_RESOURCES
IwGetTextParserITX()->ParseFile("restemplates.itx");
#endif
```

The following code provides an example of what the `restemplates.itx` file might look like. We'll discuss the different resource template types in greater detail in the coming sections; but notice how a template called `default` is defined for each type. This is so we can revert to normal loading behavior should we want to.

```
CIwResTemplateImage
{
  name         "default"

  formatHW     FORMAT_UNDEFINED
  formatSW     FORMAT_UNDEFINED
}

CIwResTemplateImage
{
  name         "rgba4444_nomipmap"

  formatHW     RGBA_4444
  mipMapping   false
}

CIwResTemplateMTL
```

```
{
  name        "default"
}

CIwResTemplateMTL
{
  name         "clamped_unfiltered"
  clampUV      true
  filtering    false
}
```

Once a resource template has been defined, it can be invoked from within a GROUP file by using the `useTemplate` parameter. This parameter takes the type and name of a resource template, searches for it and, if found, applies any settings defined in the template to any resource of the type that is loaded from then on. Here's an example:

```
CIwResGroup
{
  name "images"

  useTemplate "image" "rgba4444_nomipmap"
  useTemplate "mtl" "clamped_unfiltered"

  "./materials.mtl"

  useTemplate "image" "default"
  useTemplate "mtl" "default"
}
```

Defining material templates

A material resource template is declared by an instance of the `CIwResTemplateMTL` class and is used to provide a starting configuration for all instances of `CIwMaterial` that are created while the template is in use.

We can specify any parameter in a material template that can be applied to a `CIwMaterial` instance when processed from an ITX file. In the following table, a few of the more useful ones for template purposes are listed, but for a complete list take a look at the Marmalade documentation for `CIwMaterial`:

Parameter	Description
`colAmbient`, `colDiffuse`, `colEmissive`, and `colSpecular`	Allows a default RGBA color to be specified for the ambient, diffuse, emissive, and specular lighting components. For example: `colAmbient { 255, 255, 255, 255 }`.
`cullMode`	Specifies the back-face culling method to use for the material. Can be one of `BACK`, `FRONT`, or `NONE`.
`alphaMode`	Specifies a default transparency mode. Can be one of `NONE`, `ADD`, `SUB`, `HALF`, or `BLEND`.
`blendMode`	Specifies the blending type that will be used when drawing. Possible values are `MODULATE`, `MODULATE_2X`, `MODULATE_4X`, `DECAL`, `ADD`, `REPLACE`, and `BLEND`.
`alphaTest`	Specifies the type of alpha test to use when drawing pixels. Consists of a test type followed by an alpha value. Valid test types are `DISABLED`, `NEVER`, `LESS`, `EQUAL`, `LEQUAL`, `GREATER`, `GEQUAL`, `NOTEQUAL`, and `ALWAYS`. For example: `alphaTest GEQUAL 128`.
`zDepthOfs` and `zDepthOfsHW`	Allows this material to have an offset added to the z component of vertices when they are rendered, to force drawing backwards or forwards. Useful for drawing glowing effects so they can be forced to appear behind or in front of a 3D model. `zDepthOfs` is used in the software renderer and `zDepthOfsHW` is used when rendering with OpenGL ES.
`filtering`	Set to `true` to use bilinear filtering when rendering.
`clampUV`	If `true`, the UV coordinates are clamped within the bounds of the texture. This helps avoid the problems caused by bilinear filtering when rendering the edges of a texture, as bilinear filtering will attempt to blend between texels on the left and right or top and bottom of the image as it will assume the texture can be tiled otherwise.

Defining image templates

We can also use the resource template system to specify how we want images to be processed, which includes the ability to specify what texture format is used. To define a resource template for images we have to declare an instance of `CIwResTemplateImage`, which can be configured using the following parameters:

Parameter	Description
`formatSW` and `formatHW`	Converts any image to the requested format. The two versions of this parameter allow a format to be defined for the software renderer and another format for OpenGL ES rendering. For a complete list of texture formats, take a look at the Marmalade documentation for the `CIwImage` class, but bear in mind that some of these formats apply only to software or hardware rendering. For example, OpenGL ES does not support any of the palette-based formats, while the software renderer does not support compressed formats such as PVRTC or ATITC.
`compressForDiskSpace`	When `true`, converting textures using the `formatSW` and `formatHW` parameters will only store the converted version in the binary version of the GROUP file if it is smaller (in memory terms) than the image in its original format. Defaults to `false`.
`mipMapping`	When `true`, mipmaps will automatically be generated for the image. It can be very useful to set this to `false` for images that will form part of the UI, since these generally want to be drawn at their native size and mipmaps will not be needed.
`allowLowQualityCompression`	If using a hardware compressed format, Marmalade will not use the requested compression if the resulting texture is likely to be of low quality, for example, when using PVRTC on an image with an alpha channel. Setting this parameter to `true` allows you to force Marmalade to perform the requested compression.
`ignoreImages`	If set to `true`, images will be ignored and a 2 x 2 checkerboard texture will be used instead. Can be useful when debugging to speed up loading time.

Defining model templates

When loading a 3D model from a GEO file, we can use an instance of the `CIwResTemplateGEO` resource template to control how the model is processed. Many of the options available allow us to increase rendering performance when we know that a particular model will be used under certain conditions; for example, it will only ever be rendered using OpenGL ES or it may have been exported with normals, which are not required as the model will never be rendered with lighting enabled.

Some of the more useful settings are shown in the following table, but there are a great many more, so check out the Marmalade documentation for `CIwResTemplateGEO` for more details:

Parameter	Description
`scale`	Allows a floating point value that will be used to scale all the vertices of the model, to be specified. Can be useful to allow 3D models to be created in a modeling package with one scale and used at a different scale in the game.
`buildCols`, `buildNorms`, `buildUVs`, and `buildUV1s`	If set to `true`, the processed model data will include vertex colors, normals, and UV information, assuming it exists in the exported model. This can be useful to save memory in the game if lighting or textures are not required on the model.
`triStrip`	If set to `true`, a model will be conditioned for rendering using triangle strips. The default is `false`, which will cause triangle lists to be generated. Only takes effect if the model is being conditioned for rendering with OpenGL ES.
`calculateNorms`	If set to `true`, the model builder will attempt to generate vertex normals for lighting purposes. Useful if the source model was exported without normals for any reason.
`chunked`	If set to `true`, the model will be subdivided into smaller "chunks" for rendering using binary space partitioning. This can be useful when rendering a model much larger than screen size, as it allows whole sections of the model which are off-screen to be ignored.
`maxPrimsPerChunk`	Used in conjunction with the `chunked` parameter to specify the maximum number of polygons each chunk of the model should contain.

Defining animation templates

The `CIwResTemplateANIM` class allows ANIM file data to be adjusted when being processed. It only provides a couple of options, which are listed in the following table:

Parameter	Description
`zeroMotionTolerance`	Allows a floating point value to be specified that will be used to filter the translation part of any key frame data. When animating a model it is possible that the artist may accidentally include some small movements to the bone positions, which yields a larger output data set. This value allows movements up to the specified value to be ignored, which can mean fewer key frames have to be output.
`transformPrecision`	Another floating point value that specifies the precision to be used when animating. The default value is `4.0`, meaning that the animation mathematics are calculated at four times the world space resolution. If you have an animation with lots of subtle movements, you may want to consider increasing this value so that those movements are not lost.

Defining GROUP file templates

Finally, there is the `CIwResTemplateGROUP` class that is used for creating a **texture atlas**. A texture atlas is simply a collection of several smaller textures that are laid out within a much larger texture. This can improve rendering speed since fewer texture swaps are required when rendering.

We won't be looking at texture atlases in detail in this book, so if you want further information take a look at the Marmalade documentation page for the `CIwResTemplateGROUP` class.

Producing binary versions of resources

Previously in this book we've seen references to the fact that Marmalade produces binary versions of our resources, which are normally both smaller in size and quicker to load compared to the source assets.

Until now we've kind of glossed over this a little, but now that we know about build styles it's worth taking a closer look.

The binary versions of resources are generated automatically for us whenever we load a GROUP file, assuming we have the ICF setting `ResBuild` set to `1` and we're running a Windows debug build of our game. These files are written out with the file extension `.group.bin` into a directory called `data-ram`, which lives alongside the regular `data` directory where our source assets reside.

If we look inside the `data-ram` directory for any project, we'll discover another set of subdirectories and these are what contain the binary versions of our resources. These subdirectories correspond to the extra prefix directories that we specify in our build styles.

When the `.group.bin` files are written out, they will always be written to the prefix directory specified by the currently active build style, regardless of whether the source file was read from the standard `data` directory or from the extra prefix directory.

The relative directory path from the `data` directory will also be created in the output directory when writing out the binary versions of the files.

This makes it very easy for us to deploy different sets of resources to different platforms as we just need to include all the `.group.bin` files from one of the subdirectories of `data-ram`.

Let's illustrate this with a quick example. Suppose we have a file `data/images/images.group` that loads in a number of textures. If no build style is specified, the default is the Marmalade-defined `GLES1` style, which specifies a prefix directory called `data-gles1`. The binary version of the file will be written to the file path `data-ram/data-gles1/images/images.group.bin`.

If we now run our program again, with the `pvrtc` build style selected (as defined in the section on build styles earlier in this chapter), the images will be converted to PVRTC format and instead written to the file path `data-ram/data-pvrtc/images/images.group.bin`.

As it happens, Marmalade does not just write out the binary versions of the GROUP files, it also creates a number of other files that can be useful for debugging purposes. We won't look at these in detail in this book, but you might find them useful to take a look at if you're having problems with some resource not being processed as expected. In particular, there is a file with the extension `.group.bin.txt` that details all the classes encountered while processing a particular GROUP file.

There is one drawback to this approach, that is, you must load every single GROUP file that your game makes reference to in order to generate all the binary versions of them. This can particularly be a problem if your game has a large number of levels and you have a GROUP file for each level. A good way of solving this issue is to create a special mode for your game that can be given a list of all the required GROUP files (and potentially any dependencies between them) and will then load each file in turn to generate the binary version.

Compressing resources using the Derbh archiver

Game resources can soon grow very large in size, so it would be great if we could somehow compress these files so that they take up less space in our installation package, particularly if there are any restrictions on the maximum size an install package can have.

Marmalade provides just such a feature in the form of Derbh archives, which is very similar to compression systems such as ZIP that you will no doubt be familiar with. Derbh supports multiple compression algorithms, including the standard LZMA and also its own proprietary algorithm, which can achieve improved compression by operating over multiple files simultaneously.

The Marmalade SDK provides an API which allows us to load compressed files as easily as if they were provided as individual uncompressed files. A command-line utility called DZip is also provided to generate the archives in the first place.

Creating a Derbh archive

To create a Derbh archive, the first thing we have to do is create a **DZip Configuration File (DCL)**. This file is passed to the DZip utility to specify the source files and how they should be compressed. Here is a simple example of a DCL file taken from the Skiing example project for this chapter:

```
archive data-ram\data-gles1\skiing.dz
basedir data
basedir data-ram\data-gles1

file text\EN.str 0 dz
file models.group.bin 0 dz
file flag\flag.group.bin 0 dz
```

```
file rock\rock.group.bin 0 dz
file skier\skierskiing.group.bin 0 dz
file sound\sound.group.bin 0 dz
file tree\tree.group.bin 0 dz
file ui\ui.group.bin 0 dz
```

The first line uses the `archive` keyword to specify the name of the Derbh archive to be created, which is normally given the extension `.dz`. It is possible to create several archives at once by simply adding further `archive` entries.

The `basedir` keyword allows us to specify a directory in which to search for the files that will make up the archive. In the previous example we specify the directories `data` and `data-ram\data-gles1`.

Next we list all the files that will be added to the archive using the `file` keyword. The first parameter is the name of the file to include, which should be relative to one of the directories specified by the `basedir` keyword. This is followed by a number and a compression type. The number refers to which archive the file should be added to, with zero being the first archive specified in the DCL file.

There are a number of compression types available, although note that not all of them actually compress the source file! We can use a different compression type for each file if we so wish. The following table shows the types available:

Type	Description
`lzma`	Uses lzma compression, which generally gives the best compression ratio and has a reasonable decompression speed.
`dz`	Marmalade's own compression format, which gives a good compression ratio and decompression speed.
`zlib`	Uses zlib compression, which provides a less optimal compression ratio but has a very good decompression speed.
`zero`	A block of zeros the same size as the file will be added to the archive. Can be used for debugging purposes, for example, if we need to detect corrupted files.
`copy`	The file is included uncompressed in the archive. In the case of a file type that is already compressed, this can produce a smaller end file size for the archive than trying to compress the file.

With the DCL file constructed, we can then build the archive file using the DZip utility. This utility can be found as the file `tools\dzip\dzip.exe` in the Marmalade SDK install directory.

To create the archive, simply pass the name of the DCL file into the DZip utility, ensuring you run the command from within a directory where the `archive` and `basedir` entries can be located.

Using a Derbh archive in code

With a Derbh archive created, it is then really easy to make use of it in our game. Firstly we need to add support for the Derbh API by adding `derbh` to the list of `subprojects` in the MKB file. We also need to include the `derbh.h` file to provide access to the API functions.

To make use of our archive file we just need to add a call to the function `dzArchiveAttach`, which takes a single parameter—the filename of the Derbh archive itself. From then on any call to open a file will first check to see if it exists in the Derbh archive, and if it does the data will automatically be decompressed and returned whenever we try to read from the file. It really is that simple!

We can attach more than one archive at a time as well by simply calling `dzArchiveAttach` for each archive we wish to use.

If a request is made for a file that doesn't appear in the archive, Marmalade will then look in the `data` and `data-ram` directories.

If we want to stop using a Derbh archive for any reason, we can either call `dzArchiveDetach` to remove the last archive that was attached or we can specify the archive to detach using the `dzArchiveDetachNamed` function.

It is important to note that only files loaded from within the application code will be accessible from an attached Derbh archive. If you are trying to start a music track with s3eAudio or a video clip with s3eVideo, these files must exist as separate files as they are loaded by the operating system native methods, which obviously will have no way of accessing a Derbh file's contents.

The automatic Derbh method

For most projects there is actually an even easier way of making use of Derbh archives, which doesn't require us to create a DCL file or build a Derbh file ourselves. We don't even have to attach the archive in our code! To make use of this feature, all we need to do is add the following to the `deployments` section of our MKB file (we'll be covering this section of the MKB file in greater detail in just a moment).

```
deployments
{
  auto-derbh
}
```

With this in place, the Marmalade Deployment Tool will automatically build us a Derbh archive from the relevant files in the `assets` section of the MKB file (again, the `assets` section will be discussed shortly) and will attach it before our application code starts executing.

> Be wary of using the automatic Derbh facility if you ever deploy files that need to be modified by your code after installation. You will not be able to modify a file once it is contained within an archive, so you would instead need to make a copy of any such files in a new location the first time your application runs.

Creating different deployment types

It's now time to take a deeper look at how Marmalade handles the deployment process. If you've been following the sample code, you may be wondering how we are able to make a deployment package that contains all the necessary resource files in order to function. Or, if we're creating multiple resource sets, how do we choose which one to pair with our code when creating the installer package?

We also need a way of including icons and captions that will be used to represent our application when installed on a device.

All of this magic occurs in the MKB file, and the following sections aim to explain exactly what you have to do.

Specifying icons, application names, and other details

The `deployments` section of the MKB file is where we can set all manner of attributes that will be applied to the final installation package of our application. There are a huge number of deployment options that can be specified, some of which are global to all supported platforms and some that are operating system specific.

The following table lists several of the more immediately useful attributes, but you should go to **Marmalade | Marmalade Development Tools Reference | MKB File Settings | Deployment Options** in the Marmalade documentation for full details.

Attribute	Description
`assets`	Specifies which asset group to use in a deployment. This will be explained in greater detail in the following sections.
`name`	Specifies the name of the deployment. This name will be used for the name of the installation directory, the executable file, and the installation package file. If this value is not specified, the filename of the MKB file will be used instead.
`caption`	This is the name that will be used to identify the application once installed on the device—for example, the text that appears underneath a program icon. If no caption is specified, the `name` value will be used instead.
`app-icf`	Allows an alternative file to be specified for use instead of the default `app.icf` file.
`version`	Specifies the version number of the application. It should be provided in the form `major.minor.revision`.
`version-major`, `version-minor`, and `version-revision`	An alternative way of specifying the version number. Each of these attributes should be followed by a number representing the respective part of the version number.
`iphone-icon`, `iphone-icon-ipad`, `iphone-icon-high-res`, and `iphone-icon-ipad-high-res`	Sets the icons for use in iOS deployment. These settings specify a filename to an icon of suitable format and dimension to be used as the specified icon type.
`android-icon`, `android-icon-hdpi`, and `android-icon-ldpi`	Sets the filenames containing the icons for use on Android deployments.
`bada-icon`	Specifies the file to be used for the icon on Bada deployments.

As you can see, there are options for specifying the icon files for most platforms and indeed there are further platform-specific attributes for specifying information such as application signing keys.

You should check out the aforementioned page of the Marmalade documentation for further details on this, as you will be unable to produce final deployment packages for submission purposes without this information.

Specifying asset lists

We need some way of listing all the resource files that have to be included in the deployment package so our game can run. Marmalade allows us to do this by way of the `assets` section of the MKB file. Here's an example from this chapter's version of the Skiing project:

```
assets
{
  [common]
  (data)
  sound/music.mp3

  [normal]
  <include common>
  (data-ram/data-gles1)
  skiing.dz

  [highres]
  <include common>
  (data-ram/data-highres)
  skiing.dz
}
```

This small example demonstrates most of the functionality available in the `assets` section. First, you will notice the use of square brackets to create named groups of assets. In the example we have asset groups called `common`, `normal`, and `highres`.

Normal brackets are used to specify a directory, relative to the directory containing the MKB file, where files that need to be included in the deployment package can be located. This is then followed by the files themselves. You can have any number of these blocks of files in an asset group.

The important thing to remember about how directories and files are specified in an asset group is that the directory in brackets becomes the root path of the application's installation directory on the device. Let's illustrate this by looking at an example.

First we have the `common` asset group, which specifies that the file called `sound/music.mp3` can be found in the `data` directory. When installed on the device, the `music.mp3` file will be written into a subdirectory called `sound` in the application's installation directory.

Now let's consider the asset group called `normal`. Here the path to the file is completely enclosed in the brackets and just the name of the file, `skiing.dz`, is specified. This will result in the `skiing.dz` file being written into the application's installation directory.

There is one final feature of the assets section demonstrated by the example, which is the ability to include an asset group from within another asset group. This is done using the `include` keyword, which is enclosed in angle brackets along with the name of the asset group to be included.

Looking at the example we can see that both the `normal` and `highres` asset groups include the `common` asset group.

Creating and using deployment types

We can now look at creating different configurations for different devices. The `deployments` sections of the MKB file also allows us to create different deployment types by specifying a name in square brackets. All settings that are made after this will only apply to that deployment type. Settings can be applied globally across all deployment types by specifying them with square brackets before defining a deployment type.

It is possible to limit a deployment type to a certain set of mobile platforms by following the name in square brackets with a platform identifier or a comma-separated list of platforms in quote marks.

A full list of all the platforms supported by Marmalade at the time of this writing is provided in the following table:

Platform	Notes
`android`	Specifies the Android operating system.
`iphone`	Any iOS-based device—iPhone, iPod touch, or iPad.
`bada`	Targets the Samsung Bada platform.
`lgtv`	Specifies the LG Smart TV system.
`playbook`	For targeting the Blackberry Playbook tablet.
`symbian9`	Builds an application that runs on Symbian 9 S60 or Symbian ^3 devices.

Platform	Notes
webos	Targets the webOS platform, the best known device being the now discontinued HP TouchPad.
winmobile	Allows for Windows Mobile 6 device support. Note that Marmalade cannot target Windows Phone 7.
win32	For x86 Windows builds.
osx	For x86 Apple Mac builds (when using the Mac version of Marmalade).

It is not mandatory to specify a platform list in a deployment type. If no list is given, it is assumed that any platform is a valid target.

Once a deployment type has been specified, any attributes will only apply to that deployment type. This is particularly useful to us for being able to specify different sets of resources. By using the `assets` attribute we can specify the asset group that we want to be included in the final deployment package. The following example of the `deployments` section is taken from the Skiing project for this chapter.

```
deployments
{
  name="SkiingC8"
  caption="SkiingC8"

  [normal]
  assets=normal

  [highres]
  assets=highres
}
```

To create an installation package for a particular deployment type, all we have to do is follow the same deployment instructions provided in *Chapter 1, Getting Started with Marmalade*, of this book to start up the **Marmalade System Deployment Tool**. The second page of this application allows us to choose the deployment types that we want to create by clicking on checkboxes, as shown in the following screenshot:

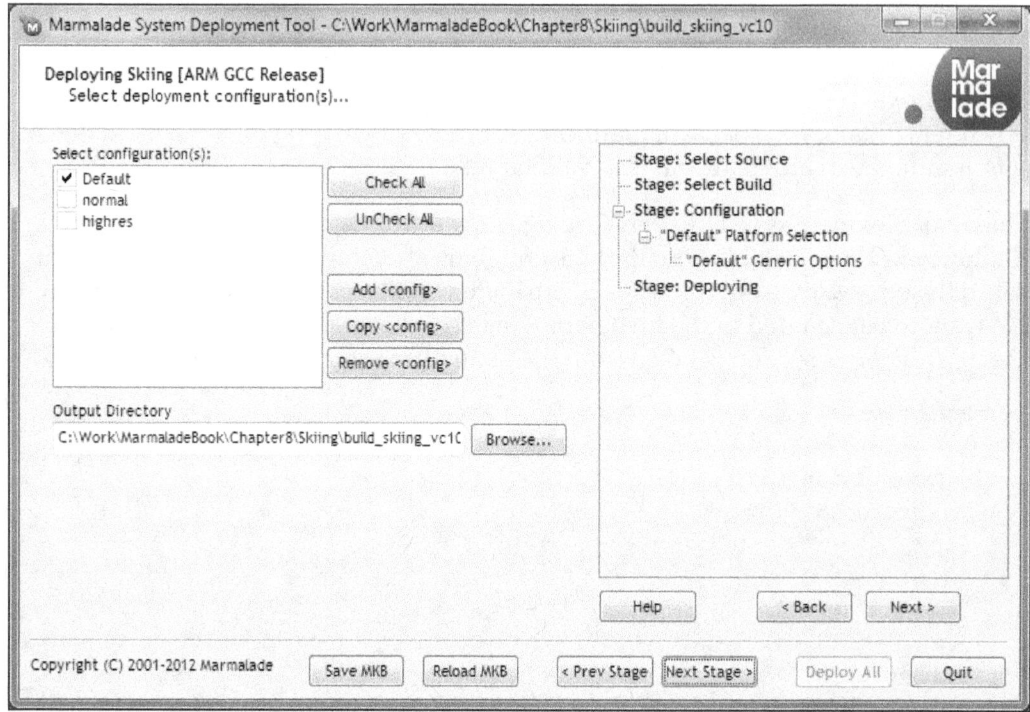

This page does allow you to create and modify deployment types by way of the **Add <config>**, **Copy <config>**, and **Remove <config>** buttons, but I personally prefer specifying them by hand in the MKB file. Using these buttons modifies the MKB file accordingly.

Once you have progressed through all the pages of the deployment tool and made the deployment packages, they can be found in the folder `build_projectname_vcxx\deployments`, where `projectname` is the name of the MKB file and `vcxx` refers to the version of Microsoft Visual C++ that you are using for development.

Example code

There are two example projects that accompany this chapter, and they are described in the following sections.

The build styles project

This is a very simple example demonstrating the use of build styles, resource templates, and deployment types. It is based on the Graphics2D example from *Chapter 2, Resource Management and 2D Graphics Rendering*.

The `resbuildstyles.itx` file defines a build style called `highres` that specifies a prefix directory called `data-highres`. If you look inside the `data` directory, you will see that the jar of the marmalade image in `data\images\textures\marmalade.png` is 256 x 256 pixels in size. A new directory for the `highres` build style has also been added, containing a 512 x 512 version of this image. This file is called `data\data-highres\images\textures\marmalade.png`.

If you now look at the `app.icf` file, you will see the new entry `ResBuildStyle=highres`. If you run the program with this line in place, the 512 x 512 version of the image will be loaded. Comment out or remove this line, and the 256 x 256 image will be loaded.

The `restemplates.itx` file shows a simple example of a resource template that will force the images to be converted into RGBA4444 format and also disables mipmapping. This resource template is used in the `data\images\images.group` file to reduce the size of the `images.group.bin` file as no mipmap images need to be stored in it.

Finally, the `BuildStyles.mkb` file declares two deployment types called `normal` and `highres`. When making an install package using the **Marmalade System Deployment Tool**, we can select either of these options to include the low or high resolution images. Note that the deployment tool will also list the default deployment type as this is always defined automatically by the deployment tool. Using the default type will not include any resources and so will not work on the device.

The Skiing project

For this chapter the Skiing project has been updated to use build styles, resource templates, and deployment types. It also makes use of Derbh archives to reduce the size of the install package.

In this instance the build styles system has been used to allow a larger size of font to be used on devices with a higher screen resolution. The `data\data-highres\ui\fonts` directory contains alternative versions of the font files `skiing.gxfont` and `skiing.tga` that will be loaded when the `highres` build style has been selected in the `app.icf` file.

No changes were necessary to any of the UI layout configuration since we used the approach of sizing controls based on the screen dimensions of the device. We just need a slightly bigger sized font to fill the larger screen area better.

To make deployments easier and to reduce the overall memory size of install packages, the Derbh API has also been used. If you look in the root project directory, you will see two new files called `skiing.dcl` and `skiing-highres.dcl`. These files list all the resources needed by the game and are used as input to the DZip tool to create the archive files. A batch file called `MakeDerbh.bat` has also been included to demonstrate use of the DZip tool.

Note that the Derbh archives can obviously not be created until the various `.group.bin` files have been generated. In order to do this you will need to run the game twice, once with the `ResBuildStyle=highres` setting set in the `app.icf` file and again with this line commented out.

The two DCL files create the target archives inside the `data-ram\data-gles1` and `data-ram\data-highres` directories, but both generate an archive called `skiing.dz`. The deployment types in the `Skiing.mkb` file include the relevant version of this file so our code becomes independent of the deployment type. At the start of the program we just have to attach the `skiing.dz` archive with the `dzArchiveAttach` function in order to access the correct resource files.

Summary

In this chapter we have learnt how Marmalade makes it easy to organize our resource files so that we can create different versions of them for devices of different specifications. We only need to provide alternative versions of resources that must be different, for example higher resolution textures. Any common files, such as configuration and GROUP files, can generally stay the same.

We've also covered the use of resource templates to allow us finer control over how our resources will be used in the game (for example, by specifying a particular type of texture compression to be used) and we've seen how to make different deployment types that include the same core code but different resource files.

Finally, we've also looked at the Derbh API to allow us to compress our resource files to save space in the installation package.

In the next chapter we'll be looking at how we can make use of social media to allow our players to share information about our game with their Facebook friends.

9
Adding Social Media and Other Online Services

Modern mobile devices are now amazingly powerful when it comes to graphics and sound, but perhaps the biggest differentiator between them and other dedicated hand-held videogame systems is that most of them are able to connect to the Internet.

While other gaming systems may be able to go online via WiFi, many modern devices can also use a 3G or other such data connections to connect to the Internet wherever the user happens to be. For this reason many games now feature the ability to connect to social media sites such as Facebook, or to share scores using services such as Apple's Game Center.

In this chapter, we will be looking at how it is possible to use Marmalade to add the following online capabilities to our games:

- Launching a web browser to display a web page
- Integrating with Facebook on iOS and Android
- Familiarizing ourselves with the possibilities for other online functionality, including advertising and in-app purchasing

Launching a web page in the device browser

Let's start our foray into the realm of the connected world by looking at the simplest way of adding an online feature to our games—launching a web page in the device browser.

Being able to direct the user to a website can be extremely useful for things such as instruction manuals, hints and tips, or technical support access. It is also great for cross promotion of titles by making it really simple to deliver a **Get More Games** button that highlights other games you have created.

How do we accomplish this magic? It's really simple! Just include the header file `s3eOSExec.h` and then make a call to `s3eOSExecAvailable` to see if the functionality is supported by the platform we are running on. Most of the platforms supported by Marmalade allow this functionality, but it is always best to check!

If support is available, all we have to do is call the function `s3eOSExecExecute` with the URL of the web page and a Boolean value indicating whether or not our application will quit. On platforms that don't support multi-tasking this parameter will make no difference, so it is usually OK to set this flag to `false` to ensure that our application is not closed down.

Here's a code snippet to illustrate:

```
if (s3eOSExecAvailable())
{
  s3eOSExecExecute("http://www.google.com", false);
}
```

The main disadvantage of this approach is that by launching the application in the device's internal web browser, it takes the user away from our game; but in the cases mentioned previously, this may be an acceptable trade-off given how easy it is to implement.

Integrating with social media

Social media sites such as Facebook provide a great way of advertising our games by getting our players to spread the word for us. There are countless examples of games which allow players to post a message to their Facebook wall or Twitter feed to show off their latest high score or boast about achieving a certain target in the game.

In this section we will take a detailed look at how we can implement integration with Facebook and we will also talk briefly about Twitter.

Using Facebook

Marmalade comes with an API called s3eFacebook that wraps up most of the tricky stuff involved in communicating with the Facebook servers. Unfortunately this ease of use does come at a price, which is that it is only supported on iOS and Android.

If Facebook support is required across all platforms, we would need to implement everything from scratch using HTTP requests via the IwHTTP API provided with Marmalade. This is a challenging task, so we'll be using the s3eFacebook API in this part of the book.

Creating a Facebook app

The first step in Facebook integration to a Marmalade project is to create a Facebook App on the Facebook website, which is really little more than a way of authenticating the source of any Facebook API requests.

When we create a Facebook App we are provided with two hexadecimal values. One is called the **App Id** (also known sometimes as the **API Key**) and the other is the **App Secret**. These values will be needed when we send requests to Facebook in order to identify our application on the Facebook servers.

To create a Facebook App follow these steps:

1. Log in to Facebook by visiting `www.facebook.com` and entering your username and password. If you do not already have a Facebook account, you can also sign up for one at this address.

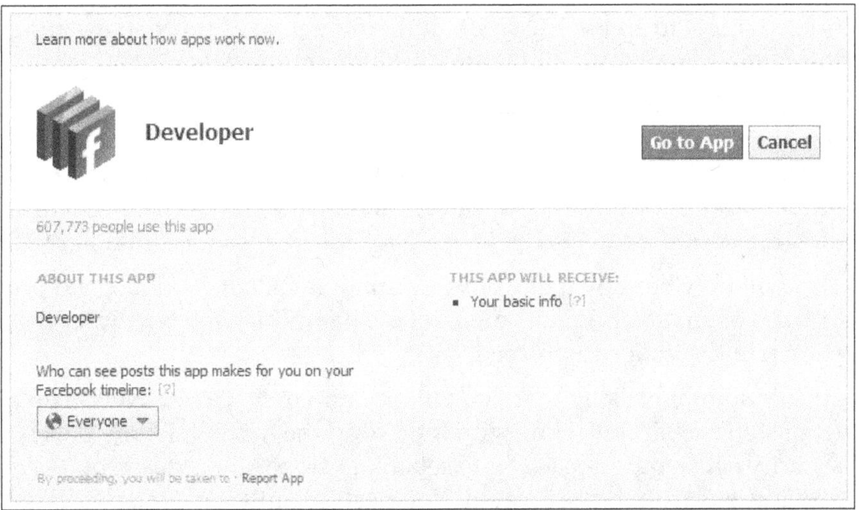

2. Once you are logged in to Facebook, visit the URL `www.facebook.com/developers`. If you have never created a Facebook App before, you will see a dialog like the one in the preceding screenshot. This screen has a single drop-down box that allows you to specify whether everyone or just your friends will be able to see posts created by the application. For now leave this set to the default value of **Everyone** and click on the **Go to App** button.

3. You will now see a screen detailing all the Facebook Apps you have created, which will be empty assuming this is the first App you have ever created! Click on the **+ Create New App** button to start creating a Facebook App.

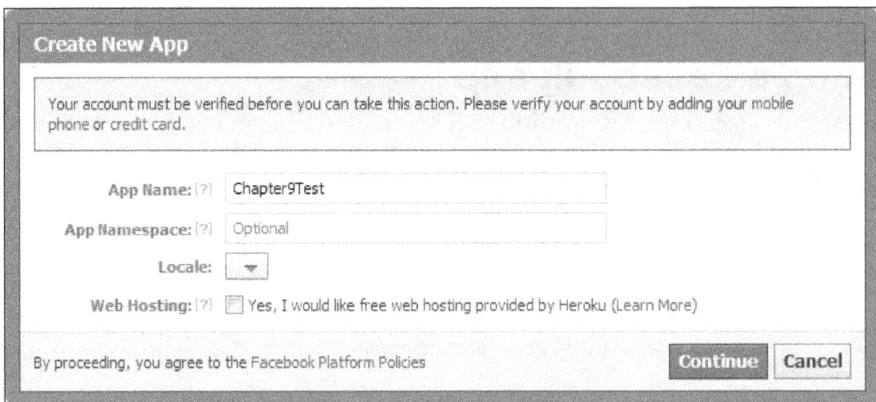

4. The previous dialog box shown should now appear, minus the pink box containing the text about verifying your account (more on this in a moment). For the purpose of this chapter all we need to supply is the **App Name** value, which is a string that will be shown to the user when our Marmalade project first attempts to access Facebook. It therefore makes sense to use the name of the game or perhaps your company name for this field.
5. Click the **Continue** button to create the Facebook App. Note that the remaining fields can be ignored for now. The **App Namespace** value is used to reference the application on Facebook as a URL or as part of an HTTP request and is for more advanced Facebook integration. The **Locale** and **Web Hosting** controls can also be ignored for the purposes of this chapter.
6. You will now be shown one of those annoying Captcha dialogs to prove you are a human and not some kind of spamming web bot. Enter the words shown in the image to proceed.
7. At this point it is likely that you will be shown the **Create New App** dialog from step 4 again, this time with the text in the little pink box. This is another security check put in place by Facebook to stop hundreds of rogue Facebook applications from being created. You need to authorize your Facebook account before you can create a Facebook App. I would suggest you click the link labeled **mobile phone** to verify your account as it is by far the easiest way. You will be asked to enter your mobile phone number so a text message can be sent to you containing an authorization code that you then enter into a dialog to verify yourself.

8. Once you have verified your account you will return to the **Create New App** dialog once again. Ensure the **App Name** value is correct and click on the **Continue** button again. The Captcha screen will likely rear its ugly head once more, so fill it in.

9. At this point the Facebook App has been created and you should now be looking at a screen similar to that shown before, which shows various pieces of information about the Facebook App. The most important are the **App Id/App Key** and **App Secret** values, which you'll need later; so make a note of them.

Creating a Facebook test user

We will obviously want to test the Facebook integration of our application out once it has been implemented, but it would be good if we didn't have to spam all our friends with test wall posts and the like. It's therefore a good idea to create a test user.

For understandable reasons Facebook doesn't really want us to create full Facebook accounts for our test users, so instead they allow us to create test users using our Facebook App. Follow these steps to create a test user:

1. Log in to Facebook and then visit the `www.facebook.com/developers` page.
2. Click on the relevant Facebook App in the left-hand pane and then click on the link labeled **Edit Roles** on the right-hand side of the **Roles** section of the page.

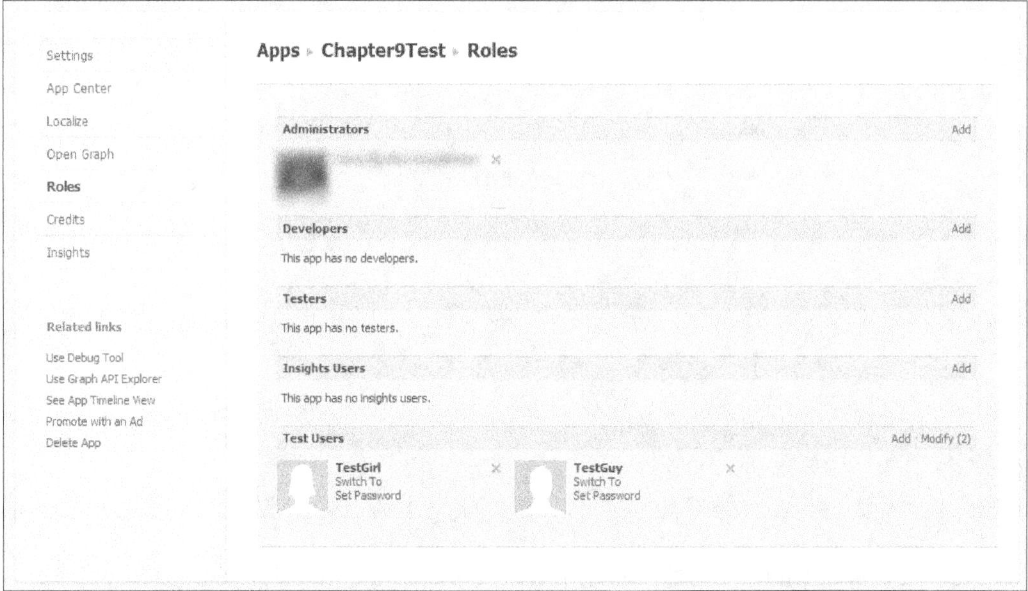

3. The **Roles** page for the Facebook App will be displayed (see previous screenshot). At the bottom there is a section labeled **Test Users**, which has a link labeled **Add** that you should click on to create new test users.
4. A small dialog box will appear with three options. The first is labeled **Number to Add** and is a drop-down box allowing between one and ten test users to be generated.
5. The **Authorize this App** checkbox allows us to determine whether the created users have already authorized the Facebook App to use their account. It's worth creating users of both types to fully test our application, but ultimately it's up to you whether you authorize now or when we first try to log in using this user account.

6. Finally, the **Enable Ticker** checkbox lets you decide whether the user will be using the Facebook Ticker interface (which is a real-time timeline of wall posts and other events) or the older standard interface. Not all users have access to the newer Ticker interface, so it is again worth testing your project using both methods.
7. Click the **Add** button to create the new users. You will return to the screen first shown in step 3, but the new users will be shown at the bottom of the page now.
8. Each test user will have a couple of links next to them. You should first click on the **Set Password** link to allow a password to be set for this user. A textbox will appear, to allow you to enter a password.
9. Next, click on the **Switch To** link next to one of the users to log in as that user and display their Facebook wall.
10. At the top right of the test user's wall, there should be a button labeled **Edit Profile**. Click on it.
11. On the **Edit Profile** screen, click on the **Contact Information** link in the left-hand side panel.
12. At the top of the screen there should be two e-mail addresses associated with the profile. One of these should be of the form `username@tfbnw.net`, which is the e-mail address we will need to use later to log in as the test user. Make a note of this e-mail address and the password you set in step 8.

Adding the s3eFacebook API to a Marmalade project

With the Facebook App and test users configured, let's get down to adding Facebook support to a Marmalade project. The first thing to do is open the project MKB file and add `s3eFacebook` to the list of `subprojects`. We can then include the `s3eFacebook.h` file whenever we need to make use of the s3eFacebook API functions.

We also need to add another configuration setting to the MKB file in the `deployments` section. The line in question looks like this and is only needed for iOS builds. On iOS our application temporarily loses focus when we log in to Facebook and this value ensures that we regain control when the login process is completed:

```
iphone-bundle-url-schemes="fb0123456789abcdef"
```

The hexadecimal value following the initial `fb` should be replaced with the 16-digit App Id generated by the Facebook App.

Checking for s3eFacebook support

As previously mentioned, the s3eFacebook API is only supported on iOS and Android, so it's good to be able to check at runtime whether we can support Facebook or not. This is easily done using the `s3eFacebookAvailable` function, which will return `S3E_TRUE` if the API is available or `S3E_FALSE` if it isn't.

Initialization and termination

Before we can call any of the s3eFacebook APIs, we must first initialize a Facebook session. We do this with a call to the function `s3eFBInit` that takes a single parameter, a null-terminated string containing the App Id of the Facebook App we want to use.

The function will return a pointer to an `s3eFBSession` instance, which we will need to use to access the Facebook API and make requests to it.

We can release the Facebook session with a call to `s3eFBTerminate`, which takes the session pointer returned from `s3eFBInit` as its only argument.

It is sufficient to call the `s3eFBInit` function the first time we want to make any Facebook request and then to use this same session information for the execution life of our application. The `s3eFBTerminate` function only needs to be called at shutdown time.

Logging in and out of Facebook

Before we can make any Facebook request, we must first log in to Facebook. This is done with the `s3eFBSession_LogIn` function, which takes five parameters. The first is the `s3eFBSession` pointer returned from `s3eFBInit`. We can then specify a callback function, which will be triggered once successfully logged in. A pointer to a block of user data can also be specified, which will be passed into the callback function when it is triggered.

The callback function can be specified as `NULL`, in which case we need to check for login to be completed by calling the `s3eFBSession_LoggedIn` function. This takes the session pointer as an argument and will return `S3E_TRUE` when the session is logged in.

The final two parameters of `s3eFBSession_LogIn` are an array of null-terminated strings listing the Facebook API permissions we want to make use of and the number of permissions in this array. Permissions allow our application to notify the user that our application wants to perform certain operations on their account, such as posting to their wall or accessing their photo collection. A full list of permissions can be found at the web page `http://developers.facebook.com/docs/authentication/permissions/`.

The following example code shows a sample callback function and how to use it with the s3eFBSession_Login function:

```
// Login callback
void LoginCallback(struct s3eFBSession* apSession,
s3eResult* apLoginResult, void* apUserData)
{
  if (*apLoginResult == S3E_RESULT_SUCCESS)
  {
    // Logged in OK
  }
  else
  {
    // Login failed
  }
}

// Log in to Facebook using the session returned from s3eFBInit.
const char* permissions[] = { "publish_stream" };

s3eFBSession_Login(lpSession, LoginCallback, NULL,
  permissions, 1);
```

This code attempts to log in to Facebook requesting the publish_stream permission that allows an application to post to a user's wall.

When a Facebook login attempt is made, our application will lose focus and the device's Facebook application will be started. If the user doesn't have a Facebook application installed, the device's web browser will be launched instead.

You will be asked to provide your Facebook account's login details, so for testing purposes enter the details for one of the test user accounts we generated earlier. Once logged in, another screen will appear detailing what our application wants to do with the user's Facebook account. In the previous example this would just be posting to the user's wall. If the Facebook App has not yet been authorized for the Facebook account, the screen will also have two buttons labeled **Allow** and **Don't Allow**, which the user can use to grant or disallow access respectively.

The Facebook login process will first look to see if a user is already logged in to Facebook by looking for a browser cookie, and will not ask for username and password details if this is the case. If the test device is also your own personal device, you will probably want to log out of Facebook before testing your application to avoid annoying those on your friends list!

After authorizing (or indeed disallowing) the Facebook App, our application will regain focus and the login callback function will be triggered to say whether the process was successful or not. If the Facebook app was not authorized or there is no Internet connection available, login will fail.

Logging back out of Facebook again is also simple. All we have to do is make a call to `s3eFBSession_Logout`, passing the `s3eFBSession` pointer as its only argument. In practice we only ever need to log out of Facebook on closing our application or if you specifically want to log off to allow different user credentials to be used instead. The session will not expire or become invalid as long as our application is executing.

Posting a message to a user's wall

We'll now take a look at one of the most common things that games use Facebook for: posting a message to the user's wall to alert their friends to a new high score or some in-game achievement.

In order to do this we'll be making use of the Facebook Graph API. There are other ways, but the Graph API is the most up-to-date way of doing so and doesn't look likely to be replaced any time soon.

For more information on the Facebook Graph API take a look at the web page `http://developers.facebook.com/docs/reference/api/`, and for details about wall posts take a look at `http://developers.facebook.com/docs/reference/api/post/`.

To begin making a Facebook Graph API request, we use the function `s3eFBRequest_WithGraphPath`. This function takes as arguments the session pointer, the desired Facebook Graph path, and the HTTP method to use (GET or POST). The Graph path and HTTP method are both specified as null-terminated strings.

The function will return a pointer to an `s3eFBRequest` structure representing the new request if it is successful, or `NULL` if it fails.

With the request structure created, we can now add the various parameters we need to it using the functions `s3eFBRequest_AddParamNumber` and `s3eFBRequest_AddParamString`. Both functions take the `s3eFBRequest` structure pointer and a null-terminated string for the parameter name as their first two parameters. The third parameter is a 64-bit integer value (Marmalade defines a type called `int64` for this) for the former function call, or a `const char` pointer to a null terminated string for the latter function.

Most Graph API values will require you to specify an access token to show that your application is authorized to make requests. The access token is provided to our application as part of the login process and we can retrieve it using the `s3eFBSession_AccessToken` function, which again takes the session pointer as its sole input. The access token is returned as a `const char` pointer.

The access token can then be added to a Graph request using the `s3eFBRequest_AddParamString` function by specifying `access_token` for the parameter name and using the return value from the `s3eFBSession_AccessToken` function as the value for the parameter.

Once all parameters have been added to the request, we can send it to the Facebook servers using the `s3eFBRequest_Send` function. This function takes the request pointer as its first input, followed by a callback function and a pointer to an optional block of data that will be passed to the callback function when it is triggered.

The function will return immediately with `S3E_RESULT_SUCCESS` if the request was sent, or `S3E_RESULT_ERROR` if there was a problem transmitting it. The s3eFacebook API will wait for the request from Facebook to arrive and will call the specified callback function with the result when it does.

When a request is completed we should make a call to `s3eFBRequest_Delete` to free any resources associated with it.

Let's look at an example illustrating all of the previous points for posting a simple message to the user's wall:

```
// Sample callback function for s3eFBRequest_Send function
void RequestCallback(struct s3eFBRequest* apRequest,
   s3eResult* apRequestResult, void* apUserData)
{
   if (*apRequestResult == S3E_RESULT_SUCCESS)
   {
      // Request successful
   }
   else
   {
      // Request failed
   }

   // Free the request resources
   s3eFBRequest_Delete(apRequest);
}

// The following code snippet illustrates how we can send a request
```

```
// to Facebook using the Graph API to post a wall message

s3eFBRequest* lpRequest = s3eFBRequest_WithGraphPath(lpSession,
   "me/feed", "POST");
if (lpRequest)
{
   // Add the required parameters
   const char* lpAccessToken = s3eFBSession_AccessToken(lpSession);
   s3eFBRequest_AddParamString(lpRequest, "access_token",
      lpAccessToken);
   s3eFBRequest_AddParamString(lpRequest, "message",
      "Hello Facebook!");

   // Send the request to Facebook
   if (s3eFBRequest_Send(lpRequest, RequestCallback, NULL) ==
      S3E_RESULT_SUCCESS)
   {
      // Wait for the callback to be triggered now!
   }
   else
   {
      // Error occurred sending request, so free it
      s3eFBRequest_Delete(lpRequest);
   }
}
```

Further s3eFacebook features

The previous sections really just scratch the surface of the kind of Facebook integration that is possible using s3eFacebook. For example, we have made no mention of processing any results sent back to our application by the Facebook API. There is a whole family of functions with the prefix `s3eFBRequest_Response` that allow the return values from a Facebook request to be analyzed.

For more information on the entire s3eFacebook API, go to **Marmalade API Reference | Extensions API Documentation | Facebook Extension | Facebook API Reference** in the Marmalade documentation.

Using Twitter

Sadly Marmalade provides no dedicated built-in support for Twitter; so if Twitter is important to you, you'll need to provide your own implementation.

One way of doing this would be to use the Twitter API directly by sending HTTP requests to Twitter's servers using the IwHTTP API. This would allow a solution to be created that should work fine on all operating systems; but this might require a lot of code to be implemented to deal with all the possible problems that can occur when working online (for example, lack of internet connection, server timeouts, and so on).

Another possibility, although it would be limited to iOS and Android, would be to use the Marmalade **Extensions Development Kit** (**EDK**) to access existing Twitter solutions on these two platforms. This may be simpler to implement since the low level Twitter API HTTP requests will have been taken care of; but the EDK is currently only supported by iOS and Android. *Chapter 10, Extending Marmalade with the Extensions Development Kit (EDK)*, of this book will be looking at the EDK in more detail.

If you are interested in supporting Twitter in Marmalade, the following web page may be of use to you:

`https://dev.twitter.com/docs/twitter-libraries#cplusplus`

It mentions a number of existing C++-based libraries for accessing Twitter that may form a good starting point for a Marmalade solution.

Connecting to other types of online services

We'll now take a quick look at some of the other types of online services that games on mobile devices typically connect to. While we won't be covering these in depth, it's still worth giving them a mention in order to form a better picture of what is possible.

Supporting social gaming networks

Social gaming networks such as Apple's Game Center or cross-platform solutions such as Scoreloop or OpenFeint have become commonplace in many mobile games. In the following sections we will look at some of the possibilities we have available in Marmalade projects for these types of services.

Using Apple's Game Center

One of the most well-known social gaming systems in the mobile games world has to be Apple's Game Center (`http://www.apple.com/game-center/`). Unsurprisingly, this system is solely devoted to iOS-based devices, so if you are developing a game for iOS this is probably going to be your first choice for support.

We cannot access Apple's API directly given that it is an Objective-C library, so Marmalade instead comes with a wrapper API for the service, called s3eIOSGameCenter.

The s3eIOSGameCenter API is far too big for us to delve into here, but it is quite a close wrapping of the standard Apple-supplied API and thus fairly simple to understand how to convert any sample code you may come across on the Internet to use the Marmalade wrappers. An example project to demonstrate its use is supplied in the Marmalade installation folder `examples\s3eIOSGameCenter` and there is plenty of information in the Marmalade documentation too, at **Marmalade API Reference | S3E API Documentation | S3E: iOS Only | S3E iOS Game Center**.

Support is provided for all the major features of Game Center, including leaderboards and achievements, multiplayer matchmaking, and even voice chat!

Using Scoreloop

The Scoreloop system is an extremely popular cross-platform solution that, at the time of writing, supports iOS, Android, BlackBerry PlayBook, and Windows Phone 7. Given that Marmalade supports the first three of these platforms, combined with the fact that the nice people at Scoreloop also supply a version of their API that can be used directly in a Marmalade project, this system is a very good choice if you want to support social gaming in a cross-platform project.

The Marmalade version of Scoreloop provides support for leaderboards, achievements, and Scoreloop's challenge system for offline multiplayer gaming.

More information on Scoreloop can be found at `www.scoreloop.com`, where you can sign up for a free developer account and download the latest version of the SDK.

Supporting in-app purchases

The current popularity of so-called Freemium games has come about because there are now other ways of charging for games besides a single up-front purchase cost. The advent of **in-app purchases** (**IAP**) has allowed us to literally give away our games for free and yet still make a profit by selling additional game modes or level packs to users after they have already played and enjoyed our games.

In the following sections we will be looking at how Marmalade allows in-app purchases to be supported on iOS and Android.

Adding in-app purchasing for iOS devices

As with Game Center, the in-app purchase SDK supplied by Apple is written in Objective-C, so we can't use it directly in a Marmalade project.

Again Marmalade solves this problem by wrapping up the Apple libraries into an API called s3eIOSAppStoreBilling.

This API allows us to obtain a list of in-app products that are available for purchase and their costs. We can then make a request to purchase a particular product and will be notified of success or failure when Apple's servers have taken care of all the behind-the-scenes stuff that needs to be done in order to process the payment.

Just like the original Apple implementation, there is no support for allowing a user to automatically download extra data when a purchase has been made. Instead we have to implement this ourselves on receipt of the purchase confirmation, which would involve either shipping all the "unlockable" data with the original application download or downloading it from our own server.

For more information on this API, take a look in the Marmalade documentation by going to **Marmalade API Reference** | **S3E API Documentation** | **S3E: iOS Only** | **S3E iOS App Store Billing**, and the example code that can be found in the Marmalade installation at `examples\s3e\s3eIOSAppStoreBilling`.

Adding in-app purchasing for Android devices

Marmalade also provides a wrapper API for implementing in-app purchases on Android called s3eAndroidMarketBilling. The naming of this API is still based on the original name of the Android store (Android Marketplace), but it works fine with the renamed Google Play system.

Sadly Marmalade hasn't been able to provide a single API that can target multiple platforms, simply because the iOS and Android systems work so differently. A good example of this is that the Google Play system does not allow us to query the list of available products for an application. This is a really strange omission on Google's part (especially given that you do have to set up a product list on the Google Play servers anyway) and it means we either have to hardcode our product identifiers into our application or provide our own server to mirror this information.

Information on this API can be found in the documentation by going to **Marmalade API Reference** | **S3E API Documentation** | **S3E: Android Only** | **S3E Android Market Billing**, and there is some sample code at `examples\s3e\s3eAndroidMarketBilling`.

Using advertising

We've just looked at in-app purchases as being one way of generating an income from your games, but another way is to make use of one of the many advertising solutions available. Just like those clickable adverts that are a common part of most websites, we can give over a little part of our game's screen display to adverts that will then provide another potential income stream.

The following sections explore some of the options available to us.

Implementing iAd support for iOS devices

As you are probably aware, Apple has its own advertising solution purely for iOS, called **iAd**. Again this requires use of an Objective-C API, so the Marmalade SDK provides a C wrapper for it called **s3eIOSIAD**.

This is a very simple API that allows you to request an advertisement from the iAd servers. If an advert is available you have control over when to show it, so the advert only needs to be visible at certain points in your game if you so wish.

Documentation on this API can be found at **Marmalade API Reference | S3E API Documentation | S3E: iOS Only | S3E iOS iAd**, and example code exists in the Marmalade installation directory at `examples\s3e\s3eIOSIAd`.

Using other advertising solutions

Since iAd can only be used on iOS platforms, we are forced to consider other possible solutions when targeting other platforms (although most of these other solutions can still be used on iOS as it happens!).

Marmalade does not provide support for any other advertising systems directly, but other developers have taken up the challenge here and have made their own solutions available for use on the Marmalade Code Community pages.

At the time of writing there are a couple of useful projects called *s3eAdWhirl* and *s3eAdNinja* that at least provide support for Android. These solutions are quite clever in that they actually target multiple sources of mobile advertising in order to ensure that an advert is shown in your application as often as possible to maximize your revenue.

The *IwGameAds* module is another open-source community project that shows how to integrate with multiple ad services and works across more platforms than you can shake a very large stick at. The full source code and documentation for it can be found at the following web address:

`http://www.drmop.com/index.php/iwgameads-sdk/`

In the unlikely event that these don't suit your needs and there is a particular mobile advertising system you would like to use, another possibility is to implement your own support for that system using the Extensions Development Kit that is described in more detail in the next chapter.

Example code

Now let's take a look at the example code associated with this chapter.

The Facebook project

The Facebook project brings together into one place all the information contained in this chapter about posting to a user's Facebook wall so you can easily see how to implement the code in a more real-world application.

On running the sample, we are presented with two menu buttons. The first allows us to log in and out of Facebook while the second allows us to post a message to our wall when we have successfully logged in. A status message will be displayed at the bottom of the screen.

The s3eFacebook API has been further wrapped into a small class called `Facebook`, which deals with logging in and out of Facebook and building up Graph API requests. This is a good approach as it provides a further layer of abstraction and keeps all the s3eFacebook API usage in one place. If the core Facebook API were to change for any reason (possible, given that Facebook could potentially change the way in which things have to be done at any time), all the code that needs to be updated is easy to find.

The message to post to the wall is requested using the `s3eOSReadStringUTF8WithDefault` function; so this example also serves as a guide to using this API.

If you want to build and run this sample code, you will need to create your own Facebook App and supply the App Id and App Secret values generated for it. The `app.icf` file contains two settings allowing these values to be specified (though currently only the App Id is actually used in the code!).

It is also necessary to modify the `iphone-bundle-url-schemes` line in the `deployments` section of the project's MKB file. If this setting is not changed, the application will not regain focus after the Facebook login process on iOS devices.

As mentioned when discussing the s3eFacebook API earlier in this chapter, this sample code will only work on iOS and Android devices.

The Skiing project

This chapter sees Facebook support being added to the Skiing project. The `Facebook.cpp` and `Facebook.h` files created for the Facebook project have been added to the Skiing project unchanged in order to support posting a message to the user's wall.

When the player reaches the "game over" screen, a check is made to see if Facebook support is available. If it isn't, the normal "game over" message is displayed and after a short delay the user will return to the title screen.

If Facebook functionality is available, a slightly different "game over" screen is displayed. This version informs the player of their score and then asks if they wish to post a message on their wall to boast about it to their friends. Buttons marked **Yes** and **No** are provided to allow the player to choose what to do.

If they click on the **Yes** button, the game will attempt to log in to Facebook and then post a message detailing the player's score. The request also references an image file and a web page link that will also be displayed alongside the wall message.

As with the previous Facebook project, it is necessary to create your own Facebook App and supply the correct values for the App Id, App Secret, and the `iphone-bundle-url-schemes` setting.

Summary

In this chapter we've taken a quick look at how to add various kinds of online services to our games. Specifically, we've seen how to add Facebook support to our titles and now know where to start looking should we want to include social gaming, advertising, or in-app purchases.

Each of these topics could easily fill an entire chapter, but unfortunately there just isn't room in this book to go any deeper. Hopefully you now have a good idea of the options available though.

At several points in this chapter the Extensions Development Kit (EDK) was mentioned as a possible way of implementing online features that are currently not supported as part of the base Marmalade SDK. In the next chapter, we will be taking a look at the EDK to see how we can access APIs that form part of the iOS and Android operating systems.

10
Extending Marmalade with the Extensions Development Kit (EDK)

In the previous chapter we mentioned how Marmalade's **Extensions Development Kit (EDK)** was a possible way of adding functionality to a Marmalade application that had not been otherwise exposed, by using the standard Marmalade APIs.

In this chapter we'll be looking at the following topics:

- An overview of what the EDK is and why it is needed
- How to extend Marmalade by creating an EDK extension for Windows, iOS, and Android to support reading gyroscope information

Why is the EDK necessary?

The Marmalade SDK manages to work its magic of being able to take one codebase and deploy it to multiple platforms by providing a set of APIs that sit on top of the APIs specific to each platform.

A deployed application executable actually consists of two separate files. Our application code is compiled into an **S3E file**, which is the Marmalade equivalent of a Windows **Dynamic Link Library** (**DLL**). This file is the same across all platforms.

In order to execute our S3E file, a Loader program is used. This program is the glue between the platform we are running on and our own code. The loader program starts up first, loads the S3E file into memory, and then passes control to the code within it. If our code needs to make a platform-dependant call, it actually makes a request to a function in the loader that will then call the correct operating system function.

The loader program is a fixed entity and cannot be changed by us, so Marmalade provides us with the EDK system to enable us to make platform-specific function calls. Certain parts of the Marmalade SDK have actually been implemented in just this manner; for example, the s3eFacebook API is actually an extension!

The only problem with the EDK is that it is not a completely cross-platform solution. At the time of writing, it was only possible to write extensions for iOS, Android, Windows, and Mac OSX.

Since this book is primarily concerned with development using the Windows version of Marmalade, we won't be looking at how to build a Mac extension here, however we will need access to a Mac computer in order to build iOS extensions since, by necessity, we have to use the Apple iOS SDK, which is not available as a Windows download. For details on creating Mac extensions, look in the Marmalade documentation by going to **Marmalade (C++)** | **Extensions Development Kit (EDK)** | **EDK Guides by Platform** | **OS X EDK Guide**.

Creating an extension for gyroscope input

To illustrate the process of creating a Marmalade extension, we'll take a look at how to add support for gyroscope input. This is a useful addition since it lets us add a whole new input method to our games yet it also demonstrates just how easy it is to extend Marmalade's functionality.

Our extension will consist of the following functions:

Function	Description
`GyroscopeAvailable`	This function is automatically generated for us by the EDK build process. It returns `S3E_TRUE` if the Gyroscope extension is supported for the current platform, and `S3E_FALSE` if it isn't.
`GyroscopeSupported`	Not all mobile devices actually contain gyroscope hardware, so this function is provided to determine whether or not we can make use of the gyroscope in our game. The function returns a normal C++ `bool` value indicating whether a gyroscope is present.

Function	Description
`GyroscopeStart` and `GyroscopeStop`	These two functions start and stop the hardware generating gyroscope input data.
`GyroscopeGetX`, `GyroscopeGetY`, and `GyroscopeGetZ`	Returns the current gyroscope data values for the X, Y, and Z axes. The values are returned as `float` values in radians per second.

The API detailed earlier provides the bare minimum functionality required to provide gyroscope support and has deliberately been kept simple in order to demonstrate the process of building an extension more clearly.

Declaring the extension API

The first step in creating an extension is to specify the functions it will contain, which we will do using an **S4E file**. This file is used to define the API of our extension and is best illustrated by an example. If you want to follow along, create a new directory called `Gyroscope` and create a file called `Gyroscope.s4e` inside it with the following contents:

```
include:
#include <s3eTypes.h>

functions:
bool GyroscopeSupported() false
void GyroscopeStart() void
void GyroscopeStop() void
float GyroscopeGetX() 0.0f
float GyroscopeGetY() 0.0f
float GyroscopeGetZ() 0.0f
```

The example starts with the line `include:`, which is then followed by any number of C preprocessor commands, include files, structure definitions, and class definitions that will become part of the extension's main header file. In our case we are just including the `s3eTypes.h` file; but if we needed to pass lots of data between the extension and the calling code, we might want to add structures or classes, enumerations, and definitions here too.

Next we have the `functions:` section of the file, which is little more than a list of the functions that our extension will contain and can be called from within a Marmalade project that makes use of the extension.

> We do not have to list the `GyroscopeAvailable` function explicitly in the list of functions. The EDK build process automatically generates this function for us by taking the name of the S4E file and appending "Available" to the end of it.

As you can see, the functions are listed almost as if they were normal C function prototypes. Each function is listed on its own line by first stating the return type and then its name and parameter list (which all just happen to be empty in this example!).

Additionally, each function in the S4E file function list also specifies a default value it will return and can be followed by a number of optional directives that control the behavior of the function, how it is added to the extension, and how it is called. Our example makes no use of these directives, but the following table shows what can be specified:

Directive	Description
`run_on_osthread`	Specifies that the extension function should only be executed on the main OS thread of the application. This is particularly important if the function performs any kind of user interface interaction, as many platforms will only allow UI calls to be made on the main thread.
`no_lock`	Disables thread-safe locking when calling this function. By default all extension functions can only be called on a single thread at any particular time and locking code is automatically generated to ensure that this happens.
`fast`	Enables fast stack switching. This is an optimization option, which means less data needs to be passed between our application and the loader when making an extension function call by using the same stack as the loader module. Normally the loader module and our application code have separate stacks.
`no_assert`	Stops an assert from being raised if an extension function is called on a platform for which the extension has not been built. The default value for the function will be returned.

Directive	Description
`order`	By default each function listed in the S4E file will be added to the extension in list order and this order is used internally to locate the correct function pointer to call. As our extension develops over time, we may want to add or depreciate functions but still keep related functions together in the S4E file. By adding `order=x` after a function declaration we say that this function will occupy position x in the function order, with *x=1* being immediately after the last function that does not specify an order value. If that sounds confusing, don't worry; for our own projects we will probably never need to make use of this feature as it is only really an issue if we are making our extension available for other people to use!

There are also a number of global directives that can be specified in the S4E file and these should be listed at the very start of the file before the `include:` line. Again our example makes no use of these directives, but for your information they are listed in the following table:

Directive	Description
`no_init_term`	Specifies that the extension needs no initialization or termination functions to be automatically generated. It is unlikely you will ever use this directive since these functions are generally required in order to set up the interface between the extension and our project code.
`errors`	Allows access to some macros that make communication of errors easier to implement by automatically generating functions, such as `GetError`, present in many of the S3E APIs that make up the low-level Marmalade API.
`globals`	Declares that the extension will require a global structure block allocated for its internal use and makes some macros available in order to support getting and setting values in this structure.
`callbacks`	States that this extension wants to make use of callbacks and will automatically define callback IDs to support this using the same approach used in other built-in S3E APIs.

Making an extension for Windows

We'll begin by creating our extension for use on Windows. Obviously it's unlikely that a Windows PC would feature gyroscope hardware (though I guess not impossible!), but starting with the Windows version is easiest as it does not require us to install any additional software or SDKs in order to build it.

Creating a Windows extension

Since we won't actually be supporting gyroscope input on Windows, our API only needs to return `false` in the `GyroscopeSupported` function and the functions for accessing current gyroscope values should always return a `0` value. Obviously the start and stop functions need to do absolutely nothing!

We've already created the S4E file, so now we'll put it to use. Open Windows Explorer, navigate to the `Gyroscope` directory, and then right-click on the `Gyroscope.s4e` file. Select the menu option **Build Windows Extension**, which will run a Python script that generates a number of new files and directories.

In the main `Gyroscope` directory three new files are created:

- `Gyroscope_build.mkf` is the MKF file for the extension that allows us to specify additional generic or platform-dependant source files that are needed for building it
- `Gyroscope.mkf` is the MKF file any Marmalade project that makes use of our extension will need to include as a subproject to access the extension functions
- `Gyroscope_windows.mkb` is the MKB file that creates a Visual Studio project that we can use to compile the extension code

There are four subdirectories created as well. We can safely ignore the `stamp` directory, which contains a file used internally by the EDK build scripts to track changes to the extension API. We can also ignore the files in the `interface` directory, which are autogenerated and should not be altered.

The `h` directory contains a single file, `Gyroscope.h`, which again we should not modify, as any changes we make will be overwritten by the extension creation scripts. This file is very useful, however, as it is the file we will include in our project sources to access the functions in the extension.

Finally there is the `source` directory that in turn contains three more subdirectories. The `generic` subdirectory contains source files that will define the default behavior of the extension if platform-specific source files are not provided. The `h` directory also contains files that are used across all platforms for building the extension code. While we can make changes to these files, it is unlikely we will ever need to.

This leaves us with the `windows` subdirectory that contains a single file called `Gyroscope_platform.cpp`. This file contains stubs for each of our extension functions that were generated from the data provided in the functions list of the S4E file.

Note however that all the stubbed functions end with the suffix `_platform`. The EDK system actually generates a set of generic functions with the exact names specified in the S4E file that calls the equivalent functions that are suffixed with `_platform`, if they exist. This is necessary so that code that uses an extension can still be compiled and executed on a platform for which an extension has not, or cannot, be created.

Implementing a Windows extension

Ordinarily we would need to modify the `Gyroscope_platform.cpp` file to implement the extension; but for our purposes no changes are actually necessary as the generated stubs provide the desired functionality on Windows.

Obviously, in this case a Windows extension is a little redundant, but bear in mind we could always create a more complex extension that somehow emulates gyroscope behavior, perhaps using a joystick or some other input device.

Building a Windows extension

To build the extension, we just double-click the `Gyroscope\Gyroscope_windows.mkb` file to create a Visual Studio project. Once Visual Studio starts up, select the **(x86) Release** build type from the drop-down menu at the top of the Visual Studio IDE, go to the menu option **Build | Build Solution** (or just press the *F7* key), and the Windows version of the extension will be created. Simple!

Making an Android extension

Now we'll turn our attention to Android. We'll need to install some software before we can begin, though, as the build process needs to be able to access Java development tools and the Android SDK.

Installing the required software for Android development

First of all you will need to install the Java JDK, which is available for download at the following address:

`http://www.oracle.com/technetwork/java/javase/downloads/index.html`

When downloading the JDK, make sure it is Version 6 that you download and not the newer Version 7. The Android SDK is not guaranteed to work correctly with Version 7.

Once the install package has downloaded, execute it and follow the instructions to install the Java development tools to your PC.

Next you will need to download the Android SDK and NDK. The Android SDK is the Java library normally used to develop Android applications, while the NDK is an additional set of libraries that allows Java Android code to interface with compiled C++ code.

The Android SDK is available at the following URL:

`http://developer.android.com/sdk/index.html`

It comes as a Windows installer file; so just execute it, accept all the default install options, and wait for it to install.

> Once the Android SDK has been installed, it is useful to set the environment variable `ANDROID_ROOT` to the installation directory. This lets the Marmalade deployment tool know where the Android platform tools can be found so that it can automatically install and run generated package files on an Android device connected to your PC using a USB cable.

Next you can visit the following URL to download the Android NDK:

`http://developer.android.com/tools/sdk/ndk/index.html`

> You will need different versions of the NDK depending on which version of Marmalade you are using. If you are using Marmalade 6.1 or higher, as expected in this book, you will need NDK version 8. For earlier versions of Marmalade, you will need NDK version 7.

The NDK is supplied as a ZIP archive, so you will need to decompress it using a suitable archiving program (for example, WinZip). The NDK should be contained in a directory named something like `android-ndk-xxx`, where `xxx` refers to the version number of the NDK. You can either copy this directory into the root of your `C:` or you can set the environment variable `NDK_ROOT` to point to the installation path.

Creating an Android extension

Now that we have the necessary development tools in place, we can create the Android extension files by again using the Windows Explorer to locate the `Gyroscope.s4e` file. Right-click on the file and select the **Build Android Extension** menu option.

The files `Gyroscope_android.mkb` and `Gyroscope_android_java.mkb` will be created in the main `Gyroscope` directory. These files will be used later to build the extension code.

The `source` directory will now contain a new directory called `android` that contains two files `Gyroscope.java` and `Gyroscope_platform.cpp`. The former is where we can add Java code that uses the Android SDK code to implement our extension API. The latter is the C++ code that our Marmalade project will call, which in turn calls the Java implementation code.

It is possible to implement the entire extension in the `Gyroscope_platform.cpp` file by using the **Java Native Interface** (**JNI**) to access and call into the compiled Java code; but this adds an extra layer of complexity and implementing the extension in Java is normally a far easier proposition!

Implementing an Android extension

To implement the gyroscope code for Android, we will need to edit the file `source\android\Gyroscope.java`. First we need to make a reference to the Java classes we'll be using; so change the list of import declarations at the top of the file to look like this:

```
import com.ideaworks3d.marmalade.LoaderAPI;
import com.ideaworks3d.marmalade.LoaderActivity;

import android.content.Context;
import android.hardware.Sensor;
import android.hardware.SensorEvent;
import android.hardware.SensorEventListener;
import android.hardware.SensorManager;
```

The first two imports allow us access to some helper functions that provide access to things such as the application's main `Activity` class (all applications in Android need to be derived from this base class). We'll need this to access some system resources.

The remaining imports are for the parts of the Android SDK that we will need to use to access the gyroscope data.

The EDK system has generated a Java class called `Gyroscope` that contains stubs for all the methods we need to implement. We will need to alter the class definition slightly, though, as we need to implement some methods that will receive gyroscope updates. Change the class definition as follows:

```
class Gyroscope implements SensorEventListener
```

`SensorEventListener` is a Java interface that our class must implement in order to receive sensor events (in our case, gyroscope data).

We'll also add some member variables for caching the gyroscope values and a flag that we'll use to handle the fact that some Android devices return gyroscope values in degrees per second rather than radians per second. Add the following code to the bottom of the class definition:

```
// Cached gyroscope values
private float x;
private float y;
private float z;

// Are the results in degrees/s or radians/s
private boolean mUsesDegrees;
```

Before we start implementing the EDK itself, we'll add a couple of private helper functions to allow us to access the Android `SensorManager` and gyroscope `Sensor` instances that will allow us to retrieve the current gyroscope data. Add the following two methods at the beginning of the class definition:

```
// Helper function for accessing the Android SensorManager
private SensorManager GetSensorManager()
{
   Context lContext = (Context) LoaderActivity.m_Activity;
   SensorManager lSensorManager = (SensorManager)
      lContext.getSystemService(Context.SENSOR_SERVICE);
   return lSensorManager;
}

// Helper function for accessing the Android Gyroscope Sensor
private Sensor GetGyroscopeSensor()
{
   SensorManager lSensorManager = GetSensorManager();
   if (lSensorManager == null)
      return null;

   Sensor lGyroscope =
      lSensorManager.getDefaultSensor(Sensor.TYPE_GYROSCOPE);
   return lGyroscope;
}
```

The `GetSensorManager` method accesses the global `SensorManager` instance by using the main `Context` class of the Marmalade application. We do this using Marmalade's `LoaderActivity` class that contains a member variable that is a reference to the main Android SDK `Activity` class instance. This reference can then be cast into a reference to a `Context` instance, since `Activity` derives from `Context`.

Once we have the `Context` reference, we use it to obtain a reference to the Android `SensorManager` class that is responsible for controlling input devices, including the gyroscope. If no reference is available, a `null` reference will be returned.

The `GetGyroscopeSensor` method lets us check for the presence of a gyroscope by requesting the `SensorManager` class for the default gyroscope handler. If a suitable handler is not found (that is, a return value of `null`), there is no gyroscope hardware available on this device.

Now we can start implementing the API by looking at the `GyroscopeSupported` method. This function needs to return `true` only if the device has gyroscope hardware. We can do this as follows:

```
public boolean GyroscopeSupported()
{
    Sensor lSensor = GetGyroscopeSensor();
    return lSensor != null;
}
```

It is now time to implement the function that will allow us to start receiving gyroscope data. Find the `GyroscopeStart` method and change it to the following code snippet:

```
public void GyroscopeStart()
{
  x = 0.0f;
  y = 0.0f;
  z = 0.0f;
  mUsesDegrees = false;

  Sensor lGyroscope = GetGyroscopeSensor();
  if (lGyroscope != null)
  {
    mUsesDegrees = lGyroscope.getMaximumRange() > 100;
    GetSensorManager().registerListener(this, lGyroscope,
                  SensorManager.SENSOR_DELAY_FASTEST);
  }
}
```

In this method we start by ensuring that the cached gyroscope values are zero and we assume that the device will return values in radians per second. We then obtain the gyroscope's `Sensor` class instance using our private `GetGyroscopeSensor` method.

To determine whether this device returns values in degrees or radians, we look at the maximum range value of the gyroscope sensor. We set the `mUsesDegrees` member variable to `true` if the maximum range is greater than 100, as there does not appear to be any more robust way of determining this.

We then set our class instance to be a listener for gyroscope data. Periodically, the `onSensorChanged` method (which we have yet to implement) will be called with new gyroscope values.

Next we will implement the `GyroscopeStop` function, which should look like this:

```
public void GyroscopeStop()
{
  SensorManager lSensorManager = GetSensorManager();
  if (lSensorManager != null)
  {
    lSensorManager.unregisterListener(this);
  }

  x = 0.0f;
  y = 0.0f;
  z = 0.0f;
}
```

Yet again we obtain the `SensorManager` class reference and tell it that we no longer want to receive gyroscope data. We also clear the cached gyroscope values just in case our code tries to access them while the gyroscope hardware is not active.

The next three methods we need to implement are those that return the cached gyroscope values. These are easy to implement and should look like this:

```
public float GyroscopeGetX()
{
  return x;
}

public float GyroscopeGetY()
{
  return y;
}

public float GyroscopeGetZ()
{
  return z;
}
```

We are now almost finished. All that is left to do is implement the listener methods that are part of the `SensorEventListener` interface that we have derived the `Gyroscope` class from. Add the following code after the `GyroscopeGetZ` method.

```
public void onAccuracyChanged(Sensor aSensor, int aAccuracy)
{
}

public void onSensorChanged(SensorEvent aEvent)
{
  if (aEvent.accuracy != SensorManager.SENSOR_STATUS_UNRELIABLE)
  {
    x = aEvent.values[0];
    y = aEvent.values[1];
    z = aEvent.values[2];

    if (mUsesDegrees)
    {
      x = (x * 3.14159267f) / 180.0f;
      y = (y * 3.14159267f) / 180.0f;
      z = (z * 3.14159267f) / 180.0f;
    }
  }
}
```

The `onAccuracyChanged` method is left empty since it must be implemented to satisfy the interface. The `onSensorChanged` method is important, though, as this will receive the new gyroscope input values. We first check to see if the passed in `SensorEvent` contains reliable data (the device itself will determine what constitutes reliable data); then, we just pull out the new gyroscope values and store them in our member variables.

If we determined that the device is returning values in degrees per second, we do a quick conversion to radians to ensure that our extension always returns consistent values.

Building an Android extension

Our Android extension code is now ready to be built and this is even simpler than it was with the Windows version. All we have to do is open Windows Explorer and navigate to the `Gyroscope` directory, and double-click first the `Gyroscope_android_java.mkb` file and then the `Gyroscope_android.mkb` file. The first MKB file will build the Java code, while the second will build the C++ code that will be called from our project code and that will in turn call the Java code.

Making an iOS extension

Building an EDK extension for iOS is a little more involved as it requires us to have access to the Apple iOS SDK and therefore an Apple Mac.

Installing the required software for iOS development

Firstly, you will need to download the iOS SDK that is bundled together with Apple's XCode development environment. Head over to the following web page, which will contain a link to open the Mac App Store where the latest version of XCode can be downloaded:

`https://developer.apple.com/xcode/index.php`

Once XCode has downloaded and you have installed it, you will then need to download the Marmalade SDK in its Mac OS X incarnation. Head over to the Marmalade website at the following URL, log in, and download the Mac version of Marmalade.

`https://www.madewithmarmalade.com/downloads`

Install the Marmalade SDK to the default location. If you only have a single Marmalade license, you will need to use the Marmalade website to release the license from your PC so you can use it on the Mac. Refer to *Chapter 1, Getting Started with Marmalade*, of this book for more information on how to do this.

Creating an iOS extension

Unsurprisingly, we create the files needed for the iOS Extension in a similar manner to the Windows and Android extensions. Just right-click on the `Gyroscope.s4e` file and select the menu option **Build iPhone Extension**.

Just two new files will be created for the iOS extension. These are `Gyroscope_iphone.mkb`, which is the MKB file that we will use to build the extension code, and `source\iphone\Gyroscope_platform.mm`, which contains the auto-generated stubs for our API functions.

Implementing an iOS extension

To implement the iOS version of the Gyroscope extension, we need to edit the `Gyroscope_platform.mm` file. This file is an Objective-C source file that also allows us to use C and C++ code in the same file. The function stubs are all standard C-style functions, but we can still make use of Objective-C classes and features within them.

On iOS, we use an Objective-C class called `CMMotionManager` to gain access to gyroscope data, so we first need to let our code know about this class by changing the list of included files as follows:

```
#include <CoreMotion/CoreMotion.h>
#include "Gyroscope_internal.h"
```

We'll also declare a global pointer to a `CMMotionManager` instance that we will use throughout the rest of our code. Add the following line after the include files:

```
CMMotionManager* gpMotionManager = nil;
```

We'll need to allocate an instance of this class before we can access the gyroscope. Luckily, the EDK build script has generated a function called `GyroscopeInit_platform` that is automatically called for us when we use the extension in our project, so this will make a good place to allocate a new `CMMotionManager` instance, as shown in the following code:

```
s3eResult GyroscopeInit_platform()
{
  gpMotionManager = [[CMMotionManager alloc] init];

  return S3E_RESULT_SUCCESS;
}
```

We also need to free the instance when our application is terminated and once again the EDK build script has come to our rescue with the function `GyroscopeTerminate_platform`. We need to modify this function so that it stops the gyroscope, if it is still active, and then releases the `CMMotionManager` instance. Here's the completed function:

```
void GyroscopeTerminate_platform()
{
  GyroscopeStop_platform();
  [gpMotionManager release];
}
```

The rest of the implementation is actually surprisingly easy, as the `CMMotionManager` class works in a very similar manner to the API we have chosen for the extension. We'll start with checking to see if gyroscope hardware is available. The `GyroscopeSupported_platform` function looks like this:

```
bool GyroscopeSupported_platform()
{
    return gpMotionManager.gyroAvailable;
}
```

Starting and stopping the gyroscope hardware is also little more than calling a method of the `CMMotionManager` class. For safety we wrap these calls with further checks to make sure the gyroscope is available and not already started or stopped.

```
void GyroscopeStart_platform()
{
  if (gpMotionManager.gyroAvailable && !gpMotionManager.gyroActive)
  {
    [gpMotionManager startGyroUpdates];
  }
}

void GyroscopeStop_platform()
{
  if (gpMotionManager.gyroAvailable && gpMotionManager.gyroActive)
  {
    [gpMotionManager stopGyroUpdates];
  }
}
```

The only thing left to do is get hold of the current gyroscope input values. The `CMMotionManager` class contains a property called `gyroData` of class `CMGyroData`, which in turn contains a `CMRotationRate` property called, funnily enough, `rotationRate` that holds the current gyroscope data.

The following code shows the implementation for getting hold of the gyroscope data for the x axis. How to obtain the y and z axes values should be fairly obvious from this!

```
float GyroscopeGetX_platform()
{
  CMGyroData* lpGyroData = [gpMotionManager gyroData];
  if (lpGyroData)
  {
    CMRotationRate lpRotRate = [lpGyroData rotationRate];
    return lpRotRate.x;
  }
  else
  {
    return 0.0f;
  }
}
```

There is one final thing we have to do before we can build the extension, and that is to tell the EDK build tools that we need to include the iOS SDK framework `CoreMotion`, as this contains the code for the `CMMotionManager` class.

To add a framework to our extensions, we must edit the `Gyroscope.mkf` file. Look for the `deployments` section for iOS towards the bottom of the file (Marmalade refers to it as the "iphone platform" for legacy reasons) and add the following line to it:

```
iphone-link-opts="-framework CoreMotion"
```

Building an iOS extension

So far, all of the previous steps for creating an iOS extension can be done equally well on Windows or Mac, but this final step absolutely requires us to use a Mac.

> We need to ensure the Mac has access to the entire `Gyroscope` directory. How you achieve this is up to you, but a good way is to share the `Gyroscope` directory out on your development Windows PC and then access this share on the Mac. This way the code is built on the Mac but all the compiled files are already in the correct place on your Windows development machine.

To build the extension you first need to open a Mac terminal window. Make the `Gyroscope` directory the current directory in the terminal window and then enter the following command line:

```
mkb Gyroscope_iphone.mkb -arm
```

This will build the extension and our work on the Mac is done. Simple, but kind of annoying that we only needed to execute one command, isn't it?

Using the Gyroscope extension

We've now seen how to create and build extension modules for Windows, Android, and iOS, but how do we make use of them in our Marmalade projects?

It's actually surprisingly easy. All we have to do is reference our extension in the project MKB file's `subprojects` section (the easiest way to do this is to provide a relative path to the `Gyroscope` directory from the main project directory), just as we would with any normal code module, and then include the auto-generated `Gyroscope.h` header file so we can call the extension functions.

The only thing to bear in mind is that because an extension may not have been created for every platform we wish to target, we must make sure the extension is available for use before we call any of its functions. This is easily done by using the `GyroscopeAvailable` function that is automatically generated for us by the EDK build scripts. If this function returns `S3E_TRUE`, the extension is available for use. If it returns `S3E_FALSE`, any call to an extension function will fire an assert but will otherwise do nothing.

There are also no special steps required for building or deploying our application, even on Android, where any code written in Java needs to be supplied in a JAR file. The deployment tool will automatically add any required extension files to the install package without us having to do a thing.

Example code

The following sections detail the code samples that accompany this chapter.

The Gyroscope project

This project contains the complete source code for the Gyroscope extension developed throughout the course of this chapter. Compiled versions of the extension have also been included so you can build the other example projects for this chapter without having to first build the extension itself.

The GyroTest project

The GyroTest project is a simple example that makes use of the Gyroscope extension. It demonstrates how to include the Gyroscope extension into a project, how to check if the extension is available, and then how to call the extension function if it is available.

The sample will be displayed on screen whether or not gyroscope support is available. If it is, the raw gyroscope values will also be displayed on screen.

The Skiing project

Our final update to the Skiing project sees it make use of the Gyroscope extension developed in this chapter as another possible control method.

As with the other input methods in the game, a class called `GyroscopeManager` has been created, which wraps up the Gyroscope extension. This then keeps all use of the extension functions in a single source file, which makes it easier to update should we ever change the API of the extension in any way.

No matter how still the device is, even if left lying on a stable surface, the gyroscope values will always have a certain amount of jitter. The `GyroscopeManager` class deals with this by maintaining a filtered version of the gyroscope inputs that are used to control the skier in the game.

In every update of the main game loop, a new filtered value for each gyroscope axis is calculated by adding a percentage of the difference between the current filtered value and the new raw value for each axis to the current filtered value. This results in the smaller effects of jitter mostly being ignored without losing the larger intentional gyroscope inputs from the player.

Summary

In this chapter we've looked at how to use the Extensions Development Kit to extend the functionality of Marmalade. As you can see, it is relatively easy to create an extension that can make use of the APIs available on each of the platforms currently supported by the EDK.

The Gyroscope extension is a good example of supporting a hardware feature that hasn't yet been exposed in the main Marmalade SDK, but extensions can also come in extremely handy if you want to use any third party libraries that may have been created directly for a particular platform using its native SDK.

As this book draws to a close, you should now have a good grasp of the power of the Marmalade SDK and will hopefully be jumping at the opportunity of developing a game and launching it on a number of extremely popular platforms. Happy coding and best of luck writing the next big gaming phenomenon!

Index

Symbols

A

B

C

D

E

F

G

H

I

J

K

L

M

N

O

P

Q

R

S

T

U

V

W

X

Z

Thank you for buying Marmalade SDK Mobile Game Development Essentials

About Packt Publishing

Packt, pronounced 'packed', published its first book "*Mastering phpMyAdmin for Effective MySQL Management*" in April 2004 and subsequently continued to specialize in publishing highly focused books on specific technologies and solutions.

Our books and publications share the experiences of your fellow IT professionals in adapting and customizing today's systems, applications, and frameworks. Our solution based books give you the knowledge and power to customize the software and technologies you're using to get the job done. Packt books are more specific and less general than the IT books you have seen in the past. Our unique business model allows us to bring you more focused information, giving you more of what you need to know, and less of what you don't.

Packt is a modern, yet unique publishing company, which focuses on producing quality, cutting-edge books for communities of developers, administrators, and newbies alike. For more information, please visit our website: `www.packtpub.com`.

Writing for Packt

We welcome all inquiries from people who are interested in authoring. Book proposals should be sent to `author@packtpub.com`. If your book idea is still at an early stage and you would like to discuss it first before writing a formal book proposal, contact us; one of our commissioning editors will get in touch with you.

We're not just looking for published authors; if you have strong technical skills but no writing experience, our experienced editors can help you develop a writing career, or simply get some additional reward for your expertise.

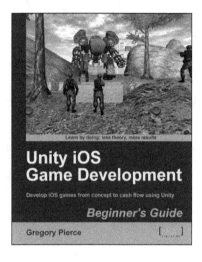

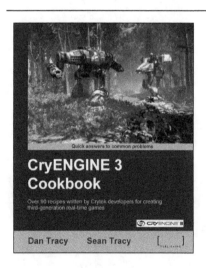

www.ingramcontent.com/pod-product-compliance
Lightning Source LLC
LaVergne TN
LVHW062307060326
832902LV00013B/2081

* 9 7 8 1 8 4 9 6 9 3 3 6 3 *